Also by Margo Kaufman
1-800-AM-I-NUTS?

THIS DAMN HOUSE!

My Subcontract with America

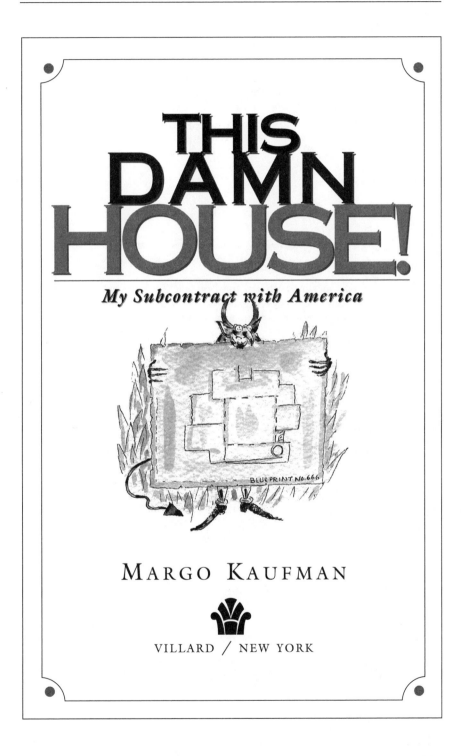

BLUEPRINT No. 666

Margo Kaufman

VILLARD / NEW YORK

DISCLAIMER

This is a true story. However, in the interest of self-preservation, I've
changed the names, descriptions, geographic specifics, and personal
idiosyncrasies of some of the participants. If you think you recognize
anyone in this book, I would consider it a personal favor if you would
just keep it to yourself.

For anyone who has looked at a bearing wall and thought, "This room would sure look a lot better without *that*." But most of all for my sister, Laurie Goldberg, who made me laugh when I needed to most.

ACKNOWLEDGMENTS

Deciding to fix up your house in order to write a book about remodeling is about as sane as deciding to write a book about terrorism then going out and hijacking a plane. That I succeeded is largely due to my innate pigheadedness and my good fortune to have been blessed with an extraordinary amount of outside help.

First and foremost I must thank my beloved husband, who to his everlasting credit never once asked why the hell I'd gotten us into this mess. I'm grateful as well to my friend, Jon Winokur, who spent so many hours talking me through every step of this project that he succumbed to the remodeling bug, too. (Now, if only I could convince him to use color in his house.) And I'm beholden to my fellow pug enthusiast, Victoria Roberts, for her charming illustrations.

This book would not exist without the efforts of my agent, Loretta Fidel; my editors, David Rosenthal and Craig Nelson; the amazingly efficient Andrew Krauss; and all the talented people at Villard Books: Tad Floridis, Beth Pearson, Dan Rembert, Margaret Wimberger, Adam Rothberg, Leta Evanthes, Diana Frost, and Deanne Adlen-Chalk. Thanks are also due to Ken Minyard and Roger Barkley at KABC Talkradio for giving me a chance to vent on the air every week.

My entire family was generous with support and advice (some of which I actually took). Much love to all and extra hugs to: Flora Pearlstein, Paul Asnes, Laurie and Ken (the Shark) Goldberg, Arthur and Shirley Mankin, Eric Mankin, Allan Pearlstein, and Bobby Pearlstein. Heartfelt thanks to my dear and encouraging friends: Marian Bach, Marjorie David, David Ewing, Nancy Hathaway, Susan Garfield, Marc Glassgold, Marilyn Hulquist, Deborah Levin, Blanche and Quentin Roberts, and Suzy Slutzky.

A round of applause to all the folks who helped put our house together—especially Walt Wozniak (whom I wish I could afford)—and to all the doctors who helped put me back together—in particular Jeffrey Eckhart, Gary Emery, Henry Mankin, Peter J. Rosen, and I. Bernard Weinstein. And a special commendation for distinguished service to my devoted Primary Care Physician, Gloria Asnes.

Finally, tummy scratches to Sophie and Clara, who didn't do a damn thing.

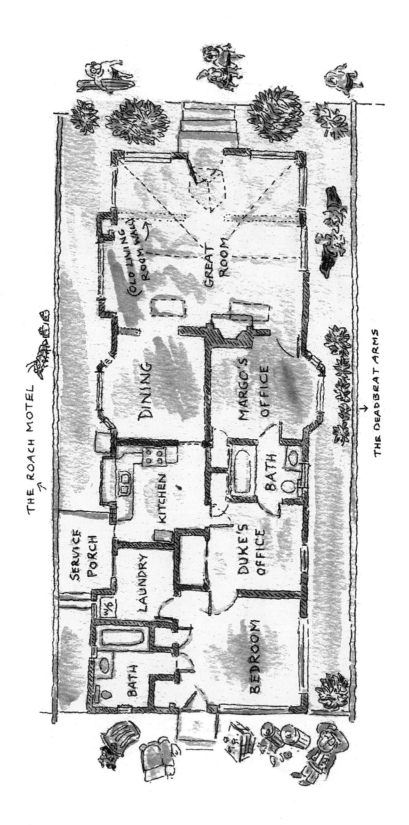

CHAPTER ONE

I DON'T KNOW what I'm going to do. My husband, Duke, and I have been interviewing architects for over a year now, and the most I can say is that it makes dating seem like fun. With a love object, what's the worst that can happen? You pick Mr. Wrong, marry, get some nice towels, realize you made a hideous mistake, have a meltdown argument, and get divorced. (Hopefully, you get to keep the nice towels.) But with an architect you risk financial ruin, mental collapse, and a potential eyesore that you've got to live in or try to unload in a shaky market.

If that's not scary enough, you have to make what amounts to virtually a blind choice, since architects don't seem to do very much in exchange for your retainer check. In a way, I envy their sense of professional entitlement. When I want to sell a book or an article, I have to write a long, detailed proposal to give an editor an idea of what he's going to get. By contrast, it seems that all an architect does is show up with an album of blurry photos, a roll of blueprints, and a list of properties whose owners just happen to be out of town—indefinitely.

"It's a lot easier when you're dealing with a friend," says my sister, Laurie, who recently bought the home of her dreams in Chicago. She and her husband, Kenny (known among contractors he has dealt with as the Shark), are remodeling their master bedroom with the help of his architect, Cousin Bernie, who started working on the drawings the day they went into escrow. "Bernie's really talented," Laurie says smugly. "He did the shah of Iran." (Laurie's not worried about losing her crown and going into exile.)

I can't decide which I envy more: the fact that Laurie and the Shark were able to buy a six-bedroom, ivy-covered Georgian pile on a tree-lined street in a bucolic neighborhood for less than the market value of our little bungalow in that bastion of lunacy, Venice Beach, California, or that all she has to do to put in a spacious master bedroom suite with a double-sided wood-burning fireplace is to pick up the phone and say, "Hey, cuz."

"An architect's a good thing to have in the family," Laurie says. "It makes things so much easier, like when you're getting married and you already have a hall."

I wouldn't know; we eloped. Besides, most of my in-laws are in the circus, so unless I'm looking for someone to juggle five burning torches or a couple to jump rope while they're standing on each other's shoulders on stilts, I'm out of luck. At this point, I'm desperate enough to pick up the Yellow Pages, look under *A,* pick out the guy who runs the half-page ad with red ink and a tacky little clip-art picture of a house, and give him the job.

It couldn't be more discouraging than the quest so far.

Our architectural star search began several years ago when we decided to renovate our ninety-year-old, twelve-hundred-square-foot beach bungalow. From the outside it looked like a storybook cottage, but inside it was a warren. On paper we had three bedrooms, two baths, a living room, dining room, kitchen, and a sunporch, but all the rooms were undersized, with low ceilings, gray industrial carpets, and so little natural light that I felt I was suffering from seasonal affective disorder. (Our windows offered breathtaking vistas into the apartments that flanked us on either side. We kept the blinds closed, partly for privacy, partly to ward off accidentally seeing something that might land us in the Federal Witness Protection Program.) What's more, after seven years of occupation by my husband, the world's messiest human, my less-than-fastidious pug dogs, Sophie and Clara (who were preceded by a pair of even less fastidious elderly pugs, Bess and Stella), and me, a compulsive dollhouse builder, folk art collector, and writer who works at home in a cramped office, the place was claustrophobically cluttered with magazines, miniature projects, books, wood carvings, and chew toys.

Not knowing where to begin, I called the only architect I knew even vaguely—our neighbor Larry, the good-looking, Nautilus-muscled, Ralph Lauren–clad heir to a dry-cleaning fortune. He'd just opened a design shop in the Valley and was looking for clients. I should have eliminated him on that basis alone. An hour into our meeting, after intense cross-examination, Larry admitted that he had never remodeled a house before.

"But I'm working on a hospital entrance," he said. I had a vision of the picket gateway that he erected in his front yard last summer. The one that looks like it was spawned by an airport metal detector.

It was disconcerting that, even though Larry has lived in our neighborhood for five years and owns a bungalow almost identical to ours, he still didn't have an inkling about what he'd do to our property. Somehow I was under the impression that architects fantasized about making over houses, the way a teenage girl daydreams about changing her nose.

"Nothing happens in big steps," Larry said, taking home a copy of the blueprints to our house. But funny, one thing did: After our first discussion, he sent us a ten-page contract and a bill for a sizable retainer. We decided to look further. Despite my increasingly threatening entreaties, Larry took ten months to send our blueprints back.

Candidate number two, Horace, was a lot more promising. He was recommended by a girlfriend who prides herself on being in the loop. Horace looked like he was sent by Central Casting. A tall, gawky, storklike man with a Georgia twang, he wore owlish Calvin Klein glasses and the kind of houndstooth jacket you can only buy east of the Mississippi. His credentials were impeccable too: he had taught architecture at a prestigious West Coast university and lived in a house built by Frank Lloyd Wright's son.

The night we met, Duke and I were filled with hope. Horace walked us up and down the narrow Venice walk streets to get an idea of what we liked. I hadn't had so much fun since I was a child circling what I wanted for Christmas in the F.A.O. Schwartz catalog. "I'd like an office in a tower," I said.

"And a darkroom," said Duke.

"Do you want a dream kitchen?" Horace asked.

"I'd rather have a dream bathroom," I said. I don't cook.

"I do want a Chinese restaurant stove," said Duke, who does. (Whatever that is, it's not in the Williams-Sonoma catalog.)

Horace nodded gravely and wrote down every word in his meticulous hand. A week later, he returned with his portfolio. The only thing we were really impressed with were his radiator-cover designs. And how often do you need radiator covers in Southern California? Still, when Horace recommended that we have his engineer look over our property to get an idea of the technical problems he'd have to work with, it seemed like a wise thing to do. It would cost $150, but we rationalized that knowledge was power.

I expected some tattooed brute in coveralls to go crawling in the sand under the house and up into the attic, poking his flashlight in every nook and cranny. So I was a little startled when Horace introduced us to Ali, a slim Iranian in a meticulously tailored, thousand-dollar Armani suit. He gingerly tiptoed through our backyard trying not to scuff his Bally wingtips. Ali's first words were "I'm in a hurry." He'd left a famous Persian architect, "the one who designed Omar Khayyam's tomb," in the car with the motor running.

That was strike one. Strike two was when, after spending only twenty minutes looking around, Ali announced he saw no reason to climb into the attic. Strike three was a toss-up between the fact that he was terrified by Stella, an obese fourteen-year-old pug who snoozed through his entire visit (and has since gone to the Great Sofa Cushion in the Sky), and his inability to figure out how to open the primitive latch on our garden gate. Not, we agreed, a good sign in a structural engineer.

Later, I called Horace to complain that we didn't get much for $150. He blithely replied, "Ali has a two-hour minimum," something he hadn't mentioned before.

Things hung fire for some months after Ali's visit. It's astounding how long you can put off making a decision when to do so will mean the total disruption of life as you know it. I developed a full-blown case of Home Owner's Denial Syndrome, which enables you to repress all knowledge of dry rot, chipping paint, and corroded plumbing. I even remained sanguine when my friend Rusty called and raved about his remodel, which was being done under the auspices of his college roommate, Bob, a brilliant architect. (The only college roommate I ever had slept seventeen hours a day.)

"Bob even helped us buy our new house," said Rusty, who sold his teeny house in Los Angeles at the crest of the real estate market and moved to Oregon, where property is relatively cheap. "He checked it out to make sure it had potential. Then once we bought it he came over and walked around the house and told us what the possibilities were. He only charged a minimal hourly fee. And he was really generous with his time. We'd make him dinner, and he wouldn't charge us even though he spent the whole time talking about the project."

Not surprisingly, Bob wasn't available for a consultation with me. Still, I couldn't help but notice that architects kept popping up unexpectedly in my life. The last time I experienced a similar phenomenon was when I was single and I decided to get married. Instantly, the Universe stopped sending me Tasmanian film directors of a certain age and began sending thirty-eight-year-old Jewish men. I could have gone to Greenland and the first person I'd have met was Benjy Sachs, M.D. Similarly, I couldn't go to a garage sale without being waited on by a card-carrying member of the American Institute of Architects.

Hands-down winner for Mr. Congeniality was candidate number three, Chuck, who came into my life when I went to buy a new pug puppy. I've been owned by pugs—those bulgy-eyed dogs with curly tails and pushed-in faces—for twenty years, and anyone associated with the breed has an edge with me. Chuck lives with a well-known character actor and noted pug breeder. I had bought Sophie, my beautiful but dim-witted two-year-old bitch, from him, and following the demise of fourteen-year-old Bess (Stella's sister), I'd stopped by his house hoping to buy another.

The actor didn't have any puppies I liked—I would later have to go all the way to New York to buy Clara, a preternaturally cunning runt—so he showed me his extensive collection of pug bric-a-brac instead. I was eyeing a loony chess set that featured black pug pieces versus fawn, when the subject turned to earthquakes. "Do you worry about your house?" the breeder/actor asked, handing me a delicate nineteenth-century Viennese bronze pug chasing a boar.

"Never," I said. "If the house collapsed, it would save us the trouble of remodeling."

The actor perked up his ears. "Are you looking for an architect?"

Enter Chuck, a peppy, happy-go-lucky set designer who moonlights as a builder and still finds time to be a surrogate father to a pack of wheezing muffinheads.

"We can't hire an architect because he loves pugs," Duke warned me when I came home and announced that our architectural star search was over.

"Of course not," I lied.

A few nights later, Chuck came to our house with his half-German, half-Iranian partner. I didn't get the clear impression either was actually licensed, but they brought thick rolls of blueprints to attest to their skill. Frankly, blueprints are like pets and children—difficult to appreciate or understand unless they're yours. From the intricacies of the plans, it *looked* like they knew what they were doing, but to me it was like viewing the visual equivalent of legalese.

"Nobody else has a problem understanding plans," said the partner, who regarded me with the high esteem that Middle Eastern men traditionally extend toward women who question their judgment.

The designers promised to send us a brochure describing their major achievements, credentials, and references. But the handsomely printed four-color, six-font booklet we eventually received attested only to their skill with a Macintosh—long on colorful graphics but still no references.

Eventually, Chuck arranged a tour of their latest project, Casa de Phone Sex, a faux Moorish castle in Brentwood, which he'd remodeled for a dominatrix who'd made a killing in 976 numbers. It was tastefully done in Upscale Bordello, with a king-sized bidet, white satin sheets, and strategically placed mirrors. Duke kept looking for hooks and strange fixtures in the ceiling. The home had an aura of theatricality and was obviously costly, but it was definitely not us.

We wanted to believe that Chuck could create something that was us—without breaking us—but he was not tossing out ideas. On the other hand, the more time we spent with him, the more we liked him. Chuck was funny, easy to talk to, straightforward, and, not least important, a first-rate raconteur of pug anecdotes.

Alas, that did him in. Chuck came back from the National Pug Championships atwitter. His masterwork, a Japanese set for the Grand Parade of Pug Champions, had been sensationally received. The pièce de résistance was an Oriental bridge, over which the wheezing, over-the-hill former pug champions waddled and vogued. Apparently, the finale was so spectacular that one of the viewers in the crowd fainted.

I nearly fainted, too, when a source that I've developed in my position as Hollywood Correspondent for *Pug Talk* magazine confided that the Japanese bridge came in three times over budget. Later, Chuck informed us that he couldn't, in good conscience, recommend doing anything to our house for under $200,000. We put the house on hold again.

Still, the Universe kept spurring me on. One Saturday, Duke and I were strolling along Ocean Front Walk with Sophie and Clara. We passed a couple dozen vendors hawking $5 knock-offs of $200 sunglasses, a pet couturier peddling leather bomber jackets, yarmulkes, and bridal gowns, and scores of gawking tourists who asked the usual stupid pug questions (Are they pit bulls? Did they run into a wall?) in five different languages. Suddenly, we noticed an intriguing construction site. A clapboard bungalow much like ours was getting the second story that I'd always wanted. I scribbled the number down on my disposable pooper-scooper.

Candidate number four, Maurice, no longer lived in Los Angeles. Like a sizable portion of the populace, he'd fled to Seattle and was commuting. But his polite, impeccably dressed young associate in Oliver Peoples wire-rim glasses assured me that the architect's absence wouldn't be a problem. He invited us to inspect the house under construction.

It was my dream addition—a cleverly designed space that was open and modern but retained the feel of a turn-of-the-century beach house. I would have written a check on the spot, even if Maurice spent his days hunting endangered species in Timbuktu. But my ever cautious husband warned me not to get excited. "You liked all of them at first," Duke said pointedly.

When I was dating, I developed a theory called the Dam of Lunacy. It went like this: There's a limit to how long even the most tightly wrapped person can maintain a façade. Behind every $100 Umberto haircut and overaerobicized body lie neuroses untamed by hair mousse and ten-K runs. Invariably, on the fifth date, the Dam of Lunacy breaks. That's when you discover that the adorable stockbroker with the condo in Maui has been seeing a psychoanalyst five times a week for the last seven years and can't have sex on the days he has therapy. It is advisable to postpone judgment until you get a reality check.

Rosy-cheeked, blow-dried Maurice flew in from Seattle, resplendent in tastefully understated $500 Matsuda wire-rim glasses, $300 Gucci loafers, and a creamy cashmere sweater without so much as a smidgen of lint (his fingernails were clean too, a disconcerting sight in a builder). He swept through our dark, narrow living room like my mother perusing a new shipment at Barney's and recited what he perceived to be our needs: "Redesign the first floor, fix the kitchen, and possibly do a second-story addition to include a master bedroom and bath." Maurice estimated that he could make it all happen for "only a hundred and fifty thousand dollars." I never expected to hear the words "only" and "a hundred and fifty thousand dollars" combined in the same sentence.

"That's more than we planned on spending," Duke said, as if "planned to spend" is a viable concept in home remodeling.

Maurice got huffy. (I suspect they teach Huffy the first semester in architecture school. Second semester they teach Attitude, and third, Arrogance. "And when they graduate, they get the expensive glasses," Duke adds.)

"I would like to see you spend that much," Maurice said dismissively. He walked us through the various phases of design: schematics, elevations, contract documents, bidding. I didn't understand a word of it until he got to the part about supervising construction.

"That means you'll make sure that the contractor doesn't put a wall in the wrong place." I've heard more than my share of horror stories from remodeling veterans. Plumbers who damage soil pans that run the length of the house . . . Contractors who drive their front-end loaders into an existing basement . . . I expected an architect to protect me from all that.

"If things go wrong structurally, it's not my fault," Maurice snapped. "I won't guarantee things I can't fix."

I could hear my little inner voice chirping, "Who the hell does he think he is?" But I told the little voice to shut up. This architect's work was remarkable, and his satisfied clients included a famous revolutionary turned politician who didn't strike me as the type to hire anyone second-rate. After a brief lecture on additional services such as interior design and permit expedition, which weren't included in his 10 percent of the project fee, Maurice flounced out.

"He didn't focus on me once," Duke complained. "And he thought he knew best what I should do."

I checked his references anyway.

The housewife, the ad man, and the restaurateur all agreed that the architect had a phenomenal sense of space, fabulous aesthetic taste, and innovative ideas. "But he's a pain in the ass," said the psychologist, whose home was two months from completion. I asked for specifics. "Well, he likes his own ideas better than yours, he's insulted when you don't do it his way. His personality is difficult." The psychologist conceded he would hire Maurice again. "I'd bring a baseball bat," he said.

"I want to talk to one more," said my husband, who detests making commitments.

I'm not foolish enough to enter into a legal agreement with a person my husband dislikes.

For months my friend Marcella had been pushing me to call Tex—the genius who had remodeled her kitchen. I was wary, since her kitchen walls are covered with quilted brown-and-white gingham, but she swore that he had nothing to do with that. Moreover, he was seventy-fourth on the list of the World's Hundred Best Architects (that doesn't seem like such an honor), he'd remodeled many of her neighbors' homes, and he had a reputation for staying on budget.

Tex insisted that our first meeting be at his office—which seemed pointless, until we arrived and discovered a building so spectacularly situated and sparsely furnished that if Linda Bloodworth Thomason was creating a hit sitcom about an architect (Mr. Ten Percent, starring John Ritter) this would be the set that would wind up in the Smithsonian, next to Archie Bunker's living room. The sleek glass expanse was nestled into a hill in a rustic California canyon. His friendly wife led us into a white trapezoid-shaped room wallpapered with blueprints, sketches, and detailed lists. Sitting behind a marble slab held up by steel girders was Tex, a cross between Sean Connery ten years ago and the Energizer Bunny, with mesmerizing green eyes and a good-old-country-boy twang. It was kind of a relief to see that his striped shirt, patterned tie, argyle socks, and plaid suspenders didn't match. And he wasn't wearing eyeglasses.

Duke and I ran through our wish list: rearrange the existing rooms to bring in more light and space, upgrade the kitchen, clean up the master bathroom, and if possible, add an extra bedroom and bath. Tex nodded agreeably and tossed off a few secrets about the Coastal Commission that he had picked up when he built a custom home on the Venice canals.

"Honey," he called out offhandedly, "can you find me a copy of that magazine article?" (*That* magazine turned out to be *House Beautiful*.) My husband asked how much such a custom home cost. Tex estimated around $125 a square foot. We must have turned a little pale because the architect smoothly switched gears and started talking about artist studios. "We can knock down your house and put up a huge studio-type space for sixty-five dollars a square foot."

Duke and I exchanged glances. It wasn't a bad idea. Actually, it was the first budget-minded idea any architect we had spoken to had proposed. We tried not to look excited. We asked for references. Tex later faxed us a résumé that read like Who's Who? in Hollywood. We invited him to inspect our property later that week.

Tex bounded out of his hunter green Bronco four-by-four, eyes darting in all directions as if he were securing the perimeter. He vaulted up a neighbor's wall to get a better sense of what the view would be like. "You think I could get up on the roof of that structure?" he asked, pointing to the looming apartment building next door. We supposed it could be arranged. (We didn't think Tex would be spooked by the reports—cherry bombs? gunfire?—that occasionally emanated from the complex.) In the meantime, we gave him a tour of our house. He was visibly unimpressed. "I can bring in a bulldozer and level this place for eight hundred dollars," he said.

You know you're in trouble when someone wants to demolish your home and you find yourself getting turned on. "We can go to three stories," Tex said, ambling down our front walk to check out the neighborhood. It happens that ours is a one-story single-family dwelling sandwiched between two oversized apartment complexes filled with tenants who would sound colorful if we were reading about them. (We have dubbed the buildings the Deadbeat Arms and the Roach Motel.) A height limit has since been passed, but Tex waved away our concerns. "I already called the city councilman's office," he said. "I'm pretty sure we can get a variance."

I was flabbergasted. The architect appeared to be hustling. But it was his next action that truly staggered me. He got down on his hands and knees on the sidewalk—a Venice Beach sidewalk!—and rummaged through the discarded hypodermic needles, unscooped dog poop, and empty wine bottles searching for surveyor tags. An hour later, after offering advice on everything from an outdoor shower (useful, after an ocean swim) to small business loans (available if we did 51 percent of our work at home), Tex asked if he could take some pictures. We said okay. He could have asked to put a Ferris wheel in our front yard, and we would have said okay.

"I can arrange for you to tour some of my studio spaces next week," he said hours later, when he finally drove off.

I couldn't wait, so I called Marcella. She arranged for us to inspect her neighbor's Emotional Mediterranean–style home (that's Realtorspeak for a stucco box roofed with terra-cotta tiles), which Tex had redesigned. The entrance was marked by a flashy terra-cotta arch. "Nice touch," Duke said approvingly.

The owner was a prominent, well-built—I know because he answered the door wearing only teensy gym shorts—divorce attorney whose role model was clearly Arnold Becker on *L.A. Law.* "If I can work with Tex, anyone can," he said, and vanished into his fully mirrored, fully equipped home gym to do another set of squats. Tex had transformed three dark boxy rooms into an open, amazingly lavish testament to the Southern California lifestyle, complete with rose-colored marble bathroom with a Jacuzzi shower, an Über-Moderne granite-and-stainless-steel kitchen as sterile and high-tech as an operating room, and a redwood deck, dripping with bougainvillea, that overlooked a David Hockneyesque swimming pool with a mosaic frieze of the scales of justice on the bottom of the deep end.

"So we can hire him?" I whispered.

"Let's wait until we see the studios," my husband said. "But I don't think we're going to do any better."

"Figure on it costing twice as much as Tex tells you," Arnie said as he walked us to the door. If that didn't create enough cognitive dissonance, he went on to inform us that 50 percent of all remodels end in divorce.

"Here," he said. "Let me give you my card."

CHAPTER TWO

THE FIRST STOP on Tex's Grand Tour was a voluminous design studio with eighteen-foot ceilings and an adjoining apartment, which he'd built for "only eighty thousand dollars." The sheer volume was dazzling—especially since I couldn't open a closet or cupboard in our house without something falling on my head. (If only they would build closets in cyberspace so I could upload all my junk into the void. When I need something, I could just click on a little screen icon and my entire winter wardrobe would appear.) On the other hand, I've never yearned to lie in bed on a mezzanine and behold a sixteen-foot drop. Also, the Bare-Bones Deconstructionist finish—no baseboards or crown moldings, uncovered concrete floor, exposed heating ducts—was better suited to a trendy restaurant than a home, at least my home, which I prefer to be cozy.

"There's something to be said for spending a little more money," Duke whispered. (Was it my imagination, or was that the point of the exercise?)

Our second stop was a top-of-the-line three-story white stucco box, or in Realtorspeak, "a spectacular Tuscan villa." The interior was sort of Japanese Minimalist Gone to Sea. Metal gangplanks with thin, almost invisible wire railings magically criss-crossed in midair. Childproof or pugproof it was not, but the skylights let in so much sunlight that you'd have to put on sunscreen to read the morning paper. The teak floors were glossier than a starlet's eight-by-ten head shot, and the slate-countered kitchen and pale-gray-tiled bathrooms were a triumph of elegant simplicity.

"*This* I like," I said happily.

"*This* cost six hundred thousand dollars," Tex replied.

We had an hour before the final stop and Duke had to drop by his office. Tex and I went out for coffee. I learned that he was a fourth-gener-ation builder who loved his job because "I get to deal with people during a happy period of life, when they're expanding." He learned that I didn't yearn for Brescia marble mosaics, custom Australian-lacewood cabinets, or veined granite counters. I just wanted unpretentious, uncluttered space that could stand up to casual beach living.

"That's what I like to do best," Tex said with bonhomie, and all I could do was grin foolishly. He offered to let me in on his secret for suc-cess. "Ask for the moon and the stars. Most artists settle for way too lit-tle."

I also confirmed my suspicion that the architect was dangerously charming. He had a habit of reinforcing cryptic suggestions like "What you really want to do is optimize the usage" with a beguiling twinkle of his sparkly oceanic eyes. He reminded me of a rake I used to date, a guy so smooth that he once drove me to the Bel-Air Hotel so he could kiss me good-bye in front of the swans. I would have been more impressed, ex-cept the swans knew him.

Luckily, Duke rejoined us for the finale, a Brobdingnagian stucco box done in Pseudo Warehouse. It was cleverly configured, with a cathedral-like living room, a loft with a bedroom, bathroom, and a galley kitchen, and a basement studio so vast that you could mount a production of *Aida*—with elephants—inside. Tex's original patron had sold the house to an agoraphobic young photographer who now longed for a cozier nest. I couldn't blame her. The structure was only four years old, but the paint was flaking off the exposed heating ducts (Tex's explanation: the owners used cheap paint) and the roof was leaking (the owners used the low-ball roofer).

Still, we hadn't seen anything to indicate that Tex was the wrong choice. Not that we had a choice. Tex was already acting like he had the job.

"Do you guys have a few minutes?" he asked when the tour was over. "I want to iron out a few details." Duke suggested that we reconvene at a nearby Chinese restaurant. "They gave us those wonderful Sichuan pickles the last time," he said wistfully.

I went to the ladies' room to wash my hands. As soon as I got away from the architect, I felt discombobulated, like I was coming down from a drug-induced high. I splashed some cold water on my face, took a deep breath, and tried to regain my equilibrium. I succeeded briefly. Then I went back to our table. My husband was holding up a napkin, and Tex was casually saying, "Four hundred thousand dollars."

"What?" I stammered.

With great ceremony, the architect handed me an intricate panoramic collage of our neighborhood that he had fabricated from his photos (all that was missing was a drunk passed out on the sidewalk). I was flattered that he'd made such an effort, but at the same time, my internal trouble detector went on red alert. My husband was staring at the collage, transfixed.

Next, Tex passed me a napkin, on which he'd drawn a quick sketch. "First, we raze the existing structure and put up a three-story residence in its place," he said briskly. "Second, we build a huge freestanding studio in the back." I don't remember if there was a "third." I was too busy gasping for breath.

Our house sits on the front half of a 30 x 120-foot lot. When Duke originally bought the property, he threw down a bunch of ratty carpets in the sandy backyard and turned it into a parking lot. Parking is at a premium in Venice, and he was renting spaces for $35 a month. By wedging cars in bumper to bumper—a particularly irritating configuration that in California goes by the name of stack parking—Duke managed to collect rent from a dozen vehicles. It didn't seem to bother him that he was frequently woken up in the middle of the night by an irritated parking tenant who needed him to move five cars, but it drove me nuts. I suggested that we triple the rent and limit the spaces.

At first, Duke was skeptical. (Not for the first time in our relationship, I felt like Eva Perón to my husband's Che Guevara.) Without consulting him, I hired an asphalt company. One morning, my husband looked out the window wide-eyed as a huge cement mixer pulled up and disgorged an astonishing number of laborers. Like laden ants, they hauled away the ratty carpets (which had not improved with age, exposure to rain, and rancid motor oil), laid down a thick coat of asphalt, and rode around on little machines smoothing it down. I even paid extra and had them draw neat yellow lines. Duke was delighted.

"All I need now is a little kiosk with a girlie calendar and a black-and-white TV with the ball game on," he said. Our little parking lot brings in enough income to pay our property taxes and our car-insurance premiums with relatively little aggravation.

Tex felt we were settling for too little. He had consulted a Realtor (no doubt the one on the bus-stop ads who proclaims himself to be "The Buyer's Friend") and learned that there was a huge market for studio space. If we built a colossal expanse in our backyard, we could make enough to cover what was sure to be our colossal new mortgage.

I considered the kind of tenants who would want to rent such a mammoth space. Musicians. Artists. A satanic drug cult. I shook my head. "I don't want tenants," I said firmly.

Tex didn't deign to reply to that. He just continued on with the pitch. "It's the best way to develop property at the beach," he said matter-of-factly. His fee for this extravaganza would be 15 percent, around $60,000, most of which we'd owe him by the end of the month.

"Impossible," I said. "We can't afford it."

"Think about it," Tex crooned. I half expected him to pull out a pocket watch and let it swing before my eyes.

"Let's think about it, honey," said my mesmerized mate.

"That's right," said Tex. "Turn it over in your mind."

I wish that we could pick up and move. I wish that we could sell the damn house and trade up to a bigger one. I wish that we never had to talk to an architect again; that we could forget all about remodeling. But alas, we're trapped by three unchangeable things: location, location, and location.

We live at the beach. Five little words, and yet they describe a luxury as priceless as a twelve-carat emerald and as seductive as Tom Cruise. Our wee bungalow is half a block from the sand, on a charming tree-lined walk

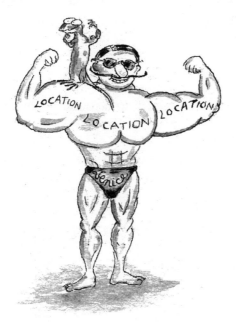

street where cars are not permitted (granted, the back of our house faces a not-so-picturesque alley where a parade of derelicts stagger from Dumpster to Dumpster, searching for the currency of the neighborhood—soda cans). Every morning I walk Sophie and Clara along the esplanade overlooking the Pacific Ocean or ride my Raleigh Beach Cruiser up the coastal bike path that runs from Redondo Beach to Malibu. We breathe the cleanest air in the city. Duke swims in the Santa Monica Bay. As city lifestyles go, it's pretty hard to beat.

Admittedly it's far from perfect. The beach I'm referring to isn't Malibu or even Hermosa but rather Venice, the floating carnival of human eccentricity and exhibitionism that is now Southern California's second biggest tourist attraction (after Disneyland), attracting more than three million visitors annually. Described by Beat Generation historian Lawrence Lipton as "that jerry-built slum by the sea," our neighborhood was born strange and has only gotten stranger.

A brief history. Back in 1905, Abbot Kinney, a Midwestern tycoon who'd made his fortune in Sweet Caporal cigarettes, decided to re-create Venice, Italy, on 160 acres of salt marsh, twenty-five miles from downtown Los Angeles. He dredged eleven canals (five of which remain) and spanned them with arched Venetian bridges. To further enhance the surreality of the place, he imported a flotilla of black silver-prowed gondolas complete with twenty-four singing gondoliers. Stars of the day, like Sarah Bernhardt, Helen Hunt Jackson, and Madame Modjeska, performed in the chautauqua hall and stayed at the Ship Hotel, a 182-foot-long replica of Juan Cabrillo's galleon (the first European ship to see this shore), which was built on pilings next to the pier. Fun seekers came from all over the city, riding on the Pacific Electric red cars to visit what a vintage postcard called "The City of Joyland." Attractions included an aquarium with seals and sea lions, two roller coasters, and in 1911, the first Ferris wheel on the West Coast.

Kinney's theme park was eventually destroyed by storms and fires, though his gaunt visage remains on a WPA mural in the local post office and his name appears on a street sign. But Venice lives on as a scruffy tribute to the unexpected. On a recent stroll I took with my mother down the infamous Venice boardwalk she beheld a shepherdess of uncertain religious denomination carrying a crook; a Rottweiler in a bridal gown and veil; a troupe of five-year-old rap singers; and a muttering schizophrenic pushing a cocker spaniel in a baby carriage. She also passed dozens of tarot readers, palmists, and psychics (the more industrious use laptop computers), spectacular murals by local artists featuring startling, larger-than-life images such as Venus de Milo on roller skates, a white-cap-filled seascape splattered with red and yellow Morse dots and dashes, and a Chagall-inspired fiddler dancing on the roof of a green wooden beach pagoda.

"For this I sent you on Dr. Bernhard's Tour," Mother sighed, referring to a six-week European grand tour designed for teenage Jewish princesses. The itinerary included stops at an Amsterdam diamond cutter, a Swiss watch factory, and the Lalique showroom in Paris.

Ever the New Yorker, Mother remained unfazed—for about three blocks. Then a steroid-fed musclehead who resembled Bibendum, the Michelin icon, sauntered by with an iguana on a leash. Mother turned to me with alarm. "Is this place safe?" she asked.

"Oh, sure," I lied. Actually, in Venice, you have to remain on guard at all times. Anything can happen. For instance, you're walking down the street, you see a cordoned-off area, a crowd of gawking onlookers, four squad cars, and eight heavily armed policemen in Bermuda shorts waving batons. And you have five seconds to make the quintessential Venice decision: Is it a murder or a movie?

In recent years the neighborhood has been featured in *Falling Down, The Doors, Point of No Return, White Men Can't Jump, L.A. Story,* and *Mixed Nuts,* plus almost every episode of the TV show *Baywatch,* or as we call it here, *Babewatch.* As for the murder statistics, well, I don't want to know (though I couldn't help hearing that there was a gang shooting on the boardwalk last week).

"Look how close you are to the ocean," Mother said tactfully.

I've repeated that particular phrase like a mantra since the day I moved in. The first six months I was dazed and revolted by the panoply of lunacy that surrounded me. I'd spent almost my entire adult life in Westwood Village, a primly landscaped, well-patrolled cluster of Spanish-style garden apartments, upscale stores, and movie theaters around UCLA. I thought nothing of walking my dear departed pugs, Bess and Stella, at midnight alone. I set terra-cotta pots of ivy geraniums and fairy primroses on my front steps, and they flourished for years. By contrast, an entire lemon tree vanished from my Venice garden overnight. The worst thing I could say about my Westwood neighbors is that a disconcerting number of them were lithe blonde coeds in denim miniskirts who zipped around on red Honda scooters. (After thirteen years, I began to feel like Dorian Gray's picture; I got older, but everyone around me stayed twenty-two.)

But those scooter girls never succumbed to an urge to dance in the street wearing nothing but seaweed, and I never overheard one recounting how she used pomegranates to simulate blood in a coven ritual—unlike my neighbors here. Ordinary life was pleasant, safe, and predictable; the closest I came to the dregs of society was on the front page.

Here, they're on the front lawn. Not too long ago, I went out to my car, intending to drive to an appointment. I found a hobo stretched out on the asphalt. "Do you mind if I sleep here?" he asked.

"Actually, I'm not nuts about the idea," I said politely, mindful of the fact that I was about to drive off and leave our home unattended. "If it's just a nap, I guess it's okay, but I'd rather you don't move in."

"I won't," he promised.

Call me suspicious, but I still didn't feel comfortable leaving. Then I had an inspiration. "Excuse me, sir," I said. "As long as you're here, could you do me a favor and watch the house?"

I don't know who was more confounded to hear those words come out of my mouth—the hobo or me. "Sure," he mumbled, and true to his word, our house was intact and he was gone when I returned. What startled me was that I took it in stride. I guess my comfort zone is wider than I think.

I wound up in Venice the usual way women wind up in places they wouldn't choose to be in a million years—I met a guy. Duke had dwelled by the ocean for so many years that for all purposes he had sprouted gills. When we met, he lived in the sloppiest apartment I'd ever seen, on the top floor of a once-charming seaside hotel gone to seed. I called it the Sty in the Sky. His flat had two notable features—a glorious view of the Pacific and the Pop-Up Panty sofa, a futon with a disconcerting tendency to disgorge lingerie and earrings that weren't mine.

At some point in our courtship—probably after I hurled my feminist precepts to the wind and washed the three months' worth of dirty dishes stacked up in his kitchen sink—I began spending weekends at the shore. In my mind, the ocean, sand, and palm trees are irrevocably linked with vacation, and I looked forward to the outing all week. Besides, my safe, upscale neighborhood made my then-boyfriend edgy. "All these children running around," Duke complained whenever he spent the night. "All these college students." (Why he was blasé about chain saw jugglers, crack dealers, doomsday preachers, and gangbangers was—and still is—beyond me.)

When we finally decided to set up house, there was no question as to where it would be. Duke already owned the bungalow we currently live in—he'd bought it in 1985 from a pair of elderly sisters in New York who had inherited it from their brother. It was the kind of place that no woman in her right mind ever would have purchased. A woman would have immediately realized that while the clapboard cottage was darling and close to the water, it was also sandwiched between two apartment buildings that were filled with—oh, how do I put this delicately?—lowlives. But the male sensibility seems to relegate lowlives to the same category as insufficient closet space—no big deal.

Duke had never lived in the house, or I could have refused to move in on the grounds of establishing neutral territory. He'd always rented it out. As luck would have it, one of Duke's tenants gave notice and the other disappeared, owing rent. The only logical thing for us to do was move in.

Back when I was single, I had a theory of dating called the Fifteen-Minute Mandate, and it went like this: Whatever you dislike in a date during the first fifteen minutes invariably sinks the relationship, be it fifteen days or fifteen years down the line. It applies to houses too. My first uncharitable thought after Duke ceremoniously carried me over the threshold was, "This place is dark and cramped."

And seven years later, it still is. Our cottage was built in 1912 as a weekend getaway for a family with a big Victorian home in Pasadena. It's not one of those glorious Craftsman-style California bungalows with an ornate hand-carved mantel, built-in bookshelves with leaded glass windows, and oak parquet floors that were built by Greene and Greene. Ours looks more like the work of cut-rate developers who put up blocks of hastily built cottages in the teens.

But unless we win the lottery, we're stuck here forever. Duke purchased the house when Venice real estate was much cheaper than it is today. It's actually less expensive to remodel—and probably even to knock it down and build from scratch—than it is to find a better place that we can afford this close to the sea.

I found this hard to believe until I talked to Artemis, an unrecognized artist who has a great following as a Realtor (her dour face is on all the SOLD signs). I called her after the debacle with Tex and asked what was on the market. Artemis stood to earn at least a new Mercedes on the deal, as she'd get commissions on the house we sold plus the one we bought. "How much were you thinking of putting into your place?" she asked. "A couple hundred thousand—at least?"

"Oh, at least," I said sarcastically.

"I'll check the multiple listings and get back to you," Artemis said with such a notable lack of enthusiasm that I asked if it was too much trouble. Apathy is a hallmark of the service industry in Los Angeles.

Artemis called me back a few days later. "Do you mind the Grand Canal?" she asked. I wasn't thrilled. By real estate standards, the tranquil canals—the remnants of Kinney's Venice-of-America development—are considered to be a step up. But to me, they're basically fetid, albeit scenic, sewers several blocks from the ocean where upscale Bohemians who swore they would never live in suburbia have erected multimillion-dollar glass, brick, and concrete monuments on thirty-by-ninety-foot lots. Parked out-side are the nineties versions of the station wagons they also swore they'd never own—monster four-by-fours with custom paint jobs, CD players, cellular phones, and talking car alarms that warn, "You are too close to the vehicle!"

One advantage to living in the Canal Zone is that if you want to bor-row a cup of sugar from your neighbor, you can paddle over in your in-flatable boat. The other bonus, the chance to share your yard with scores of loud and not especially fastidious ducks and geese, was eliminated when the Fish and Game Department announced that the waterfowl had contracted a deadly form of herpes and had to be destroyed.

The neighbors hastily organized an early-morning march to protest the quacktastrophe, and they appeared en masse brandishing mugs of de-signer coffee. (Curiously, these designer coffees have names once associ-ated with other mind-altering substances: Kona Delight, Thai Surprise, Colombian Gold.) The Save the Ducks movement made the national news, confirming everybody's worst suspicions about Venice Beach. Next, the residents called in their high-powered lawyers and obtained a tempo-rary restraining order. They spirited the ailing ducks away to a farm in the Valley for quarantine (in whose expensive jeep, I wondered?). Eventually, the order was overturned, and in an action that was condemned as an atrocity on the order of Kristallnacht, the Fish and Game Department rounded up the ducks and put them to death. The neighborhood mourned with a candlelight vigil.

Venetians will protest almost anything. When I first moved here, Duke took me to a rally. "It's a good place to meet the neighbors," he said. That should have been my first clue. A large crowd of ex-hippies waving home-made placards marched up the boardwalk. The leader began chanting, "What do we want?" I was expecting maybe shelter for the hundreds of homeless who had erected a large tent city on the sand.

But the crowd yelled, "Parking spaces!"

I tried to keep an open mind and asked Artemis for more details about the house.

"It's a Victorian charmer," she said, and I silently translated, "decrepit wreck." "Fourteen hundred square feet, two bedrooms, one bath, break-fast nook, fireplace, French doors, and a bonus room." A bonus room is Realtorspeak for a room that was built without permits, in this case a claustrophobic attic crawl space that could be used as an office (or a jail cell). It didn't seem promising. We already had three bedrooms (granted, two are too small to hold a queen-sized bed), two baths, and a fireplace.

Guess how much it was going to cost to get French doors and two hundred square feet?

"Only four ninety-nine," Artemis said. "It needs tender, loving care."

It may be difficult for a reader outside California to imagine what half a million dollars buys in local real estate—though if you pictured a one-story stucco box cheek-to-jowl with another stucco box on a crowded street, you'd be pretty close. I realize that most home-related expenses seem to be figured in some inflated Third World currency like lire, which have no relationship to the dollar as one knows it. But California prices are particularly surreal.

For instance, in the winter of 1992 our Lilliputian cottage was said to be worth over four hundred thousand dollars—down from half a million because the market was depressed. If we were to sell it and join the migration up Pacific Coast Highway, we could get an old mansion in downtown Portland or a gentleman's farm in the country with a custom-built three-thousand-square-foot showplace with acres of land around it. We could even move to Manhattan and get a one-bedroom, one-and-a-half-bath apartment, in a doorman building with a Fifth Avenue address. But Duke and I wanted to stay in Los Angeles. As long as we could live at the beach, that is.

I asked Artemis what else was on the market. "Nothing *that* cheap," she said. "If I were you, I'd build. In a couple years, if the market rebounds, you can probably get back what you put into it."

Probably is not a word I like to hear when I'm talking about our chances of recouping a huge investment. Though as Venice locations go, we're on a good street. (Translation: Nobody's been killed on it this year—knock wood.) It was easy to understand why Tex was eager to build a structural monument to his ego. All of the Los Angeles architects-of-the-moment have buildings within walking distances. Some of the landmarks within five hundred yards include Frank Gehry's Chiat Day headquarters, featuring a porte cochere in the form of drive-through forty-five-foot-high Claes Oldenburg binoculars; Brian Murphy's corrugated steel house for the actor Dennis Hopper; and Arata Isozaki's Bjornson house, a prism-shaped concrete structure on our block that reminds me of a "cootie-catcher," the folded paper fortune-telling device I made in third grade. Duke calls it "The Virus."

Santa Monica's Main Street, with Yuppie watering holes like Wolfgang Puck's Chinois on Main and Arnold Schwarzenegger's deli, Schatzi's on Main (or as the locals call it, Nazi on Main), is only a few blocks away, offering us the rarest of Los Angeles rarities—a pedestrian environment.

Unless I'm going into town for business, I can walk, skate, or bike to the bank, the video store, the post office, and the gym (Venice is the Vatican of physical fitness, with three huge bodybuilding gyms in a four-block radius). In a way, it's like living on an island. It would be paradisiacal if the island didn't boast seven panhandlers per city block. (You know times are tough when you go to Mexico City on vacation and think, wow, there are hardly any beggars in the street!)

To my husband, the sleaziness is part of the neighborhood's charm. "Venice tends to be hard on real estate speculative types," Duke says. "People who buy property the way some people get married—because they think someone has great potential and they're going to change them—have a hard time. This neighborhood doesn't change. The seediness is amazingly resistant."

Seediness is also not a word that inspires me to go into debt.

We put the house on hold—again—and flew back to my hometown of Baltimore for my nephew Adam's bar mitzvah. It was a little depressing. My sister was showing off pictures of her new four-bedroom, three-bath residence—a home to die for, with ivy creeping up the faded brick, a sunroom, family room, basement, deck, and patio. I was weak from envy. "Big kitchen, central air, beautiful rustic neighborhood with tree-lined streets, all-natural wood floors," said Laurie, who isn't averse to rubbing it in. "And we have two walk-in closets in the master bedroom."

I was secretly pleased to learn that Cousin Bernie, the master architect, had let them down. "He felt that since he wasn't charging me as much as he'd charge a stranger, he didn't need to spend a lot of time," my brother-in-law, the Shark confided. "The first time I used him it was an okay experience. But this time, he was harboring resentment that I wasn't aware of. For five months, when we thought he was working on our project, he wasn't. Finally, he said, 'We need to talk about money.' I said, 'Where's the product?' and he said, 'Well, I need a retainer first.' I said, 'Then why didn't you tell me?' He wouldn't talk to me about his bill. He wouldn't take my call. I guess he knew I was the Shark."

Of course my brother-in-law got even. "My cousin had a young associate who was privy to this information and kept trying to move the project along," the Shark said. "At some point, I fired my cousin and asked the associate if he wanted to bid on the job. He felt a little uncomfortable, but I said, 'I don't give a damn about your relationship with my cousin. Do you want the job or not?' "

Laurie told me that Bernie had stopped speaking to them and the associate was very talented and doing a marvelous job.

"You want to live in Chicago?" asked Duke.

No, but I wanted to be house-proud too.

I've always been a compulsive nester. Like an oriole, who weaves an elegant, orderly nest out of grass, fabric, floss, and cellophane, I have a constant yen to buy furniture, organize cabinets, and hang pictures. I suspect this is a trait that I inherited from my mother, who is religious in her pursuit of ambiance. "I even have baby pictures of you in a little flowered baby sack, sitting on flowered sheets," says Mother, who raised me to be fluent in textiles, color swatches, and antiques. "I took you to the decorating showrooms in New York when you were very young. I'd ask what you think of this fixture or that coffee table. You always had an opinion."

Duke claims I am always making nesting DNA, and this is true. I was the only person in my freshman dorm (and this was back in the early seventies, when any self-respecting coed was out demonstrating) with yellow gingham curtains and a matching spread.

I do not require a large sum of money, real estate, or even a vacant space to satisfy my lust for built-in bookshelves, fancy moldings, and oak peg-and-groove floors. Scattered around the country—and my house—are elaborate dollhouses that I started building fifteen years ago, when I was living in a small apartment. People questioned my sanity when I installed tiny, working crystal chandeliers and wired them to a transformer with threadlike filaments, laid thumbnail terra-cotta tiles and weensy shake shingles, and exulted when I made Austrian pouf window shades out of old lace handkerchiefs. But I have no apologies. I was retreating from a synthetic world of linoleum parquet and fireplaces with fake logs that glow when you turn on a gas jet.

Back at the bar mitzvah, my brother, Bobby, who owns a miniature art gallery that I built, tried to comfort me by telling me his remodeling horror story. Why do people feel compelled to share these nightmares? I'd much prefer they give me their banker's name or their contractor's, or better still, a large chunk of cash. Instead, I hear tales that make me cringe at the thought of changing more than a lightbulb.

Take Bobby's misadventure. Once upon a time, actually, only a few years ago, he lived with his wife, Robbie, and their two kids in a spacious two-story Pseudo Antebellum set in an unspoiled wood. Their mortgage payments were reasonable, and he had a lucrative, seemingly invulnerable management position in a family company. Then Robbie got pregnant, and they decided it was time for an architectural as well as a human addition. Bobby took out a second mortgage to build another story.

No sooner had they finished their addition than the unthinkable happened. His company decided to liquidate. "Within thirty days, I had no income and double the mortgage," Bobby recalled. He was forced to take a job he didn't like to meet his new payments.

"I got to the point where I hated the house," Bobby said. "It was too much to deal with. It was the combination of the money and all that room. The addition made the house so big that no maid wanted to clean it. They'd rather change an old guy's bag than clean three stories." It took him two years to get rid of his dream house. "Don't make the same mistake," he warned me. "Keep your nut small."

I had no desire to paint myself into a financial corner. But there was no denying that our house needed major surgery. I vowed that when I returned home I would find a way to hire Maurice, the personality-impaired but aesthetically gifted architect. I didn't like him, but I trusted him with the job.

Alas, fate intervened in the form of a fax from Tex, the master charmer. In it, he said he hoped he hadn't muddied the water with probably premature discussions on immediate and long-range financial overviews. Of course our existing house could be remodeled and expanded to meet our needs within an appropriate budget. Of course he would be happy to be our architect. Of course the final project would be great. He hoped we would consummate our agreement so that he could prepare conceptual designs.

"He does have the most experience," Duke said.

"But he has strange hypnotic powers," I argued.

"We can always fire him," said Duke. "Let's give him a shot."

At that moment, the pain of not making a decision seemed greater than the pain of going with Tex. Against my better judgment, I called and told him that he had the job.

"I've been waiting for this call for a month," Tex said with such joy that I was positive we had made the right choice. This moment of absolute certainty would vanish in a flash.

Fortunately, I didn't know it at the time.

CHAPTER
THREE

MY STOMACH began churning the day the contract arrived. Like all the other architects who'd preceded him, Tex sent over the AIA Standard Form of Agreement Between Owner and Architect, twelve pages of boilerplate that seemed to state that if an architect turns the front of your house into a flashy Las Vegas casino with an erupting volcano and burns down the back, he isn't responsible. And what's more, he can bill for his time and you're legally obligated to pay. Unlike all the other architects, Tex had drawn a neat line through any clause that offered us the faintest hope of coming out of the remodeling with our credit rating intact.

Gone was the bit about "The Architect shall submit to the Owner a preliminary estimate of Construction Cost based on current area, volume or other unit costs" and the part that says, "The Architect shall advise the Owner of any adjustments to the preliminary estimate of Construction Cost," and even the clause that says "following the Owner's approval of the latest preliminary estimate of construction cost. . . ." To make matters more unsettling our project was described as a "New Residence" instead of as a remodel.

"We can't possibly sign this," I told my husband.

"It's no big deal," Duke said blithely, "I'm sure we can work it out."

I haven't been so dumbfounded since he made the pugs an omelet. I've never known him to be blasé about something that could cost him money. That's my role in our relationship.

As with most couples, my husband and I have somewhat different values. To put it bluntly, he's cheap and I'm not. Last year, for example, our dishwasher became incontinent. Duke fixed it himself, triumphantly, but not before the linoleum floor tiles, which were a hideous (I didn't pick it) aqua-colored brick pattern to begin with, became unglued, creating a slip-break-your-neck-and-sue zone in the most traveled room of the house. "Honey," he said, on his way out the door to work, "maybe *we* should do something about this."

We called around. After getting a $700 estimate from an installer who was soused at ten in the morning, and a $500 estimate from a chain-smoker who showed up two hours late and kept calling me "hon," *I* finally located a pleasant lady who offered to send her brother out right away to do the job for $300, including materials. I called my husband at the office with the good news.

"That seems like a lot," Duke said. Mind you, he says that about everything. I suspect he comes from the Ninety-Nine-Cent Planet because he has outlandish ideas about what things should cost. (A haircut for $7.50? A new shirt, all cotton, for $12?) "I bet she'll do it for two-fifty."

"No way," she said, and after a few more calls, I concluded she was right. Undaunted, my husband announced plans to do something creative—"temporarily" staple the loose tiles down. After reflecting on how pleasant it would be to go into the kitchen in the middle of the night and a) trip and b) have a staple go through my bare foot, I scheduled an appointment behind his back. I figured I could do something creative too, like write a check for $250 and take the rest out of the cash machine. Our new floor was being buffed when Duke called. "What's that whirring sound?" he asked.

"Oh, it's the pugs," I replied. (And when he got home and saw the new adorable red-and-white floor, he didn't seem to mind.)

Still, I was nonplussed when he took Tex's contract demands in stride. "We've got to show this to a lawyer," I said. Not that I've ever known an attorney to significantly improve a contract negotiation. They usually suggest a few minuscule changes, which never seem to increase my income, and then bill me $400 for their time. (Billing hours invariably include a phone call during which the given attorney solicited my advice on restaurants or the upside potential of an affair with a personal trainer.) Even so, I was scared to proceed without legal counsel.

"It can't hurt to check," agreed Duke, who had no intention of doing the checking.

I called Josh, a superconnected, highly regarded Beverly Hills entertainment lawyer whom I theoretically have on retainer. I had to leave several increasingly panic-stricken messages with his secretary before he called me back. Not that I blamed him for stalling. I met Josh a few years ago through a mutual friend when a production company offered to option an idea I had for a television pilot. The deal seemed a little shady, so I decided to have an attorney check it out. Josh gave me a choice: He could bill me by the hour or take 5 percent of my future TV earnings. His hourly rate was $300, so I chose B. Lucky thing. Not only did the first deal vaporize, but so have several others. I reckon Josh has invested at least twenty billable hours in my career and recouped only his Xerox costs.

He finally got back to me on his way home from work, as he was driving through Beachwood Canyon, where car-phone reception is practically guaranteed to be problematic. I hurriedly explained about Tex's contract. "Is it the really long form or the short one?" Josh asked through crackling static.

"Is twelve pages considered short?"

"Actually either one totally protects him and leaves you open. You're going to be at his mercy if you sign it."

Naturally, the lawyer had a remodeling nightmare that he was all too eager to share. "We had a little cottage in the woods . . ." he began.

I felt a full-blown anxiety attack coming on.

"We loved the location, and when we got pregnant we decided to do an addition. I hired this architect, who came highly recommended. He'd done movie directors, artists, he was supposed to be the best. I told him that I wanted the addition to blend into the house. He said, 'I can do it. I can do it.' Then he went away and he brought back these drawings, which basically turned my cottage into a wall of stucco. I said, 'But this isn't the style I wanted.' He got all huffy and said, 'Well, this is the style I work in. This is my interpretation of your house.' "

"So, did you get someone else?" I asked, as a wave of nausea crashed over me.

"Hell no. I put the house on the market, found another house that had exactly what I wanted, bought it, and we moved. And I refused to pay the architect because he didn't do what I wanted. Of course, I could do that, because I didn't sign anything, so I wasn't locked in."

Luckily for my blood pressure, a sunspot erupted and we were cut off. I called my brother-in-law. The Shark recalled that he had signed the contract, with a slight modification. "I told the architect, look, I trust you, I know you're going to do a good job, but if you screw me over, you should know that I'll find you and kill you.' I thought that was incentive enough." I thought so too. The Shark, a gun fancier, has an arsenal in his house.

"Honey, why don't we just call Tex and tell him what's bothering us?" Duke asked. "I'm sure *we* can straighten this out."

Whenever he begins a sentence, "Honey, why don't we . . ." I know I am in trouble. The traditional division of labor in our household goes like this. Duke makes the sweeping executive decisions—for instance, a while back he said, "Honey, why don't we jack up the house and build another story underneath?"—and then he dashes off to work and leaves me to implement the details.

"Don't worry," he said, speaking of the home-raising. "It won't be intrusive."

I pictured myself sitting in my study, trying to meet a deadline while the floor below me was slowly being hoisted ten feet in the air. Duke, safe in his office at the university downtown, miles away so he couldn't possibly come home and supervise, would call every ten minutes with another helpful suggestion about the way it should be done (not that he's ever done it), which he'd want me to pass along to a less-than-receptive contractor. And just when I had the situation under control, my husband would toss another ingredient into the wok.

I took a deep breath and gave Tex a call. I don't know why I was so wary. Well, actually I did have a clue. Right after we hired Tex, no more than an hour after our check had cleared, he confided that one of his great pleasures in life was playing an industrial-strength truth-or-dare game. I had never heard of this amusement.

"Seven to ten people sit in a room," Tex explained, "and for two hours we take turns beating one person up verbally. Everyone gets their turn in the hot seat." This sounded like hell to me, but Tex insisted I'd enjoy it. "We try to keep it from being too destructive," the architect said.

"We have a few questions about the contract," I began hesitantly.

"Sure," Tex said. "Shoot."

"It says 'New Residence.' But it's supposed to be a remodel."

"My mistake. We'll add, 'Or Remodel.' Anything else?"

I felt guilty for thinking that he wasn't reasonable. "We're not crazy about the fact you've crossed out all the money clauses."

"Well, I can't change that," said Tex. "Only a fool would change that."

"But it's part of the standard contract. Every other architect we've talked to has let it stand."

"If they knew what they were doing, they wouldn't have done that. It's not possible for any architect worth his salt to tell you what something will cost."

That wasn't what I'd call a reassuring argument. "Then how can we budget?" I wondered.

It bounced right off him. "There are more lawsuits over prices. Architectural firms are going out of business because of that clause. I can't control the price. Contractors control the price, and they can charge whatever they think they can get."

"Yes, but can't you give us a clue?"

"Let me give you a for-instance," he continued without taking a breath. "I can look up in books what the current cost of framing and concrete is and get one hundred and fifty thousand. And I could be on target. But when we bid it out, one bid could be one twenty and another could be two hundred."

Even speaking hypothetically he was over our budget. "We'd feel a lot more comfortable if there are price controls."

"Hey, I know what things cost and I can guide you, but to put it in a legally binding document, I can't do that," said Tex.

"I don't think our lawyer will let us sign this," I said. Not that our lawyer was calling us back. (In fact, our lawyer moved soon after and "forgot" to notify us.)

"Almost all the lawyers I've known personally have been bastards," Tex replied.

I hung up, exasperated. "He doesn't listen to a word I say," I complained. "He just says what he wants over and over until he wears you down." This is a strategy all too familiar to me, as my mother uses it with stunning success. For instance, a couple of years ago I was in New York on business. I was scheduled to fly home on a Saturday morning. On Thursday night, my mother, who lives in the city, called to tell me that a big blizzard was predicted for Saturday morning. I decided to fly back Friday night.

"You can't," Mother said. "I've made dinner reservations."

I pointed out that we'd had dinner together every night that week and I didn't want to get stuck in the snow.

"But I've made dinner reservations," she said again and again and again.

I stayed for dinner and got caught on the runway at Kennedy when they closed the airport due to the blizzard. Not for the first time, I felt that being reasonable was a handicap in life.

"I'll handle Tex," Duke assured me. "I'm sure I can straighten this out."

Forgive me for being dubious, but interpersonal communication is not his strong suit. My husband believes that if he thinks something really hard, then the other person hears it. And when it comes to receiving information, well, most of the time Radio DUKE is off the air. On the other hand, it's not like I was making any progress.

The next day Duke proudly announced that Tex had agreed to tack on an addendum to his standard form. "You just have to wait him out when he goes on like that," said my husband. I was impressed for about five minutes—until the updated version arrived by fax. All it did was further protect Tex. "The Owners understand that contractors determine construction cost estimates and that the Architect cannot accurately project construction cost," read the most notable addition.

Tex had also talked my husband into a budget of "only a hundred and seventy thousand dollars," a sum we did not possess. "Relax," said Duke, which only made me more nervous. "We can borrow it from my credit union at work and only increase our monthly payments by three hundred dollars. Admittedly, math is not my strong suit, but I didn't see how that was possible.

I was certain the architect had three little sixes branded on his body somewhere.

"Honey, let's just sign it," said Duke. "Trust me. It's going to work out fine."

I reminded myself that we still had the right to fire the architect on seven days' notice. Against my better judgment, I mailed Tex a thousand-dollar retainer. Forty-eight hours later, I opened the mail and discovered a $3,700 bill from a surveyor I'd never heard of, let alone hired. I called Beelzebub in alarm.

"Oh, you weren't supposed to see that," Tex said cheerfully. "I put the bid out to four people. He's the highest." The surveyor he really wanted to use was "only fifteen hundred."

I asked if it was necessary to survey our property so soon. "It has to be done at the beginning so whatever the design thinking is, it doesn't take in account property that isn't yours," said Tex. "If a property line is five feet different, then that could greatly affect what plans could be."

It seemed sensible. On the other hand, I dislike having four-figure bills appear in my mailbox without warning, and since we hadn't gotten our miraculous loan yet, it was wreaking havoc with our monthly budget. "Do we need any other preliminary investigations?"

"Maybe a geologist in the future. And we could get a soil engineer to dig down and take a soil sample. And a structural engineer, depending on the complexity of the building."

"What are we looking at, money-wise?"

"One, two, three thousand dollars," Tex said airily. "But we can wait on some of that."

"Good," I said firmly. "Wait."

The next day I got a call from Dan, our designated surveyor. He wanted to set up an appointment later in the week. "I'm free Thursday," he said.

"I'm on deadline Thursday," I said. "I'll be pretty busy."

"We won't bother you. You won't even know we're there."

He got that right. I didn't hear a peep out of him because he never showed up. It was a different story the next day, when Dan, a tall, gaunt, praying mantis–like fellow and his taller, scrawnier partner, Don, finally arrived. I was all agog, elated by the thought that after all the thinking, the planning, and the agony of indecision, our remodeling was about to begin. I remembered the stirring opening paragraph from Tracy Kidder's masterpiece, *House*, when the surveyor opens a mahogany box, removes an antique steel-and-brass transit that looks like a spyglass, and dramatically mounts it on a tripod in the middle of a New England hay field.

Reality was anticlimactic. Dan set up a "total station," a computerized gizmo on a tripod that looked like an expensive camera. He explained that it was an electronic theodolite and that it measured horizontal and vertical angles by bouncing a signal off a prism glass. "In the old days, when George Washington was a surveyor, they used a transit," Dan said.

I stared blankly. I have the science acumen of a flea. I'm not sure whether this is due to the fact that I spent my formative years at an arty private school where the science teacher refused to teach until the Vietnam war ended or simply that I was born without the part of my brain that governs the ability to learn mathematics and physics.

Don persisted, and I finally grasped that the transit was basically a compass and a telescope mounted on a carpenter's level. He should have quit while he was ahead, but he felt that it was important for me to understand fully.

"Old George Washington would look through his scope, point the way he wanted to go, and copy the numbers down," he said. "Then, in the late forties and fifties, they developed the theodolite. Instead of having to manually read the numbers, they automatically came up on a screen and the surveyor wrote them down. Now everything is done electronically. I don't read anything. I just push buttons."

Fifteen hundred dollars seemed like a lot to pay someone to just push buttons. But I thanked him for the information and went back into the house. I may not have understood much about surveying, but I did master the first two rules of remodeling.

Rule Number One: Everything costs at least a thousand dollars.

Rule Number Two: Everything is intrusive.

I was sitting at my computer trying to finish a story when I noticed a long arm outside my window. "Building corner," hollered Dan, holding out a reflector glass.

"Got it," cried Don, who was manning the computerized doohickey in the backyard.

"Tree," Dan shouted.

"Got it," Don bellowed back.

"Sidewalk."

"Got it."

"Wall."

"Got it."

After an hour, I'd had it. I went outside. "What's going on?" I asked casually, as if I wasn't ready to strangle them both.

"Oh, I'm just telling him what to write in the data collector," said Dan. I got the feeling that he needed something to do. After all, the measurements went straight into an electronic data collector, which plugged in to a Hewlett-Packard PC back in his office. Then Plotting Software turned the points recorded in the field into dots on a map. All Dan had to do was print them out.

But I've never known a man to minimize his effort.

"We have to spread the map out on a drafting table and hook up the dots, you know, like the follow-the-dots game you play as a kid," Dan said gravely. I was reminded of a Betty Crocker commercial in which a housewife takes credit for brownies she baked from a mix that only required her to add an egg and some water and stir.

A week later Dan dropped off a beautiful map, with our names neatly hand-lettered in block print. Duke and I beamed with pleasure. It looked so official. "I delivered a copy to Tex this morning," the surveyor said, and I imagined the architect hunched over his drafting table, sketching furiously.

There was just one thing I kind of wondered about. On our surveyor's map, the outline of our house was marked by a very faint dotted line.

"Oh, we do that when the architect plans to tear the house down," Dan said. "That way he can design around it."

"But this is a remodel," I said. "He's not going to tear the house down."

"Are you sure?" Dan said. "Usually on a remodel Tex asks for specific measurements on the existing structure. I'm sure he plans to knock it down."

It was not a good sign.

CHAPTER
FOUR

I'VE WORKED the plans up two ways," Tex said as he unrolled a sheath of giant tissue paper and spread it out on his big marble desk. I could barely focus on his words, I was so dazzled by his mastery of the line and by the sight of our names, exquisitely lettered on the preliminary drawings. "Here's what happens if we remodel the existing floor and put on a second-floor addition."

It was a contractor's bonanza. Tex wanted to scoop out our house like it was a Halloween pumpkin, then flip the existing floor plan so that the bedrooms would be in the front of the house and the living and dining rooms would be in back (and virtually everything in between would have to be replaced). Our current front and back doors would be closed off and replaced by an imposing side entrance. The coup de maître, a second floor with a master bedroom suite and an extra bedroom, would be built over the back on pillars, so as not to tax the existing foundation.

"It's ingenious," Duke marveled, walking his fingers over the state-of-the-art kitchen, adjoining pantry, and the covered carport. "You managed to fit in everything we want."

The maestro glowed with the pride of creation. "It gives you more light, high ceilings, an extra bedroom, a big kitchen, a big master bedroom and bath, and a deck."

I hated to inject a note of reality, but it didn't look like anyone else would. "How much?"

"I'll get to that," Tex said with ill-concealed annoyance, and continued on with the show. He flicked his wrist and unfurled another set of drawings. "Here's what happens if we knock the house down and build from scratch."

To my untrained eye, the new structure looked a lot like the remodel, though according to the cross section it would be built on four or five lev-

36

els. "When you enter, you'd walk downstairs to the bedrooms," said Tex.

I'm intensely claustrophobic and detest the idea of sleeping underground.

"It's just a few steps," Tex said, making a little dismissive gesture. He diverted my attention to a roof deck with a circle icon, which I learned was the universal symbol for a Jacuzzi. A pair of parallel lines indicated a fifth level, where the architect envisioned a tiny widow's walk. "It will give you a sea view."

Maybe if we were giraffes . . . The building next door is four stories high, and an even taller complex impedes the sight line down the block. "Do you have a picture of what the house will look like?" I asked.

"It's all here," Tex said, indicating the blueprints.

"No," I clarified, "a sketch of the outside. So I can tell what style the house is and how it will look from the street."

The architect looked at me as if I were out of my mind. "I didn't do that," he said. "We never do that."

It was a singular but fortuitous lapse in salesmanship. Had he shown me something that I could visualize, then I might have fallen in love. And if I'd fallen in love, I'd have moved heaven and earth to manifest my heart's desire. Luckily, there was no way I could get emotionally attached to a set of technical drawings, though my husband was salivating as though he were reading a menu, anticipating a savory meal. Then again, Duke could have just been thinking about lunch, which along with dinner, breakfast, and snacks are among his favorite subjects of contemplation.

I pointed to a suspicious-looking square in our backyard labeled "Future Dwelling."

"That's the studio rental," said Tex. "I estimate you can rent it out for around twelve fifty a month."

I could have sworn we'd already had this conversation. "But we don't want tenants," I said.

"Tenants might be okay," my husband murmured supportively.

At any given moment, there are at least six FOR RENT signs on our block.

"Studios are different," said Tex. He told us about an old warehouse that he converted into studios.

"I don't want tenants," I repeated, adding a little chill to my tone.

It bounced right off him. "If you think about it, you'll see I'm right," Tex said.

Suddenly, I had an epiphany. We were looking at a fancy rendition of the plan that the architect had drawn on the napkin in the Chinese restaurant. "It's the napkin," I whispered to my husband.

But Duke was far removed from reality. He was drifting on a cloud of insulation foam through Home Owner's Never-Never Land, where steel framing costs pennies and if you open up a wall, you never find dry rot or faulty wiring. He didn't even flinch when Tex produced a list of estimated prices and we learned that the beautiful showcase remodel behind door number one would set us back $257,000. And the designer home behind the curtain, complete with studio work space (and six starving artists waiting to move in and trash the place) could be ours for a mere $352,000.

The estimates came with a comforting disclaimer:

THE SQUARE-FOOT COSTS ARE THE ARCHITECT'S GUESS OF THIS PROJECT'S CONSTRUCTION COST WITH MINIMAL FINISHES. THE ARCHITECT DOES NOT DETERMINE COST.

I lost interest immediately. It was like reading *Architectural Digest:* Nothing was affordable, so where was the fun? Given the conventional wisdom that remodeling costs twice what you anticipate, we could be looking at a $700,000 project—and that wasn't even including our original mortgage. And it's not like we had anywhere near this kind of money tucked away in the bank.

"I guess the next step is to get financing," Duke said enthusiastically.

Maybe he had a secret bank account in the Cayman Islands.

Tex offered some parting advice about variable rates, brokers, and take-out construction loans. "There's a lot of ways to do this," he said. "You've got to be creative." We filed out, a study in extremes. Duke was elated and I was so furious that if you could have harnessed the anger pulsing through my body, it could have lit up New York.

"It's the napkin," I sputtered. "He's probably going to charge us thousands of dollars for those drawings, and we got the same damn napkin."

"It's a really elegant cloth napkin," Duke said ruefully. "Folded into a swan."

"He's the devil," I said.

But he's good with napkins.

A few days later, I was having breakfast with Anna, a colleague. She asked me how the remodel was coming, and I almost cried. "I don't know what I'm going to do. The architect wants to build Six Flags Over Venice in our backyard. He's three times over budget, and we haven't even broken ground."

"Are you certain you need an architect?" she asked. "Maybe all you really need is a contractor with a good sense of design." I suspected what we *really* needed was a winning Lotto ticket, but I desperately wanted to believe that remodeling wasn't the impossible dream.

"I should put you together with our contractor," Anna said. "Walt's wonderful. He just completed our kitchen, and I'm crazy about the guy. He's polite and artistic, literate and wise. He's even neat."

If I didn't know better, I would have sworn she was having an affair with the guy. "Is he expensive?"

"The first time we used Walt, he was the middle bidder," Anna said. "We don't bid jobs out anymore, but we gave Walt's name to a couple of friends and they both said he came in next to lowest. He's wonderful about working within a budget, and all the subcontractors who work for him are pleasant."

Three days later, Walt, my would-be savior, knocked on the door. I was relieved to see a large, sturdy, sandy-haired man with broad fingers like joists, who looked like he could hold up a building. Actually, he bore a startling resemblance to Pops Larson, the fictional sage of Builder's Emporium. Walt inspected our house like a doctor examining a new patient. He even had a doctor's disconcerting habit of muttering cryptic remarks.

"It's concrete on sand," he said.

"Is that good?"

"It's okay if the sand's not moving. Old foundations. Probably can't bear on them. Could be termites."

I had to smile. A few months after we were married, I noticed a pile of black poppy-seed-like pellets on our bedroom windowsill. Duke explained that they were termite droppings. "Damn," he said. "I had the house tented a couple years ago." He wasn't enthusiastic about moving out for three days while it was tented and fumigated again.

A few weeks later, I noticed a newspaper ad hawking the latest weapon

in the war against termites—electricity. A "termite-elimination technician" would come to my house with a souped-up stun gun and shoot a
lethal current down the tunnels to shock the queen. I couldn't figure out
how the current found the queen (as opposed to say the maid and the
princes), but I was in favor of any nontoxic system. I suggested that we
make an appointment for a free consultation.

"It's not necessary," said Duke. "I can do it myself." He claimed that
all he needed to rig up a probe was an extension cord and a couple of
screws.

Those films they showed in grade school about the hazards of playing
with electricity made a big impression on me (though my husband has
been known to check for gas leaks with a match). By the time Duke got
to the part about first wetting down the wood, I was howling like a car
alarm.

"Are you out of your mind?" I screeched. "What if something happens? What will I tell your parents?" I did not look forward to calling my
in-laws and saying, "Sorry, but your son died electrocuting bugs."

"If it makes you feel better, you can stand outside and hold the master
switch, just in case," Duke said. "There's no danger if you're wearing
sneakers." (I wouldn't bet my life on that.)

I made him promise that he wouldn't try this until I had a chance to
take out a sizable insurance policy on his life. But a few days later I was on
the phone talking to a radio producer when my eye wandered up to the
windowsill and zeroed in on two fresh singe marks. "Excuse me," I said
hastily, "but my husband tried to electrocute the termites." I slammed
down the phone and hurried through the house expecting to stumble
upon my beloved's corpse. Duke was lying on the couch, covered by a
blanket of pugs, watching his favorite TV show, a Korean soap opera. (He
had wisely resisted the temptation to play dead on the floor to give me a
little scare.) "The current wasn't strong enough," he said with a sigh.

So I didn't have much hope when Walt, the contractor, mentioned termite damage. But I wasn't depressed. Unlike the architect, who spoke an
incomprehensible structural argot, the contractor talked cold cash. He
made remodeling seem as straightforward as going to the market and
picking up a few provisions. If there's one thing I understand, it's shopping.

"Normal construction costs are a hundred dollars a square foot for a
new house," he said plainly, "but for a place as old as this, you've got to
figure one fifty—at least."

We showed him Tex's blueprints and explained that we wanted to remodel, as opposed to building from scratch. "It makes no sense to keep this place," the contractor said, though he did concede that remodeling would give us an advantage with the banks. To my horror, he concurred with Tex's estimates and offered no discount solutions. (He did offer to take the plans off our hands, to use in a new house that he wanted to build, but Tex's contract prohibited that.)

"Building a house is an endothermic reaction, like fusion," Walt explained. "You've got to pump energy into it. Until you get into the hundred-thousand-dollar range you don't see a heck of a lot. But for two hundred thousand you get four times as much work."

For $200,000 I could get a brand-new house. All I had to do was leave California.

"Do you want to know what a generic house costs?" the contractor asked.

"Why not?"

The prices below don't include landscape, skylights, air conditioning, fancy finishes such as mahogany wainscoting, Javanese carved cabinetry, or hand-thrown tiles. Or whimsical personal touches such as the deluxe "Gift Wrapping Room," complete with custom built-ins to hold wrapping paper and tape, that nest-featherer extraordinaire Candy Spelling installed in her Beverly Hills mansion.

Generic House-Cost Breakdown	
Appliances	$ 2,000
Carport	$ 2,000
Concrete	$ 4,000
Contractor's Fee	$ 45,000
Demolition	$ 5,000
Design, Engineering, Permits	$ 10,000
Doors and Windows	$ 9,000
Drywall	$ 6,000
Exterior	$ 10,000
Fireplace	$ 1,500
Fixtures	$ 3,000
Floor Covering	$ 1,000
Hardware	$ 1,500
Hardwood Floors	$ 8,700
Heating	$ 3,500

Insulation	$ 1,000
Kitchen Cabinets	$ 10,000
Labor	$ 10,000
Lumber	$ 10,000
Millwork	$ 1,500
Mirrors	$ 1,000
Plumbing	$ 8,000
Paint	$ 9,000
Sheet Metal	$ 800
Shower Door and Enclosures	$ 1,000
Simplified Roof	$ 5,000
Supervision	$ 25,000
Tile and Labor	$ 4,000
Tile Material	$ 1,500
Wiring	$ 8,000
Grand Total	$ 208,000

Notwithstanding the $45,000 contractor's fee, the additional $25,000 for a supervisor whom Walt assured us would also do "a little finishing carpentry," the fact that kitchen cabinets cost the same as labor, and the grand total, it all seemed completely reasonable—if you had the resources of Donald Trump.

"Who does the design work?" I asked out of curiosity.

Walt explained that he worked with various designers, some more creative than the rest. "For this project I'd bring in our meat-and-potatoes guy," he said, and Duke and I visibly winced. If we were going to wind up in the poorhouse, it wasn't going to be for meat and potatoes. "I'll need around two thousand dollars for him to get started."

For the first time, I found myself thinking charitable thoughts about Tex, who had just sent us a $2,500 bill for his stupendous napkin. I loathed the idea of all of that money going to waste. "Tell me," I said. "Are there *any* advantages to using an architect?"

"Well, if you're going to go up over three stories, you need one," the contractor conceded. "And if you're the kind of person who really cares how something looks."

I shuffled my feet guiltily. How superficial am I? I buy everything—from the toaster to my computer—on the basis of how cute it is. And one of the things I love most about my husband is that he's aesthetically particular (I could never have married a man who liked gold shag carpets). We thanked Walt and promised we'd be in touch. Then we did what we always do when we're in a jam.

We left town. (Our marriage is held together with airline tickets.)

On the Friday before the Fourth of July, we tossed the tube of plans into the trunk of the car and drove up the coast to Santa Barbara to visit Duke's folks. I figured if anyone could talk my husband down from his home owner's hallucination it was his father, Earl, arguably the world's most maddening human. Not that he's unkind, quite the contrary, but he enjoys being difficult. (There could be a game show where contestants are locked in a booth with him and timed to see how long it takes them to lose their cool.) A typical exchange: In preparation for a family picnic, Earl asked, "Do you think we have enough bottled water?" Duke checked the supply and decided, "I better buy more." "Why?" his father responded. "We have plenty."

I was cheerful and relaxed after a lovely drive up Pacific Coast Highway. We pulled into my in-laws' driveway, and Earl opened the car door, hugged me, and offered to take us to dinner at the Sizzler, where he had a two-for-one coupon. "So what are your plans?" he asked.

Duke shrugged. "I don't know yet. We just arrived." He kissed his mother and followed her into the kitchen to heat up a bowl of her special lentil soup. After consuming this delicacy my husband traditionally falls into a comalike sleep.

"Why doesn't anyone tell me their plans?" Earl groused.

"Because we haven't made any," I said evenly. And for good reason. Earl has never heard a plan that he didn't feel compelled to change. "We'll probably visit with you for a while, then go take the pugs for a walk on the beach." Clara loves to chase seagulls, a passion she can't indulge in on Venice Beach, where a pug on the sand can result in a $36 fine from the Animal Police (who, curiously, are on horseback).

"I need to know your exact plans," said Earl. I asked if he had anything scheduled that could pose a conflict of interest. He shook his head and then pressed for a timetable again. "I didn't even know when you were coming," he complained.

My blood pressure shot up sharply. Unlike my husband, who has been known to call me and say he'll be right home and then show up five hours later, I am compulsively prompt. The night before I'd called my mother-in-law and told her that we'd arrive around two-thirty. Then, just to be on the safe side, when we'd passed most of the Malibu beach traffic, I'd called from the car and told Earl that we would arrive by two-fifteen. I checked my watch. "It's two-seventeen now," I snapped. "So give me a break."

Earl batted his eyes innocently. "Why does everyone pick on me?"

Duke awakened from his coma before I did any physical damage. "Speaking of plans," he segued smoothly, "would you like to see what we're thinking of doing to the house?" He went to the car and brought in the tube of drawings, or, as I referred to it, the Tube O' Cash.

I chewed my thumbnail. As a rule, my husband and I aren't inclined to give in-laws (or anyone else) a window of opportunity in which to meddle. But with our house, we had no choice, because Duke's parents were on the deed. When my husband purchased it, they lent him $20,000 toward the down payment, not because he needed it, but because they didn't think he should tie up all his available cash. It was impossible to refinance without their cooperation. "I'm sure there won't be a problem," Duke assured me.

I had doubts. Sometime after our first anniversary, Earl offered to sell me their share of the house so my name would be on the deed, too. At the time I was broke, but I thanked him for the opportunity and promised to keep it in mind. Not that there was any chance of forgetting; whenever he saw me he nudged. "Ask your parents for the money," he urged. I didn't want to. "Then take out a loan. You should be on the deed."

I couldn't argue, especially since I was paying half the mortgage and expenses on a house that wasn't considered joint property. And a year later, when I came into an inheritance, I told my father-in-law that I'd be delighted to write him a check. To my stupefaction, Earl seemed stunned—affronted even—by the suggestion. "I can't negotiate with you," he said. "It wouldn't be fair to my son."

A while back the newspapers ran a shocking story about a woman who checked her ailing father out of a nursing home and then abandoned him at the local racetrack. Suddenly, I was filled with empathy for the woman. "Hollywood Park," I muttered menacingly under my breath. I closed my checkbook and refused to discuss the matter again.

"You're overreacting," Duke said at the time. "Earl is just trying to be friendly."

Indeed, in the long run, my father-in-law did me a terrific favor. My husband didn't want the house to come between us, so he put me on the deed in exchange for half of his initial investment. (This is embarrassing to admit, but we have a somewhat Byzantine financial system of His, Hers, and Ours accounts.) However, his parents remained on title, too.

With great fanfare, Duke spread Tex's handiwork out on his parents' dining room table. Earl seemed rather impressed. "My, you certainly put a lot of thought into this," he said. "And money."

"Not that much," Duke said defensively. His father taught him that he'd go to hell if he paid retail. (Earl, a self-described tightwad, is the kind of zealous bargain hunter who believes reversible clothes are a great idea.)

My mother-in-law looked furtively for a box marked NURSERY. "Oh, good, there's an extra bedroom," she smiled.

They both agreed that the plans were spectacular and that remodeling as opposed to building from scratch was the way to go. "Are you sure it's not cheaper to buy something else?" Earl asked pro forma.

"We can't buy anything better," Duke said. I had to agree. In the spring of 1993, Southern California real estate prices went into free fall. But lower prices seemed to apply only to the house you wanted to sell, not the one you wanted to buy.

"It's a good time to refinance," Earl noted. "Interest rates have never been lower." He asked if we wanted him to stay on title.

"If you wouldn't mind," Duke said. "It will make it easier for us to qualify for a jumbo" (a loan over $203,150). He hastily assured his parents that we'd have no trouble making the payments and reminded them that we'd never required financial assistance.

Earl smiled graciously. "Whatever you need, just let me know," he said. "I'll do whatever I can to help." He even put aside his Sizzler coupon and took us out for sushi.

I returned home in a dither, afraid I'd lost all my powers of discernment. I felt guilty for thinking my father-in-law would be uncooperative. I felt guilty for being negative about Tex. I felt guilty for believing that my husband was out of touch with reality. I was so distressed I placed an emergency call to Dr. Pangloss, my longtime therapist. He's of the eclectic California school of psychology (cousin to California cuisine) and advocates an exotic blend of cognitive therapy, Buddhism, Sufism, and New Age mumbo-jumbo. His most recent theory is that the behavior of humans is mirrored in their automobiles (coming soon, Car Therapy). I couldn't scoff though; the starter on my Audi was on the blink.

"It sounds like the architect, your husband, and your father-in-law are operating in sort of a delusional state," Pangloss said. "But delusional states can be very powerful." (Only in L.A. could a mental health professional say this and seem rational.)

"But we can't afford it."

"It's a waste of energy to try and stop them. Why don't you give up control? You might be surprised what they can accomplish."

I'd be shocked. But that night, I had a chat with God. I asked Her to give me a clear sign that we should proceed with the remodel. Positive omens could include a three-picture deal at Universal. The discovery of gold or oil in our backyard. Or maybe I could save William Gates's life. I let go and prepared to wait.

It didn't take very long.

CHAPTER FIVE

I WOKE TO Dennis Weaver's voice on my clock radio. "Have you been dreamin' of havin' enough money to fix up your home?" he drawled over some saccharine, pseudo-Copland western music. Apparently, the bank that Dennis shills for was itchin' to fix me up with a low-interest/no-cost/no-points home loan. True to my vow to relinquish control, I hit the snooze button and went back to sleep.

Duke and I had agreed that he'd be in charge of the loan-application process. I have no natural aptitude for high finance, get panic attacks just reading about conforming rates, qualifying ratios, and jumbo loans, and above all, I detest haggling. By contrast, my husband has bought and sold a couple of houses and likes nothing better than to wrench a few extra dollars from a salesperson.

"Leave it to me, honey," he said. "It's a man's job, to go out in the forest and hunt down the quarry."

Usually I'm a big fan of gender stereotyping when it saves me from doing something I dislike, like changing the oil in my car, but in this case I was wary. My husband, the big-picture guy, invariably sticks me with the grunt work. I wouldn't mind if he said, "Good job, honey," after I've made a million phone calls and gotten all the ducks in a row, but instead he points out the flaws. I do more grunt work, he pays no attention, until the very last minute, when he steps in, performs a high-profile glamour task, and hogs all the credit. I believe that people's occupations mirror their behavior.

And Duke spent years as a newspaper editor.

Then again, my sister let *her* husband handle the financial end of home buying, and she had nothing but raves. Granted, Laurie is a publicist, who habitually puts a positive spin on things (she recently left me the perky message, "Hi, guess what? I have a mild concussion"), and the Shark is a trial lawyer who thrives on confrontation. (It also didn't hurt that his family owns a bank.)

"It was a complete luxury," Laurie raved. "He put together all the paperwork and just told me what he needed. I never could have done it myself. I was petrified. I've never been very neat about my finances. He said stuff like 'I can't believe you didn't keep all your payroll stubs.' "

This was disquieting, since my sister makes four times as much as I do and has no reason to be insecure about finances.

Though maybe everyone has a reason to be insecure about finances.

"I had a problem with American Express eight years ago when my old company didn't reimburse me for my expenses," Laurie said gravely, like she had kidnapped a child. "I had a major black dot. Oh, and they wanted to know why I was late on my Saks bill in June 1990. To tell you the truth, I didn't know. I had to write these little letters explaining why I had these problems. 'I am sorry I was not as responsible as I should have been. I really didn't mean it.' "

Hawkeye the Loan Hunter made a couple of high-profile phone calls, and the next day our mailbox was stuffed with bulging envelopes from our neighborhood lending institution, First Bank of the Boardwalk, and his company credit union—supposedly our financial ace in the hole. His plan was to make a test run on our local bank to expose our weaknesses before he zoomed in for the kill. It sounded sensible. Yet for three weeks the bulging envelopes lay unopened on the sideboard.

"I'll get right on it," said Hawkeye when I asked about the paperwork. Then he fried up a mess of potstickers, setting off every smoke alarm in the house, plopped down on the sofa, and channel-surfed between a Mexican telenovela and an Armenian variety show. Clara, who has elevated begging into an art form (Duke says the pugs' original hunting instincts have mutated into begging), sat at his feet, glaring at the dumplings, emitting indignant little yips until he relented.

"I'm giving it top priority," Duke assured me a few weeks later, as he huddled in front of his glowing computer screen, monitoring a flame war on the Internet.

Clearly, he was counting on another one of those miracles that happen around our house on a regular basis—like the miracle of the dirty shirts, which arise from the crumpled wad under the bed, drag themselves to the dry cleaner, and then hang themselves up in his closet, shrouded in plastic, neatly pressed. At the 1939 World's Fair, GE displayed a wondrous House of the Future, powered entirely by electricity. Our wondrous House of the Future is powered by me.

The loan applications consisted of seven pages of increasingly depressing and anxiety-provoking questions designed to send anyone without lifetime job security and a financial cushion the size of Roseanne into the Slough of Despond. (Moreover, each bank phrased the questions differently, so I had to review my inadequacies again and again.) I remained upbeat throughout the name, address, and social security number sections, then apprehension set in when I had to write in the amount we wanted to borrow. I get distressed owing Visa more than $250; the idea of being several hundred thousand dollars in debt rendered me catatonic—especially since the application thoughtfully included a little table that revealed that over thirty years we were going to have to pay back half a million bucks.

Next came "Assets," and the only boxes I could check were "Savings Accounts" and "Cars." Life insurance? No. Vested interest in retirement fund? Not yet. Stocks? Not worth mentioning. Net worth of business owned? Ha! Do you receive primary income from a trust? Oh, how I wish! I regretted each Bohemian life choice that had brought me to this moment—not listening to my mother and marrying a doctor, not listening to my father and getting an MBA, choosing journalism over a lucrative career in the television situation-comedy joke mines.

"Need any help, honey?" asked Hawkeye, who was nestled on the sofa, eating a confection that he'd whipped up with nectarines, yogurt, granola, and dried cranberries, watching Korean wrestling on channel 18.

"Shoot me," I replied.

The ultimate humiliation was the request for copies of the last two years' federal income taxes, which was required because I'm self-employed. As luck would have it, the years in question were the worst of my life: the year I lost my job as a columnist and the year I had breast cancer and had to be hospitalized twice (not for complications, thank God, but for a mastectomy and subsequent reconstructive surgery. Being successfully remodeled myself only made me more eager to make over the house).

"Don't worry, it'll be fine," said my gainfully employed husband, whose powers of denial are infinitely greater than mine. As long as I was filling stuff out, he kept ordering more and more bulging envelopes from supposedly eager lending institutions. Each bombarded the airwaves with sensational offers for no-cost, no-points, low-interest loans, yet I couldn't help noticing at the bottom of each application was a request for $300.

"It's the last bastion of bait and switch," Duke said disgustedly. "You see all these glowing offers and you phone up and find out that the loan in the ad is totally nailed down. You cross-examine them and eventually learn that you'll get two thirds of the money you want for twice as much interest." Holding firm to principle, Hawkeye called First Bank of the Boardwalk and bullied them into waiving the $300 charge.

I mailed the application and awaited judgment. I figured we'd hear right away, since Dennis Weaver and all the other radio pitchmen promised overnight credit decisions. Of course Dennis didn't specify *which* night they'd decide.

Three weeks passed. Hawkeye suggested that I make a follow-up call (naturally, he was too busy putting out fires at work to perform such a low-profile task). After six tries, I reached Joey, our designated loan officer, or as he styled himself, our loan counselor. "Gotta run," he said, by way of introduction. "I'm in the middle of a really big deal and took your call by mistake." In another mistake, our file had inadvertently wound up on the wrong person's desk, but Joey promised he'd get right on it.

Two weeks later we were still waiting, but my financial inferiority complex prevented me from making too big of a fuss.

Meanwhile, Tex checked in, eager to get started. "We've definitely ruled out building from scratch, and we're trying to see if we can get enough financing for the remodel," I said.

"It will wind up being cheaper to build a new house," he argued. "Especially if you go with a rental unit."

It was all I could do to keep from shouting, "We don't want a new house! We don't want a rental unit!"

"We can always do a condominium," he said.

Even if I liked Tex's structural monument, I'd have questioned the wisdom of building it on our lot. Our ever transitional neighborhood had taken a giant lurch toward the brink. One morning, I woke with an awful revelation: I was waiting for half my neighbors to crack up or overdose, as it was the only way they'd go away.

What prompted this epiphany was Elise, a drop-dead gorgeous, seriously unbalanced nymphet who lives down the block. Elise is the sort of person that men describe as "a little troubled" and women describe as "a nut case." I was on the phone with an editor who held my career in his hands when I idly looked out the window and noticed Elise, more scantily clad than usual, in our yard, punching our jacaranda tree. "Excuse me," I said hurriedly, "my neighbor is hitting my tree." (Statements like this do wonders for my professional credibility.)

It wasn't the first time that Elise had acted a wee bit strange. A few months before, I'd found her crawling in our parking lot, gathering bits of glass and newspaper. "What are you doing?" I asked.

"Clearing your driveway of plutonium," said Elise, with no trace of irony.

Now what could I possibly say, except, "Please put it in the trash when you're through"?

"Please leave the tree alone," I said, on the occasion of her latest breakdown.

"Shut up, bitch!" she replied. The jacaranda tree survived.

But it was Isaac, one of our more prominent local eccentrics, who sent me over the edge. Isaac resembles a calendar Jesus and he orbits our block hourly, like Sputnik. The pugs and I were walking back from the video store when I noticed Isaac behind me, staring at the disposable pooper-scooper in my hand. "Can I see that?" he asked.

I let him fondle it for a minute or two, then took it back and continued walking. To my great consternation, he trailed me. I turned around. "May I help you with something?" I asked nervously.

"Where did you get the scooper?"

"At Nature's Grooming. The pet store on Main Street."

Isaac considered this. Finally he asked, "Is it just for dogs?"

"Here," I said hastily. "Take this." I waited until he was out of sight, sprinted home, and locked the door.

Living in Venice, a Mecca for the homeless much like the streets of Manhattan, strains my social conscience. On the one hand, I respect the intelligence of any person down on his luck who chooses to set up camp on the beach as opposed to, say, skid row. On the other hand, after seven years of constant proximity, I'd kind of like to have neighbors who only want to borrow a cup of sugar.

Naturally, as soon as I began daydreaming about the suburbs, I got a call from our loan counselor. "It looks like it's possible that we could do a jumbo, given that your in-laws are on title," Joey said. But to be absolutely certain, he wanted to run a prequalification. "It's a dry run through the system to see if the money you require is the money you qualify for," he explained. (Wasn't that what he was supposed to be doing all this time?)

The upside? We wouldn't have to shell out the $300 fee for our no-cost home loan (the same fee that Hawkeye had gotten waived) until we knew we had a decent chance of being approved. The downside? My in-laws had to fill out a set of application forms.

"I'm not getting involved," I said instantly.

Duke removed his hands from the computer keyboard and gave me a hug. "There's not going to be a problem, honey," he said. After only a few days of stalling, he called his father. According to what Duke told me later, when I debriefed him, the conversation went smoothly. My husband told his father that we'd qualify for the loan if he cosigned, and again, assured him that we could handle the monthly payments. Apparently, Earl was eager to help. "No problem," Duke said cheerfully when he hung up the phone.

I mailed my in-laws the application, then we both left town for a week on business. We anticipated good news when we returned, but instead, I found a plaintive message from our loan counselor. (Some enterprising soul should open a halfway house where returning travelers can decompress before facing the inevitable statement from the gas company threatening to cut off service or audit notice from the IRS that must be handled the instant you get home from the airport.)

Joey sounded irritated. "Your father-in-law doesn't want to be on the loan," he said. In our absence, Earl had called the bank and announced that he didn't want to cosign; he wanted us to pay back the $20,000 plus interest during escrow, at which point he'd quitclaim the property. (Because Duke is his first-born son, he eventually forgave $5,000 of the interest.)

"Nice of him to tell *us*," I said, but I wasn't particularly surprised. A home loan brings out the control freak in even the most hands-off parents. It's their last chance to treat independent grown-up children like kids.

"At our wedding, my father-in-law told everyone he was buying us a house," Laurie said consolingly. "Kenny lived in a transitional neighborhood and his father thought it was okay for him to live there, but not for me. So he really pushed us to move. First, he said he was going to buy the house for us. Then he decided he'd give us fifty thousand dollars as a wedding gift to help buy the house. Then, when we were ready to buy, all of a sudden the gift became a loan. And not a casual one either. We had to sign legal documents."

"I'm sure it must be a misunderstanding," Duke said.

In a way, Earl did us a favor. Our relationship with Tex was doomed.

Joey offered to see how much Duke and I would qualify for without his parents. Weeks passed. I couldn't turn on a radio or pick up a newspaper without being wooed by Dennis Weaver and his fellow banking sirens. But in reality, it took twenty unreturned follow-up calls to Joey's bank to learn that the person in charge of the step we needed done was on vacation and my husband's credit union had put a freeze on refinances because they were already too tapped out in the risky market. Duke refused to shell out $300 to another bank before we knew where we stood.

"Why don't we try a loan broker?" I suggested meekly. Our accountant had told me that brokers are like travel agents; they do the legwork for you and collect a commission directly from the lender. "It's like the difference between having an agent book a hotel room versus calling the hotel yourself." Perhaps this was not a convincing argument to make to a man who has been known to stay up until three in the morning faxing hotels on the other side of the world.

My friend Debbie had been in loan hell for eight months, trying to get financing to buy a renovated turn-of-the-century Santa Monica cottage four blocks from the beach. I would have thought she'd be a good risk since Debbie, a cartoonist representative, earns over $50,000 a year and had almost six figures in savings. "The loan market is tough," Debbie told me. "I've already been turned down by three banks, two mortgage brokers, and two direct lenders."

But what about all those ads on the radio? "Nobody qualifies for those loans," she said. Even her father, by profession a direct lender, had turned her down, though she understood his hesitation. "It's a quarter-million-dollar fixer-upper in one of the weirdest places in the universe," Debbie said. Her dream house also lacked floors or closets, though it did boast a spectacular ocean view from the toilet.

Debbie's last hope was Bradley, a twenty-five-year-old former theater arts major who got a job at a mortgage company to put himself through school. "He made so much money, he dropped out," Debbie said. "He drove up in a BMW 850, wore an Armani suit, and had a ponytail. He told me that he knew what I was going through because he just bought a nine-hundred-and-fifty-thousand-dollar house but couldn't move in yet because he was knocking the house down and building from scratch. Of course he told me all this while he was sitting in my Venice apartment that I'd lived in for fifteen years. I deserve the loan just for listening to that story."

Bradley didn't handle refinancing, so instead Debbie suggested that we call Barry, the Beverly Hills Loan Broker, whose motto is that if he can't get you a loan, no one will. I was a little leery, since he had turned Debbie down, but she assured me it wasn't his fault: her property was unconventional (isn't everybody's?). Best of all, there were no fees up front: We didn't have to pay the broker unless we got a loan.

"Great concept," said Duke, who made the call.

Twenty minutes later a messenger knocked on the door with an application the size of the Yellow Pages. We were asked to supply tax returns for the last four years, bank and credit-card statements for the last three months, *and* proof of our identity (as if an impersonator would have gone up in the attic and stolen all the shoe boxes filled with our financial records). The following day brought forms from an escrow company, the day after that forms from a title company, and Barry's assistant promised an appraiser by the end of the week. However, he never appeared, and without warning Barry slipped into radio silence.

I of course took this personally until my father called and straightened me out. "Your attitude stinks," said Dad, who has never been known for his sensitivity. "Don't go in there expecting to get skinned. You're doing them a favor, giving them a mortgagee."

"But I didn't make much money last year," I confessed.

"Who cares?" said Dad. "Your husband's working. You have any unpaid bills?"

"Nothing major."

"Equity?"

"Plenty."

"Then I'm telling you, everything you have is positive. You have all the cards. Play them."

I didn't know whether to be amused or consoled. My father has extensive real estate and banking experience. In fact, he co-owned a savings and loan. On the other hand, he was indicted for what he insists were completely ordinary and conventional banking practices. I looked on the bright side. He understood how to get money out of a bank.

"Don't go to one bank, go to five," he counseled.

"But we can't afford fifteen hundred dollars in application fees," I said.

"Tell them you have no intention of paying their fees," Dad said. "You can't let them put you in a corner."

I hung up feeling like I could convince a mortgage lender to pay *me* points. Fortunately, I didn't have to test my skills, because within an hour both Barry and Joey called with good news—we qualified for a loan; how much depended on the appraisal and the interest rate.

"We let it float to where the rate gets to a place that's comfortable and appealing," Joey explained. I suddenly had a revelation. The reason lenders don't call you back is they're waiting for the interest rate to rise.

All Joey needed to "maybe" make this happen was the $300 fee, the same fee that supposedly had been waived. Not only would this not be refunded if we were turned down; we couldn't use the appraisal report to apply elsewhere. Barry still didn't want any money, so we went with him.

His designated appraiser, Biff, was a skinny blond surfer from Newport Beach in baggy shorts with a shark's skull logo and a Wave Warriors T-shirt. He spent about twelve minutes in our house, long enough to inform me that because it was legally considered a duplex—the back used to be a studio apartment—he was able to increase his appraisal fee. He also ascertained that the property had dropped a hundred thousand dollars in value in the past year. "The California real estate market is in the toilet," Biff said comfortingly. "Anyone who bought after 1989 when the market peaked is screwed."

Duke had bought in 1985, so we were still ahead of the game. But in case we needed a reminder that remodeling was risky, that night we had dinner with a couple who were wallowing in the lowest level of financial hell thanks to the vagaries of the real estate market. "Don't make a mistake that can harm you," said the wife, who insisted on remaining anonymous. And then she sadly recounted the Ultimate California Real Estate Nightmare.

"In the beginning, I bought a house that was too small for me, because I'd sold an apartment in New York and needed to turn over the money," she said. "I planned to do a small renovation and move in when the building was done. But then our relationship heated up and we decided to get married. This meant the house was way too small. So we decided to do a bigger addition and borrowed money to do it. The plans got more and more complex until it would cost us the same price of the house to do the addition. So having put several thousand dollars into the plans, we abandoned them. We took the money that we borrowed to build with and used it as a down payment on a bigger house, which still needed work. The rationale was the market was going up so fast that we should soon be able to sell the first house and pay off the loan. The interest rate against House A was huge, twelve percent, but we were assured that we could negotiate the loan because of the rising value of these properties. In the meantime, we decided that we would rent House A."

The real estate victim continued: "We did the building on House B, which cost more than we expected, but it was okay, because it should have added a hundred thousand dollars' value. Then the bottom fell out of the market. House A was suddenly worth less than what I paid for it, let alone with the loan tacked on. House B was worth a hundred thousand less than we paid for it, even with the addition. So now we can't sell House A because we can't pay off the difference, and we can't renegotiate the loans because we have two worthless properties."

"Thank you for sharing that," I said weakly.

I was inclined to give up on the loan and forget all about remodeling, but just my luck, Barry heard me on the radio (I'm a weekly guest on a popular morning show, "The Ken and Barkley Company") and suddenly realized it might be in his best interest to expedite our paperwork. No sooner had the show aired than Barry called and promised that we'd have a lender by the end of the week. "Maybe you can talk about what a great loan broker I am," he added.

"Maybe," I lied.

Four weeks passed. Lender Number One turned us down because it was concerned that if our house burnt down it might not be able to get a variance from the Coastal Commission to rebuild; Lender Two passed because we didn't have a carport; but Lender Three agreed, and Barry faxed over our approval. It seemed rather unbelievable, getting thousands of dollars just for filling out a lot of papers and making phone calls, but I was euphoric.

We went out for sushi to celebrate. Duke looked up from his salmon-skin salad and said, "I think I'll give Joey a call and see if I can get a better deal." I began to screech. After a few minutes of our traditional money argument in which my husband accuses me of throwing money at a problem to make it go away (isn't that what money's for?) and I accuse him of being a tightwad, he landed the winning blow. "Honey," Duke said, "are you a good bargainer?"

"Oh," I said, realizing. "It's like those shoes in Hong Kong." My husband once made me walk away from the most adorable shoes I'd ever seen so the salesman would run after us and meet Duke's price. (It was a lucky thing he did, or my husband would be dead now.)

After an agonizing wait, Duke convinced Barry to knock off a couple of points and waive a bunch of fees, and thus it came to pass that four months after we began the loan-application process we were finally in escrow. We had managed to pull $50,000 cash out of the house; unfortunately, half was earmarked for my in-laws.

"I'm sure Earl won't want all of his money right away," Duke said, but sure enough, Earl did.

We went to Beverly Hills to sign the papers. It was disconcerting that an escrow company, which routinely handled hundreds of thousands of dollars, was furnished with cheap desks marked by cigarette burns. But I don't know why I was surprised. After all, they routinely handled deed filing too, and they certainly didn't manage to do that on the right day (and I also seemed to be fielding an astonishing number of last-minute calls and faxes). To Duke's chagrin half the fees that he had managed to knock off had reappeared. "It's like picking fleas off a dog," he complained. "Every time I go back to the document, new fees have popped up."

I signed without looking. When we got home, we learned that Malibu had caught fire. We went down to the beach to watch the firestorm eating up the coast. It looked like a scene out of *Apocalypse Now.*

"Damn," said Duke. "Now we'll never be able to get a contractor."

CHAPTER SIX

A S A RULE I don't like firing people—you don't become a writer if you have a knack for managerial decisions—but I had grave doubts that my husband would ever be able to let our architect go. At the very mention of Tex's name, he turned into a zombie. "He's tremendously talented," Duke sighed when I railed that Tex was a fast-talking snake charmer. "If I had lots of money, I'd give it to him and see what he could do."

That was all I needed to hear to pick up the phone. "Sorry it's taken so long to get back to you," I began, "but getting financing turned out to be a lot harder than we thought."

"For everyone," Tex said amiably. "Times are tough."

"So we're not going to be able to do this project, much as we'd like to." I ticked off the major points. We didn't qualify for a jumbo loan. Our neighbors were having a collective nervous breakdown. The economy was depressed.

"You can't let the gloomsayers and doomsayers get you down," Tex said. "Sometimes it's a matter of taking a leap of faith."

"There hasn't been a single good sign since the project began," I said. "Besides, we don't have the cash."

Tex remained sanguine. "We can do the remodel in stages," he said. "We'll get the first floor rearranged, and then in a year or two when the economy turns around, we can go up another story."

The last thing I wanted was to have our future earnings earmarked for construction. "No thank you," I said.

"Here's another thought," he continued, talking faster. "We could go back to the idea of doing a warehouse. Basic structure. Great shapes."

"No warehouse," I said. "We're talking twenty thousand dollars' worth of improvements, no more. A job too small for an architect of your abilities."

"All jobs are small jobs these days," he said so lightheartedly that I wondered if I'd misjudged him. "I could come over and do some sketches. It would be cheaper for you guys to have something to show the contractor."

I could have, would have, should have, bid him adieu. But almost against my will, I heard myself asking, "How much would it cost to do a sketch?"

"I like to be paid for my time," he said pointedly, as if we had not written the gigantic check for the cardboard tube in my closet that was filled with drawings we couldn't use. He said he would charge us his usual rate of only $80 an hour. "I'll do everything in my power to keep it down."

"I have to talk to my husband," I said.

"Keep me posted," Tex replied.

"I knew you wouldn't be able to fire him," Duke said that night, scarfing up a platter of tangerine beef (my husband eats like a seagull). "He's like Freddy in *Nightmare on Elm Street*. You can't kill him. He keeps coming back."

Perhaps it was a classic case of throwing away good money after bad (or as Tex put it, "good teeth after gums"). But we didn't think it could hurt to have him do some sketches now that we were clear on just how little we had to spend. Though I wondered: Tex had been designing houses for forty years. Why didn't he advise us to wait until we knew exactly how much we had to spend?

Duke unrolled his favorite French catchphrase: "To ask such a question is to answer it."

I invited the architect to come over with his sketch pad. He said it would be simpler if we came to him. "If you can say, here's what we want to do, I can probably put together a sketch where we can get prices."

"Don't you need to measure?"

"Trust me," he said. "I know your house like the back of my hand." He gave me a stern lecture about prioritizing. "It's nice to think about steak dinners, but that's not what you do when you buy groceries. First you buy vegetables and bread."

It seemed nervy, Mr.-Let's-Build-a-Condominium preaching about the basics, but when Duke and I filed into his office we had one goal: clean up the back of the house.

The streets around Venice Beach are laid out in an alternating series of "avenues," picturesque walk streets where cars aren't permitted, and "courts," trash-filled alleys that are open to traffic. According to a local historian who peddles his research from a stand on the boardwalk, Venice founder Abbot Kinney instituted this arrangement for economic reasons.

"You have to remember, at the turn of the century, these were summer homes," the historian told me in exchange for a quarter contribution. "They weren't figuring on someone living here year-round. There was a certain amount of ocean frontage, and they found if they went to little walk streets, little sidewalks, they could squeeze more streets in. It was also safer for children, who didn't have to worry about being run over by horses."

Our front door faces one of the loveliest walk streets in the area, but these days most visitors arrive by car and come in through the back door. If they look overhead, they can observe a natural phenomenon I've never seen outside of Venice—the Trash Stream, an air current that causes plastic garbage bags to float ten feet in the air. The back door opens directly onto the master bedroom, with a clear view of the rumpled bed, Duke's leftover coffee cups, and a pile of old newspapers. The ten-by-ten bedroom used to be the living room of an add-on studio apartment. Neither of the house's original bedrooms was large enough to hold a queen-sized bed and bedside tables, so when we moved in, we cut a door through the connecting wall and annexed the space.

The adjoining six-by-eight-foot bathroom (only a Realtor would be able to call it a master bath and keep a straight face) looks like something you'd find in a trailer park. As for the five-by-four-foot cubby that served as the apartment kitchen, we shoved a looming Maytag washer and dryer through the door, wedged in a dresser, and called it the laundry room.

We hoped that Tex could dream up a clever way to reconfigure the space. We sat expectantly in his office, waiting for him to pull out his sketch pad. Instead, he pulled out his calendar and asked when we were free. "I need to come over and measure," he said, strumming his suspenders like an air guitar.

The diplomas on Tex's walls may have come from a reputable architectural school, but I was certain that his real alma mater was in Haiti, where he learned to control men's minds. I was convinced he had taken a fingernail clipping from my husband and had woven it into a little doll.

"We've got to get rid of him," I said on the drive home. "He's going to eke out every dime he can get for his skills."

"At least he has skills," Duke countered.

Tex showed up the day before Thanksgiving, brandishing a piece of folded paper but again no tape measure. With great ceremony, he sat down at the dining room table and placed the paper facedown. "Now here's a little something I worked out," he said. He flipped over the paper and presented a drawing marked "Minor Interior Remodeling." Duke's eyes grew wide and dreamy. In the backyard Tex had colored in at least eighty thousand dollars' worth of landscaping and of course, a Jacuzzi.

The drawing looked familiar, in fact, I could have sworn it was virtually the same floor plan—the dreaded napkin!—that Tex had proposed in his "Major Home Remodel." Again, the master bedroom had been moved to the front of the house, our living room to the back, and the kitchen, bathroom, and dining room had also been transposed. I could only imagine how many $80 hours he would claim it took to transfer the drawing to a smaller piece of paper. "This is completely unacceptable," I said.

"It's not so bad," said the Zombie.

I asked the Shaman how he planned to move every single room in our house for $20,000.

"What I propose is that I bring in laborers, carpenter types whom I assume have green cards," Tex said.

"You mean illegal aliens?"

"These kind of people know wall changes," Tex said. "A guy can come here and frame in a week. He's not the most brilliant, not the most legal, otherwise he'd have licenses and businesses, but he can do the job. You can organize a whole bunch of these people and turn them loose."

"Remember Pedro and Martín," Duke said.

How could I forget? A few years ago, my husband (who can tell a plumber he's putting the toilet in the wrong place in eight languages but who unfortunately is at work all day) arrived home with Pedro and Martín, two illegal immigrants from Mexico City, and announced that they were going to paint our house.

It took a month—counting disappearances—but the memory that stands out is the day they spray-painted the iron bars on our windows. Not only did I have to endure the clouds of toxic fumes wafting through the house, but the next morning I discovered that someone had sprayed large initials on our side fence. At first, I assumed that a local homeboy had helped himself to a can of paint. But then I looked at the enormous *P* and the gigantic *M* and looked at Pedro and Martín and put two and two together. "They couldn't have," my husband said, when I called him at work and insisted he come home right away.

"Sí, señor," Pedro and Martín confessed sheepishly. I reminded myself there was probably a logical explanation.

Duke posed the question in Spanish and translated the response: "They had to test the spray paint to see if it worked."

My Spanish has improved considerably since then, but I wouldn't want to bet my house on it.

"How much would a real contractor charge?" I asked.

"Contractors are a great institution, like any other," Tex said. "But they mark up a minimum of twenty-five percent, plus they take labor that costs twenty dollars and charge sixty because they need to cover extras, like insurance."

Insurance didn't strike me as an extra that I cared to skip.

The Zombie and his master were busily discussing how they could hide the trash to foil the building inspectors when I had this funny feeling that I was missing something important. I studied the drawing again. I realized there *was* a difference between this drawing and the previous version. Tex had eliminated an existing bathroom.

"What happened to my bathroom?" I asked indignantly.

"Look, honey," the Zombie said, "he turned it into a pantry."

I squealed: "I want my bathroom back!"

"Why?" Tex said, "You only need one."

Has anyone in the history of home remodeling ever *removed* a bathroom? "I want two bathrooms!" I screeched.

"Tell me," Tex said, "why do you need two?"

It was all I could do to keep from shouting: "This is a nonnegotiable issue!"

"But it's a more efficient use of the space," Tex said.

I looked around for a heavy object I could throw.

"I think you better put the bathroom back," Duke warned him.

Tex reluctantly penciled it in. My husband suggested that maybe in the interest of economy we should leave the rooms in the general vicinity of where they were and concentrate on what we had asked him to do: fix up the back of the house.

"Oh, what does that mean, the back of the house?" Tex scoffed. "If you go through a lot of work, you might as well have something worth doing."

I had to admit he had a point, which is probably why I disliked him. He kept waving things in front of me that I'd love to have but simply couldn't afford.

We should have fired Tex on the spot, but as fate would have it, I opened the door to let the pugs out and noticed that the faint sound of running water, which I thought I'd heard earlier emanating from the side of our house (the one my husband couldn't hear), had blossomed into a full-blown leak. Naturally, it was five o'clock on the Wednesday before Thanksgiving. Has there ever been a house emergency during normal business hours, when things are cheap?

Duke leapt from the table and hurried out the door to get to the hardware store before it closed. My husband is the only Jewish man I have ever known who likes to plumb. When we first moved in together, our garbage disposal broke. I waited for him to call a plumber. To my astonishment, instead he borrowed a snake to clean out the drain. I called his mother and demanded to see his bar mitzvah kiddush cup.

"You're probably going to have to replace all the old plumbing," Tex said as he let himself out. He told me he'd incorporate our suggestions into a new set of drawings.

Later, after Duke had fixed the leak and come out of his trance, I showed him the earlier drawing. "They're almost identical," he marveled. Then he had a revelation. "Tex really didn't listen to what I said."

As every woman knows, this was a far more serious transgression than the architect not listening to a word *I* said. It is like the difference between right and wrong. Even so, I sensed that Duke was ambivalent. Thanksgiving Day we drove to Desert Hot Springs, an agreeably seedy little town near Palm Springs with hot mineral tubs and businesses with quaint names like "The Alibi" and "Suzie-Q" that seem to be sealed in a time capsule, complete with freeze-dried clientele. Duke procrastinated until we were hiking in the back country of the Joshua Tree Monument. "Do you have your cellular phone?" he asked.

I'm ashamed to admit that I carry it everywhere, even into the wilderness.

"Give it to me," he said, settling himself in the crevice of a rounded boulder. "I'll fire Tex." This was sheer bravado, as there was no cellular way station in the middle of the desert and so of course the call couldn't go through. Hours later, when we got back to the Stardust Motel, my husband left a message, asking the architect to stop work until we spoke to him again. When we arrived home on Sunday night there was a message waiting from Tex.

He'd already done the drawings.

Duke called and asked him to fax them over, but Tex insisted on showing them in person (at his usual hourly rate). "I've got something Margo will like," Tex said.

I felt like I was being held hostage.

"Architects are all hopelessly stupid," said my friend Claire, an interior designer, who had just completed a kitchen remodel. "I work with them every day, and I'm telling you. They dress really well, they have great apartments, lots of fabulous ideas, but no idea of what buildings cost. I tell all my single friends not to date them."

The architect who designed her kitchen mismeasured by a foot. "And the whole thing is only eighteen feet, so what was the percentage?" Claire said. "By the time we discovered he mismeasured we'd already ordered the cabinets, the window was in a certain place, the hole for the sink was all cut, but when the cabinets arrived, it didn't line up. Now the sink will never fit under the window. And keep in mind, the architect said we could do the kitchen for thirteen thousand and it cost thirty-five."

We went to the meeting prepared to fish or cut bait. For a moment, it looked like Tex had redeemed himself. The sketch he presented, Minimal Remodel Three, was a triumph of ingenuity. He had moved the washer and dryer outside and turned the crowded laundry room into a spacious walk-in closet. (Later, when we measured this at home, we discovered that the washer and dryer couldn't fit on the side porch.) He pushed the kitchen out three feet (okay, so he removed a bearing wall) and cut out the dining room wall to create a bigger space. He also eliminated the wall between our long narrow sunporch and our long narrow living room to create a bigger space, and as an afterthought penciled in vaulted ceilings.

"I think it's as simple as you can be and still get a good house," Tex said.

The Zombie's eyes were shining. "Doesn't this seem encouraging?" he said.

It seemed wonderful, desirable, brilliant, even. It just didn't seem cheap. "Is there any way to get a bid on this to see if you're in the ball-park?" I asked.

Tex shook his head. "Well, you don't want to do that," he said. "What you want to do is get the drawings complete first. You want me to do a door-and-window schedule. You want me to specify everything in this drawing that we want down to floor finish."

Call me a killjoy, but it seemed silly to pay him to do more drawings that we might not be able to afford. "What if we just show it to a contractor to get some idea as to price?"

Tex frowned and shook his head again. "What you want to do is get the drawings complete. And then you want to go to three to five contractors and get firm prices from them. One contractor's price would be unrealistic. You want to get a bunch bidding together, that's the way you're going to keep their pencils short. That way, they're trying to keep their costs as low as they can to get the job. If they don't get the part, they'll never play Hamlet."

"Yes, but before you do all those drawings, I'd like to have an idea of what it will cost."

Tex dropped his pencil on the desk. "You want to go over this a third time?" he snapped.

"Well, yeah," I said testily. "We need to know."

Duke jumped in to smooth the waters. "It's not like it's the first time you've ever put a job together," he said. "What we're looking for is a good-faith verbal estimate that you think this will actually come in at. Just give us a range."

"The only way I could do that is to spend a couple of days going through it, looking at materials, and I don't think you want to pay for that," Tex said.

Duke asked how much it would cost for him to do the drawings. Tex refused to tell us until we mailed him a thousand-dollar retainer check (we had applied the last one to pay off the balance for the first set of unfeasible plans). Duke actually sent the check (rationalizing that we probably owed Tex most of it), and as soon as it cleared Tex revealed that working drawings would cost $5,600 (and we'd have to pull all the permits ourselves). It seemed like a high price to pay for what was billed as a twenty-thousand-dollar project. I faxed the drawing to Walt, my Dream Contractor, for a reality check.

"You're looking at seventy thousand dollars," Walt said. "And that's going in; we haven't opened the wall and found dry rot, termites, or sewage."

My husband, a man who has been known to become homicidal if he sees an advertised price for a car stereo that is $6 cheaper than the price he paid three years ago, took Tex's $5,600 fee in stride. "Everything is negotiable," he told me. "I'll take care of it." But when he called and tried to get the architect to lower his price, Tex replied, "I should have charged you twice that."

"Believe me," Duke said ingratiatingly, "it's not that you're not worth it." But the architect refused to come down.

So there we were, after six months of machinations, with a loan-enhanced bank balance, a thick tube of unusable plans, and no architect. We considered our options: Find another architect. Fix what was broken in the house. Leave the house alone and continue to live in squalor.

"Let's go to Asia," Duke proposed one evening, as we walked down to the beach to admire the sunset. My husband is currently studying Cantonese, perhaps the least melodic tongue on the planet and one even he calls insanely difficult. He was hoping for a chance to practice his Cantonese tones.

I saw no advantage to his possessing this skill. Not only did it increase my chances of winding up on Duke's dream vacation—a trip to the mysterious island of Hainan, off the coast of Vietnam, where the winter home of Mao Tse-tung's actress wife (sometimes known as the White-Boned Demon) has been converted to a resort hotel. It's also ruined one of the great joys of my life—going out for Chinese food.

It used to be that we'd go to a restaurant, tell our waiter, "Twenty-four, sixty-two, hold the MSG," and sit back and leisurely sip our tea. But now Duke orders in Cantonese, an accomplishment so spectacularly useless and affected that it was parodied in the movie *Wayne's World*. He and the waiter have a long chat while half the staff looks on admiringly. Invariably, someone asks *me* a question in Cantonese, which I cannot understand, let alone answer, or, worse, I automatically answer in Spanish, the only foreign language I know. The waiter gives Duke a sorrowful look, as if lamenting that someone so bright should be burdened with such a fool.

The fool agreed to go to Asia, but I drew the line at Hainan Island, after a guidebook that I trusted noted: "There's nothing for the tourist on Hainan Island" and *The New York Times* travel section published a traveler's warning about thievery. Unlike our home remodel, where we frequently pulled against each other, with travel plans we behaved like two synchronized swimmers. In a matter of days Duke had decided on an itinerary (Singapore, Malaysia, and Hong Kong), I located an advantageously priced Circle the Pacific fare, and we purchased tickets for a departure date four weeks hence, in mid-January.

We tried to forget about Tex, but he kept haunting us. After reading a book called *The Underside of Malaysian History,* in preparation for our journey, Duke discovered a Malaysian term that described his relationship with the architect—*latah,* which refers to the reaction to being startled that involves a loss of control or will. The *latah* person will follow commands given by others.

"I had architectural *latah,*" said Duke. "I see a blueprint and I become totally suggestible."

"Do you think we'll need malaria shots?" I asked.

CHAPTER SEVEN

TWO WEEKS before our departure for Singapore, we had dinner with the Horrible Home Owners, a couple whom Duke knew vaguely and wrongly assumed I would enjoy meeting. They'd just completed a mega-remodel, which the wife, Suzy Homebuilder, had been overseeing for several years. (Life's too short to spend several years living in a work-in-progress.) To say this woman is a control freak is like saying that Hitler was a little aggressive.

"You should have done it yourself," Suzy said archly, when she heard about our travails with Tex.

Hank beamed. "Suzy was our architect."

"I also designed the house, drew up the plans, acted as the general contractor, and did the finish carpentry," she added. (She probably cuts her own hair too, I thought uncharitably.)

Home improvement was just a sideline for Suzy, who was also writing a rock opera even though she was tone deaf. She had taken an empowering vacation at Yestermorrow, an owner-builder school in Warren, Vermont, that teaches laymen how to design and build their own shelter in just two weeks. "They try to demystify the home building process," said Suzy, who spent her mornings learning drafting and design. In the afternoon, she strapped on her tool belt and worked on a construction site building a shed. She couldn't wait until her next vacation, when she had signed up for courses in electrical wiring, solar heating, and faux marble painting. And there I was, counting the days until I would be ensconced in a luxury hotel in Singapore.

Suzy's experience sounded about as appealing as a week in Outward Bound, that survival school where they deposit you on a cliff with a match and a box of raisins. Call me unadventurous, but there are things in life that I don't want to know. How to pull my own teeth, how to change the oil in my car, how to excavate a foundation and pour concrete. Possession of such knowledge increases the odds that you will actually be tempted to use it. I prefer to limit my construction abilities to dollhouses, where if I make a mistake mitering a quarter-inch crown molding, I can pull it out with a razor blade and replace it for under a dollar. With dollhouses, I also don't have to worry about dead loads, bearing walls, and the environmental impact of heating fuels.

However, Suzy said one thing about her alma mater that truly impressed me: "Most people approach remodeling like they buy cars. They see how much they can get for their money, without considering how they want to live. But I learned to ask myself, what do I really want in a house?"

My expectations had been so diminished by economic reality that I was willing to settle for a home that was no longer in disrepair. My only goals were to take up the carpets, refinish the wood floors underneath, and install tile and a decent-looking vanity in the back bathroom. Duke had come to the conclusion that all our problems could be solved with paint— "if not new, at least freshly painted," he said, quoting an old Russian proverb. Still, before I went to sleep I commanded my subconscious to reveal its secret longing. Upon awakening, I realized there was an improvement that would make me truly happy—a large sunny room where we could entertain friends and just hang out.

We could actually achieve this goal without building an addition, if we removed the wall between the long narrow living room and the narrower sunporch and raised the ceiling to the rafters. "It certainly would give the most bang for the buck," said Walt, my Dream Contractor, when I called for another reality check. We hoped that Walt could manifest the bang, sans architect, but alas, this wasn't the case. "You need structural drawings to get the necessary permits," he said, and my heart sank.

"I'm sure your guy wouldn't charge much for that," Walt said.

I was sure Tex would. "You wouldn't happen to know an architect who isn't an egomaniac and has some idea of what things cost?"

And that's how Brandon came to control our lives.

Ten days before we were supposed to leave for Singapore, the thirty-year-old architect rapped on our door, prompt to the nanosecond, résumé in hand. He bore a striking resemblance to the Bob's Big Boy icon, down to the cowlick and the starched white T-shirt, but his demeanor was painstakingly professional. I asked how he got interested in architecture.

"That's kind of a funny thing," Brandon said. "I didn't initially mean to. I wrestled in high school and was interested in sports. I went to the University of San Diego and wrestled Division One and decided I was never going to make it and got tired of wrestling, so I went to business school. I got my bachelor's in business management, but at that time I wasn't good in math. Then I had to take calculus, and I did well so I decided I could be an architect. I'd always had fears about math and design . . ."

By the time he got around to naming all the architectural schools in the country that allowed students with different undergraduate degrees to get a professional degree in architecture, my eyes were glazed with boredom and I was doodling fanciful pictures of a Bekins moving van. Still, as my husband later pointed out, a slavish attention to detail was not a bad quality in an architect, though it did make for stultifying meetings.

"In architecture, you have to be a jack of all trades," Brandon continued. "If I was good at estimating, I'd be a contractor. If I drew really well, I'd be Jonathan Borofsky."

Alarm bells went off. I explained that we had a firm budget of $20,000. "Don't think if you design something fantastic, we'll finance it," I cautioned. "This isn't *The Fountainhead*."

The architect winced. "I consider myself good at estimating costs," Brandon said, puffing himself up like a blowfish, "but I've got to tell you. An architect has no control over a contractor's selection and management of subcontractors. An architect has no control over the contractor's work performance, price, waste, speed, luck, or efficiency . . ."

Why did I get the feeling that they taught that speech in architecture school?

On the other hand, Brandon was sympathetic when he heard about Tex, or at least he was eager to prove his superiority. "Historically, architects after World War II kind of ran amok," he said. I was gratified that he had begun his explanation in the 1940s, not the 1540s. "They got the idea that they could change the world and make a better place, and they became very egocentric. They believed the client wasn't important; their vision of the community was important. That's why the guy didn't listen to you."

Brandon promised that if *his* design turned out to be too costly, he would fix it for free. His references assured me that he was creative, easy to work with, and not an ax murderer (Brandon would later advise me never to believe references). We didn't have any desire to go on another architectural star search—look where the last one got us—so we put him on retainer without inspecting his work. My Dream Contractor's word was good enough for me. Besides, I was frantically making arrangements to leave town.

Eight days before our departure for Singapore, after spending half the afternoon crawling over and under our house with a measuring tape, Brandon appeared at our door at 7:00 sharp, clutching a spiral notebook, a roll of tracing paper, and a battle plan. I offered him a Diet 7-Up, and he shook his head (it would take him months to lower his guard sufficiently to accept a beverage). "You can see by my notes that I've got a bunch of stuff to cover," he said briskly, opening the notebook to an acutely detailed outline. We must have looked startled because he hastily explained, "I keep this notebook, it's kind of the equivalent of doctor's notes."

How comfortingly compulsive, I thought.

"Before we begin, I have a general question for you. Do you mind if I put a sign out on your front wall somewhere so people can see?"

I squinched up my nose, trying to understand.

"I want to advertise my architectural services out on your front porch. Is this a problem for you?"

"Of course not," said my husband, who'd be safe in his office downtown when passersby began to knock on the door with questions.

"Wait," I said. "Is it a big sign?"

"Yes," he said proudly. "Eighteen by twenty-four."

I saw no reason to put a billboard in my yard. But I compromised. "During the active chaos, it's okay, but not now. Not when we're about to leave the country. Not in this neighborhood."

A new pair of lunatics, Sid and Ian, had recently moved into the Roach Motel. Sid was a polite, skinny, rodentine little nebbish who wanted to be a screenwriter and never caused any trouble until he brought home Ian, an oily lout with glittering eyes whom I pegged as a sociopath from a hundred yards away. Ian claimed to be a psychologist, but he had set up a tarot-reading stand on the boardwalk using plastic lawn furniture that he had "borrowed" from our backyard. One day, Ian confided that he also ran a business at home. He handed me a brochure for a mail-order penis-extension kit.

"Thank you for sharing this," I muttered, as I darted into the house and locked the door. Duke, ever tolerant, gave Ian the benefit of the doubt until the first night the police came. It was 2:00 A.M. when we heard Sid banging on the door, hollering, "Ian, open up, it's me." For a moment, I hoped that Ian had done away with himself, but no such luck. He and Sid had a quarrel, and Ian had barricaded himself inside the apartment (we would subsequently discover this was his defense mechanism of choice). Sid alternately banged and begged for a couple of hours until finally an LAPD officer arrived and threatened to break down the door. A few days later Ian blithely offered an explanation: "Sid accidentally let my dog out, and I went berserk." Then he asked if he could borrow my housekeeper for a few hours to clean up the mess. (I turned him down.)

A week later, the police returned again. Ian had decided to barbecue spareribs on a portable grill, only instead of using charcoals he used newspaper. Sparks and burning papers were flying over the Roach Motel, and open flames could be seen above the flimsy wood fence that separates our property. ("If it burns down, they'll never be able to get a permit to rebuild that many apartments," Duke said hopefully.) The smoke got so thick that even the drunks in the apartment above Ian interrupted their nightly chug-a-lug contest long enough to holler, "Put out the goddamn fire." Again, Ian barricaded himself in the apartment and refused to come out, even when the inebriates threatened to throw the grill through his open window. Duke casually aimed a hose over the fence and sprayed it down.

"I hear what you're saying about the neighbors," said Brandon, making a neat check next to the outline entry: Ask About Sign. "Okay, next, we're going to prioritize our design goals."

In our initial meeting, Brandon had introduced us to a concept called the Economy of Scale—"The more work you give someone to do, the less expensive the per capita cost." He suggested that we let one contractor do all the repairs in the house instead of calling in a bunch of specialists. I suspected that Brandon wanted to have a hand in all our home improvements, but we were delighted to relinquish control.

I handed the architect a list of what needed to be done.

Brandon looked crestfallen when he saw my feeble attempt at organization. "Well, you saved me some things to do," he said, shaking his head. "I had made my own list." He handed each of us a copy of a far more dazzling, computer-generated chart. It was then that I realized that we had hired the human Day Runner.

"Now let's go down my list and make sure I've got your wants and desires correct," Brandon said.

"Why not use my list?" I said. "It's already prioritized."

"We can do your list first and then we'll do mine," Brandon said, as if I were a balky third-grader. He carefully changed the "II: Prioritize List" in his spiral notebook to "IIA: Prioritize Her List" and "IIB: Prioritize My List." "And then we'll organize the final priority list with costs so we'll have it in front of us."

The upshot of the two-hour exchange was that Brandon estimated

<u>Margo's List</u>

1. Rebuild the back steps and the side steps. (The wood had rotted and the stairs swayed.)
2. Fix up the back bathroom.
3. Take up the carpets and refinish the hardwood floors.
4. Pray that there are hardwood floors under the carpet.
5. Take out the wall between the sunporch and the living room and make a big room, with cathedral ceilings.
6. Fix the fireplace so smoke doesn't pour into the living room when you light it. (My husband maintained that the fireplace worked, which technically was true. But I had to sit in front of the fire with a fire extinguisher, which really killed the romantic mood.)
7. Get rid of the ugly louvered windows in the kitchen, dining room, and living room. Put in nice windows with translucent glass to block the view of the Roach Motel.
8. Paint the house, inside and out.
9. Build a bike shed, so we can move the bikes out of the living room. (Duke hated to be separated from his sporting goods, but I didn't see any reason his bicycle should be a design element.)
10. Put more storage space in the kitchen. (The National Home Builders Association recommends at least seventy-two running feet of wall cabinetry. We have four feet.)
11. Fix the heaters. (We have four gas heaters. Three don't work.)

that it would cost around $5,000 to remodel what he insisted on calling "the great room." He also gave us permission to redo the back bathroom (as long as we didn't get fancy), refinish the wood floors, and give the kitchen "a mini-face-lift" by adding a greenhouse window, more cupboards, and a new counter. However, he insisted that we remove fixing the heaters and repairing the fireplace from his construction budget. Brandon didn't seem to realize that even if we took it out of his construction budget, we'd still have to pay for it.

"Just for a point of information, architectural fees aren't considered to be hard construction costs," the contractor said. "And neither are permit fees, which could be several hundred dollars."

Brandon's List
1. *Cosmetic repair of the kitchen.*
2. *Remodeling of the kitchen.*
3. *Cosmetic repair of the bathroom.*
4. *Cathedral ceiling at entry.*
5. *Cathedral ceiling at living.*
6. *Combining entry with living.*
7. *Make fireplace focal point.*
8. *Wood floors.*
9. *Translucent windows.*
10. *Repaint exterior.*
11. *Repaint interior.*
12. *Repair back stairs.*
13. *Repair side stairs.*

We were so pleased that he was paying lip service to our budget that we let it slide. Besides, I was feeling a little under the weather. My left leg had been bothering me since we went hiking in the Thousand Palms Oasis, outside Desert Hot Springs, and Duke had insisted on taking a short cut up a steep vertical slope. I figured that I had pulled a muscle.

On his way out, the architect noticed the acoustical tile on the living room and dining room ceiling. He froze in his tracks. "Those could have asbestos in them," he said, adding that if there was asbestos, then we would have to hire a bunch of men in space suits who specialized in toxic-waste removal. The guys in space suits would charge thousands of dollars to come and hermetically seal the house, remove the tile, and haul it away. "That could blow your budget," Brandon warned. "You better have it checked."

Seven days before our departure to Singapore found me frantically calling laboratories around town, looking for an independent technician who was not affiliated with an asbestos cleanup operation. I finally located a company in the Valley that could analyze the ceiling by mail. A sepulchral-voiced technician gave me the kind of explicit instructions you give to a novice landing an aircraft after the pilot has had a heart attack. Somewhere between the part where I had to dampen the ceiling to prevent damaging particles from harming my lungs and the part where I had to extract a chunk without touching it, I had a brainstorm. I waylaid Duke on his way out to work. "Honey," I cooed, "could you do me a little favor?"

Three days before our departure, in between packing, last-minute gamma globulin shots, and making reservations to board the pugs at Blanche, my pug breeder friend's house, I called the lab for results. I was put on hold for five anxious minutes. "There's no trace of asbestos," said the sepulchral-voiced technician.

"Thank God," I sighed happily. "Our house is negative."

"I was pretty sure it wasn't asbestos," Brandon said smugly. "But it was a good thing that you checked."

That evening, the architect presented three framing plans for the great room. "You've got a one-by-six ridge and a two-by-six hip, which is good," he began. "If the ridge beam were longer, it would help us in our quest, but it's not. We've got this dormer frame, two-by-four; for the purposes of structural analysis it isn't really a factor."

I didn't know what he was talking about. I assumed that it was attic stuff.

"Where the hips meet the corner, there's not a lot of space," Brandon continued. "I made some three-dimensional drawings that you'll see later, but I wanted to present this in a certain order."

"You've understood everything so far?" my husband whispered.

"Not a word," I whispered.

"I didn't understand that much either," Duke confessed. He stopped Brandon in the middle of a riff about the hip roof—how we had one, how Frank Lloyd Wright loved them, how it differed from a gable.

"What's the main problem we have to solve?"

Brandon gets flustered when he's stopped in the middle of a lecture. I watched him strain to fast-forward his mind, like a sluggish tape recorder that needs fresh batteries. "It boils down to that in 1912 when they built this place they didn't have to support the hip with some sort of structural piece, but now we're in 1993 and we do," he said finally. "If life was simple, then your desires would be that you'd want a big post in the middle of your great room. But you don't, because you want furniture."

Eventually, he produced axonometric drawings—three-dimensional sketches—that he had made of the different kinds of beams that could do the job. Brandon is a deft draftsman, able to knock off a quick sketch in a heartbeat, and communication became simpler. Exhibit A, a great truss beam, looked like a large triangle and spanned the width of the room. Exhibit B was an equally gigantic beam that ran lengthwise and bisected the fireplace. Exhibit C featured two columns on either side of the door.

"The triangle," I said.

"I don't have a problem with that," Duke said.

"Wait," said Brandon, who was armed with at least another hour's worth of debate. "Don't you want to go through the whole exercise?"

We speedily okayed a fireplace design, a strut detail, and rejected some attic niches. Our architect was shell-shocked. "You guys don't argue," he complained. "The last couple I had doing a house got into a tiff about where their house was going. You know what I did? I told them to be quiet for a couple minutes, then I spent the time outlining the choices. I said, 'Here are the pros, here are the cons.' Then I sent them home and told them to figure it out. That way, they don't feel like they have a confrontation in front of me."

"It would be stupid to get in the position of a husband and wife competing for the favor of the architect," Duke told me later. "You wind up with a house that no one likes, and the marriage is shot too."

Two days before our departure for Singapore, Brandon brought over a schematic design for the living room. He wanted approval before we left so he could work on the construction documents while we were gone. "What I assume is that you'll take the documents on your trip," he said. "You'll get a chance to look at it, and you may call me and say, 'Gee Brandon, your original design for the fireplace, that's the one we want.' "

I was too busy packing to pay much attention. And my sore leg was still bothering me. "It's important to make changes during the planning stages instead of during construction," the architect said. "That's where you really get creamed."

I promised that we'd fax him if we changed our minds.

"Good," said Brandon. "Upon your return we'll wrap up the details and start bidding."

Oh, would that that were the case.

A LETTER FROM SOUTHEAST ASIA

Dear Reader:

I was sitting in my wheelchair, minding my own business, when a stranger approached our table at the sidewalk café. "Wouldn't you feel terrible if you left Singapore without trying something that could make you walk?" she asked. I rolled my eyes. Ever since my husband and I had arrived in Singapore, the first stop on our three-week Southeast Asian vacation, people had been trying to heal me.

"I have special health food from Beijing," the stranger said. "It can make you well." I explained that I wasn't sick: I'd injured my leg. "What happened?" she asked.

I didn't have a clue. The day before we had left Los Angeles, my sore left leg began to throb. I'd been having twinges since we hiked in the Thousand Palms Oasis outside Desert Hot Springs, when I scaled a steep slope on my hands and knees. But I wasn't alarmed. My friend Allan, the radio sports-medicine doctor, had examined me and announced with great certainty that I had sprained my ilio-tibular band. He gave me some Naprosyn and assured me that I'd be okay. "Try to stay off of it for a couple days," he advised.

No problem. The flight to Singapore was eighteen hours.

My husband, who has never been known to minimize a medical problem (at least when it's happening to him), was also optimistic. "As soon as we get to the airport you'll be miraculously cured," Duke predicted. I wanted to believe that Los Angeles International Airport was Lourdes, but in fact I limped to the gate. A stewardess suggested Tiger Balm, a salve that I later learned was like the aspirin of Asia. By the time we landed in Singapore I reeked of camphor and eucalyptus, but my cruising radius had dropped to two hundred yards.

We checked into a nineteenth-century shop house turned luxury hotel on the border of Chinatown. Down the street was an acupuncture clinic. The receptionist promised that the acupuncturist, from Beijing, could alleviate my pain with a few treatments.

Which was more unsettling? I wondered. The examining room fitted with yellow plastic garden furniture, or the electric whirligig that the acupuncturist stuck in my ear? Supposedly, all the organs have auricular points and the whirligig hums at a different frequency, depending on the diagnosis. "Heart and lungs, good," she said. "Kidneys weak." She poked a point in my forearm and added, "Leg, bad." She tapped needles (disposable, I paid extra) into my hip, forearm, and shin and marched me around the room. "Much better," she said. To show my appreciation, I offered her a stick of Dentyne. The acupuncturist recoiled. I had forgotten that chewing gum is illegal in Singapore. I apologized, made another appointment, and tottered back to the hotel.

The next day, the leg was much worse, which the acupuncturist claimed was proof that the healing energy had been released. My husband advised a different approach. "Walk through the pain and it will go away," Duke said.

I walked, make that hobbled, first to the Maxwell Road Hawkers Market, where Duke wolfed down local delicacies like fish-head curry, squid noodles, and roti, then on to a handicrafts mall, where I was too uncomfortable to bargain for silk lingerie (not a good sign). I heard myself whimpering, "Honey, can we please take a bus tour?" (And I detest buses.)

Duke looked up from his hokkien fish balls and suggested a river cruise. He directed a cabby to drop us at the quay. Alas, it was the wrong quay and I had to trudge seven agonizing blocks. When I finally stepped up on the right dock I doubled over, screaming. I felt like a rag doll whose leg was being ripped off.

A boatsman in short shorts, a diamond ring, and a Rolex hurried over with a jar of miracle salve, from Beijing, and began massaging my thigh. The ticket taker, not to be outdone, produced what he claimed was a superior ointment from Hong Kong and rubbed me more. Despite their ministrations, I couldn't walk.

But I was glad I'd shaved.

Back at the hotel, the manager produced a house wheelchair (my revised definition of "luxury hotel" now includes this amenity) and summoned Dr. Yuk, the house physician. He arrived carrying a traditional black bag laden with anti-inflammatory pills, muscle relaxants, and his liniment—everything but painkillers, which he deemed unnecessary, and a precise diagnosis. Dr. Yuk wavered between a muscle spasm and a severe sprain. "You can go home in a few days," he said.

"Home?" Duke exclaimed. We had been away less than seventy-two hours.

"You don't want to go back to Los Angeles?" asked Dr. Yuk.

We weren't in that big a hurry to return to our remodel. Still, we considered it. Then we turned on the television and saw a CNN special bulletin about the Los Angeles earthquake. As we watched endless footage of devastation, fire, homelessness, and traffic jams, a bum leg didn't seem so bad. The next day, we received a fax from Brandon, assuring us that our house was okay. We decided to continue on.

On Day One, my husband left me in the room and went sightseeing. He thoughtfully called in every few hours to rave about the glorious botanical gardens, the delicious hokkien fish balls, the big steamed fish that I was missing. "And how are you?" he added.

Well enough to want to kill him.

So the next day, the hotel lent us the wheelchair and Duke took me out on the town. Singapore is remarkably accessible, with plenty of ramps and cut curbs, and we managed to visit the shops on Orchard Road, the noodle stands in Chinatown, and the Hindu Sri Mariamman Temple, where a devotee looked at me with grave concern. "Rub oil on it," she said.

"Is there some kind that's best?" Duke asked. We waited for her answer, sure that it would be a subtle essence passed down by the sages of the Ramayana.

"Deep Heat is very good," she said.

The biggest drawback was that I was at my husband's mercy. When we went to the zoological gardens, a lavishly landscaped open zoo where moats replace bars, Duke was rolling me past the orangutans when he spied a bunch of elephants in the distance, ambling down the road. He sprinted after them.

"Oh no," I shrieked, as the chair and I hurtled toward the pack. The mahout was waving his arms frantically, motioning us away. I felt like the hapless *Saturday Night Live* character Mr. Bill, a feeling I would have repeatedly as my husband dashed across streets trying to beat a red light or parked me in the middle of a crowded sidewalk while he disappeared to peruse a restaurant menu.

My sense of powerlessness increased tenfold when we traveled on to Malaysia, a country somewhat less enlightened about the needs of the disabled. I was reluctant to go, since I still couldn't walk, but the hotel doctor maintained that I was on the mend. "Sometimes when people experience a painful injury such as yours they become phobic about walking," Dr. Yuk said. (If my mind hadn't been addled with pain, I would have heard the warning bells chime.)

Singapore Airlines treated me like heavily insured cargo. An attendant met us at the curb with a wheelchair and pushed me through Customs to the gate, where I was transferred to a narrower, stripped-down chair that rolled aboard the plane and down the aisle to my seat. (I tried not to think of what would happen in the event of an emergency landing.) I didn't panic until we landed in Kuala Lumpur and an attendant wheeled me outside, where my husband was waiting with a rental car and bad news. He couldn't find a place to rent a wheelchair.

"Trust me," said Duke, who wouldn't be the one who couldn't get out of the car to sightsee or go to the bathroom. "It will be okay."

We drove three hours to Melaka, a lovely old city with Dutch Colonial architecture, Portuguese stone walls, and virtually no cut curbs. Luckily, I had taken the precaution of making a reservation at a hotel with a wheelchair. It wasn't as comfortable as the one in Singapore (I would henceforth remember all our stops by their wheelchairs), but it worked—well, as long as we stayed inside.

That night, citing a hankering for fried dumplings, my husband pushed me into the cobblestone street. I found myself staring into the headlights of an oncoming tour bus and being dragged like a sack of potatoes over a sewer grate. In the morning, my husband installed me in a trishaw, a rickety pedicab powered by Baba, an amiable driver with muscles in his legs like steel cables. I rode like a maharani, while Duke trailed us on a rented bike.

Our most memorable stop was the Chong Hoon Teng Temple, the oldest Chinese temple in Malaysia. Duke rushed inside to take pictures. I was sitting forlornly in the trishaw, feeling like an abandoned pet, when a monk came over and helped me hop inside the exquisitely carved shrine. He whispered an order, and an acolyte appeared with a wicker bar stool, which I used as a walker to hop around with relative ease. So great was my delight that the monk insisted I take the bar stool with me. Baba strapped it on the back of the trishaw, and off we went.

Thanks to the bar stool, I enjoyed our vacation—well, as much as you can enjoy a trip where you can't walk and sleeping is painful. When we drove from Melaka to Ipoh to Penang (when I was between hotel wheelchairs), I could drag myself to the gas station bathroom, not that I really wanted to, or look around a market. It also did wonders for my triceps.

Still, I couldn't help noticing that my left leg looked like it was getting shorter. I called the hotel doctor in Singapore. Dr. Yuk maintained that I was healing on schedule. "You're just a little anxious," he repeated.

This time, I heard the warning bells and went to a Penang clinic. "It's obviously something anatomical," Dr. Rama scoffed. "There's displacement at the level of the femur." He wasn't sure if it was a muscle spasm or the hip was out of its socket, but he recommended that I go to Gleneagles Hospital right away and see the orthopedic surgeon.

Duke was more attentive on the drive over and only mentioned that he was hungry twice. Gleneagles Hospital was clean and efficient, with signs in four languages and three alphabets. The admitting nurse took my passport instead of my insurance card.

Dr. Kanagesvaran, the orthopedist, or Mr. Kanagesvaran as he preferred to be called, following the British tradition, felt my problem was likely a strained abductor muscle, and he promised that he could lessen my discomfort with a shot, just as soon as I had an X ray. He dashed behind the lead curtain, and suddenly I heard him cry, "I can't believe it."

"What's wrong?" I asked.

"Your hip is broken." He showed me the film. It wasn't one of those subtle breaks you need a degree in radiology to read. I could see the fracture from across the room.

If I wasn't so shocked, it would have been satisfying to see my husband's face turn pale. I could see him mentally reviewing my activities of the past two weeks. The traditional Malay massage, where the masseur tried to pull my leg over my head. The pool aerobics. The temple steps that he cajoled me to climb. (My mother would later point out that I had enough moral capital to win any marital argument for the next ten years.)

Mr. Kanagesvaran explained that I needed surgery immediately. He offered to operate then and there. Kind as he was, I considered it for a heartbeat, then insisted on returning home. He gave me painkillers (finally!) and a note for the airline.

Just my luck, I thought, as Duke checked our luggage and my bar stool through to Los Angeles. There I was, with a guilt-stricken husband. If I'd been in any other city I could have had anything I wanted just for the asking. A Chanel suit. One-carat diamond studs. No problem. But I was in Penang, hardly a shopping Mecca.

"Want some squid noodles?" Duke said.

Painfully yours,
Margo

CHAPTER EIGHT

UNDER ORDINARY circumstances, I'd have gone straight from the baggage claim at LAX (where my beloved bar stool was going round and round on the luggage carousel) to the emergency room at Saint John's. But when I called my orthopedist from Penang, he told me the hospital was closed due to earthquake damage and the neighboring medical facilities were so overcrowded they looked like M.A.S.H. units—without Alan Alda. (He also guessed that I'd aggravated a stress fracture.) Several days passed in a Vicodan haze before a bed opened up at UCLA Medical Center and my doctor could put a steel ball joint in my left hip. If I had a dollar for every visitor who invoked Bo Jackson, the patron saint of hip replacement, I could have covered my medical expenses.

Even as I awaited surgery, our house demanded attention. It had ridden the most devastating quake in the city's history and dozens of aftershocks like the Good Ship Los Angeles. By contrast, my dollhouses looked like a miniature disaster area. In the English Tudor, dime-sized dishes had shattered into microscopic shards, diminutive books had flown off dwarf shelves, and a six-inch occupant was crushed when an eight-inch armoire overturned on the bed. (Unlike virtually every other person I talked to in the city, the luckless doll hadn't gotten up in the middle of the night to get a drink of water right before the quake hit.)

Our big home may have survived the quake, but it couldn't escape the temblor's power over the building-department bureaucrats. Hours after we landed I was on the phone, begging my mother not to get on the first plane to the Coast (it would have been easier to tell the earth to stop moving) when I heard the front door open. Duke had gone to the pharmacy to replenish my painkiller supply, and I was alone with just the bar stool for protection. "Who the fuck is it?" I snapped.

Our architect bounded in like a Saint Bernard puppy, a camera flung around his neck. "Oh good. You're back," said Brandon, who later confessed he thought I was going to pull a gun on him. "We have a problem with the structural engineering. The plan checkers want to see lateral analysis of the south wall."

I could blame my vacant stare on pain and jet lag, but I rarely understand him even when I'm lucid. "Excuse me?" I stammered. He didn't seem to notice that I couldn't walk.

"There's no modern calculable way to figure out why your house resisted the earthquake," the architect said. "We don't know how strong the redwood siding is or what kind of nails they used. And between the time we started your project and the time we went to get a permit, we had a major quake. The plan checker correctly determined that what he would have let slide before the quake, he wasn't going to let slide now."

"How much?"

"At least a thousand. I need to design a shear wall to contain the Forces of Overturn."

I was in no position to argue with the Forces of Overturn.

My orthopedist had promised that hip replacement surgery would be a cakewalk, compared to my vacation, and in a way, this was the case. The postoperative pain was minimal, but the inconvenience was excruciating. I had to spend the next two months tottering up the supportive-device evolutionary ladder—from a walker, to crutches, to one crutch, to a cane, then blessedly back to my own two feet. For fear of displacement I couldn't bend more than ninety degrees, which ruled out playing with the pugs, taking a bath, or tying my shoes. (It's hard to feel in control when you can't put your socks on). To add to my indignity, for the first six weeks I was forced to use a Brobdingnagian toilet seat. Not only did it rule out extended social engagements, it engendered sophomoric wisecracks from anyone who entered the house.

"Nice potty," said Brandon. "My three-year-old has one just like it."

And that was self-empowering, compared to not being able to drive.

At first, I had a steady stream of visitors, but most people's general capacity for altruism is limited to about two weeks, and besides, everyone knew someone who had lost their home in the quake whose suffering was far worse than mine. I found myself calling my fellow freelancers, the only people who were home during the day, begging them to take me out for a ride. Usually, my liberator would drive me someplace less than scenic, like the hardware store or the bank (never Neiman-Marcus), crack the window open, and say, "Wait here, I'll be right back." Then she'd disappear for the world's longest bank transaction or key duplication. One Saturday afternoon my husband left me in a supermarket parking lot for half an hour. I felt like Fluffy, the pet poodle. I did, however, become a lot more popular when I got my handicapped-parking sticker.

At least the house was always there for me, whether I liked it or not. An earnest physical therapist—is there any other kind?—taught me how to go up and down stairs on crutches. Up with the good leg; down with the bad. I could manage as long as the stairs in question were even and stable, but our back steps were so rotten, they swayed. When my friend Jon brought me home from the hospital, he had to carry me inside. There I was forced to remain, until I found someone to carry me back downstairs (Duke was away at work all day) or I found a carpenter to come and fix them.

It would have been easier to find a mint-condition Leica M-3 at a garage sale. The earthquake was God's gift to construction workers, what with four hundred injured buildings in nearby Santa Monica alone and an estimated thirty billion dollars' damage citywide. I placed a series of increasingly frantic calls to carpenters who just the month before could hardly make their rent. Two turned me down flat, two didn't return my calls, and one left a recorded message on his machine saying he had moved to Kansas where the ground didn't shake and all he had to worry about were tornadoes.

Lenny, a cabinetmaker, was my last hope. Before our trip, he'd come by to give me an estimate on restoring the sash weights on our ninety-year-old double-hung picture window. His eyes lit up when he saw the window like a car enthusiast spotting a vintage '66 Mustang convertible, but he declined to name a price. "It costs what it costs," he'd said airily. (I subscribe to this philosophy only when it comes to the pugs' veterinary care.) I'd written Lenny off as a flake and was flabbergasted when he rearranged his schedule to come and rescue me.

So great was my gratitude it was lucky that he wasn't one of those Chippendale calendar-boy construction workers who inspire erotic fantasies (then again, it wasn't as if I was able to assume too many positions in the Kama Sutra). He looked like a cross between a Belushi and a beaver, with a long matted ponytail, low-riding jeans that barely covered his ass, buck teeth, and a slow, waddling gait. ("He doesn't seem to be happy unless he's working on the dam," Duke noted.)

I thanked him profusely for coming. "Sounded like you were in bad shape," said the Beaver, lighting the first of thousands of Marlboro Lights that would eventually mulch our cactus garden (is there a construction worker alive who has quit smoking?). He picked up a pry bar and began dismantling the steps.

I beat a speedy retreat, as speedy as you can beat on crutches.

My sister, who was visiting from Chicago, watched with grave trepidation. "He seems wholesome," Laurie said, "but I bet he's in a recovery program somewhere. A lot of these addictive people prefer to work for themselves. They were hippies in the sixties, and the carpenter life goes with that."

She should know. Her husband, a recovering everything, belongs to so many Anonymous groups that I'm surprised he still knows his last name. ("That makes me sound like I'm an overeater," protests the heavily muscled, *svelte* Shark. "I worked hard to be a drug addict.") His fellow addicts—the A's, Laurie calls them—had remodeled her bedroom and bath.

"We not only had the addiction group, we had the international A's," Laurie said. "We had Chinese addicts doing the electricity, Swedes painting. One night, I looked up and noticed you could see big numbers through the paint. There was a big sixty-two over the lamp. I don't know why there were numbers. I think it was for the wiring, but they hadn't had the foresight to erase the numbers or thicken the paint."

The Shark defended his hiring policy. "All the contractors that bid the job were associated with twelve-step programs," he conceded. "Not that you get a better rate, but most of the people in twelve-step recovery have an obligation to themselves to be honest," he said. "They may be incompetent, but they're generally honest, so that's important."

Whatever his substance-abuse history, the Beaver proved to be my ideal worker. He didn't want to chat, he didn't want to use the phone, all he wanted was to build his dam (and occasionally use the bathroom). I wasn't subjected to an irritating radio serenade of "Sooner or Later Love Is Going to Get You," "Time After Time," and "Maggie Mae;" he favored National Public Radio. By the end of the first day, the old steps were gone, the new posts were set in concrete, and the frame was taking shape. I brought him a Diet 7-Up—Duke had ingeniously strapped my bike basket onto my aluminum walker—and complimented him on the job.

"I love wood. It's my favorite thing to make money out of," he said. "Though it beats me where we're getting it from—Siberia, maybe. It's sort of a dilemma. I belong to every environmental group on the planet and yet . . ." He suddenly ran out of words, tugged up his jeans, and drove away.

He did open up a little as the job progressed. One day I asked him what to do about Jason, a thirteen-year-old whom I'd hired to walk the pugs after Laurie went home. I've heard stories about dogs who sense that their master is ill and become solicitous, but the ever-opportunistic pugs tried to cull me from the pack. The devoted Clara, accustomed to accompanying me on all my errands, transferred her allegiance to Duke when she realized that I was no longer able to chauffeur her around. (Clara's need for public adulation rivals Judy Garland's in the drug years.) The dim-witted Sophie yapped incessantly at my walker and later charged my crutches, which she viewed as her enemy. Even if the pugs hadn't forgotten everything they learned in obedience class and actually heeled by my side instead of tangling me in their leashes like I was a maypole, I would have been hesitant to take them down to the Venice boardwalk. A woman on crutches was no match for panhandlers, tarot hustlers, whizzing cyclists, and string bikini–clad Rollerbladers.

So I was dependent on the dog walker, but young Jason had an irritating habit of not showing up.

"Tell him you'll hire someone else," the Beaver said.

There was no one else. My friends were at work. Even John, my blond, chisel-featured, muscle-bound, 100 percent gay neighbor, who lived off a trust fund and spent his days watching soaps and talk shows, couldn't manage afternoon pug duty, though he thoughtfully stopped by every morning to pick up the shoes, wet towels, and newspapers that Duke had left on the floor in my path. "I can't miss Miss Winfrey," John explained.

"The kid doesn't know that," the Beaver said. "Lie." In a further elucidation of his child-rearing philosophy, he told me that his thirteen-year-old was overheard by his teachers saying, "We dropped the acid at ten, so it should hit by noon."

"What did you do?"

"I told him not to get caught." The Beaver extinguished his cigarette in the dirt beside the prickly pear cactus and turned the saw back on.

He originally estimated that it would take a couple of days to build the back steps. In fact it took a week—but he honored his price and even Brandon couldn't find fault with the finished product. "You could let him do the side deck too," our architect said magnanimously. I had already given the Beaver the job.

Brandon's pomposity was lightened by his dazzling efficiency. While I was convalescing, the living Day Runner—Duke called him the reincarnation of Bismarck—redid our structural drawings, ran them by an engineer, and picked up our coastal waiver, an administrative permit. Living fifty yards from the beach, we have to clear any building projects with the Coastal Commission, a watchdog environmental agency designed to protect Malibu from developers and Santa Barbara from oil drilling. According to Brandon, the bureaucrats stopped Cher from building a house for her mother on her Malibu property.

"Since you didn't want to change the characteristic of the neighborhood or cut off anyone's view, I just had to go in front of a staff person, not the whole commission," he reported. "It was a good thing too because otherwise, if your neighbors wanted to complain, they could have hung you up on a skewer."

I certainly didn't want to mess with the neighbors. The landlord of the Roach Motel was trying to evict Ian, the mail-order penis enlarger, for not paying his rent. Meanwhile, in Apartment C, a gaggle of Eurotrash was having a turf war with the surfers in the apartment building on the other side. They lobbed cherry bombs at each other over our roof.

"Chill, lady," said a German tippler when I implored him to hold fire. "We're just trying to have a little fun."

What could I possibly do? Wave a crutch at them?

Brandon was impatient to nail down the design details so we could interview contractors and begin bidding. (Frankly, I was surprised he didn't follow me to the operating room with blueprints.) Propped on pillows, I made it through a forty-minute debate on whether the new beam in the living room should be wrapped in drywall (we said no, Brandon argued eloquently for and against, then we said no again), a twenty-minute treatise on the trusslike patterns of steel webbing, and an hour-long comparison of aluminum, vinyl, and wood windows, before I pleaded exhaustion.

"God is in the details," our architect said sternly.

The devil is in there too. Remodeling is a license to be pedantic. There are countless teeny decisions to make about things I've never thought about. How many conduits do I want? Where do I want them? (What are they?) And each decision is supposed to impact your life. I don't think it's healthy to attach my ego to kitchen cabinets. Yet that's exactly what you're encouraged to do. I couldn't pick up an issue of *House Beautiful* or *Better Homes & Gardens* without being admonished to express my personality by selecting a vinyl floor that looks like antique flagstones (maybe I'm crazy, but it seems like the message behind this choice is that I'm a total phony) or to bring glamour into my life by purchasing a commercial-quality range.

In the case of the windows, Duke and I knew exactly what we wanted—plain, wooden, double-hung windows. I didn't care if they turned the wall into a work of art or if they had special tempered glass that had gone to the moon. Brandon alleged that wooden windows were expensive and difficult to pop into an existing space. I felt ashamed for doubting him—his knowledge of building trivia was so exhaustive. But the day my stitches came out, I had Duke take me to a window showroom. I faltered in on crutches and found a brand that Brandon had never heard of at a price we could afford.

On that same shopping trip, I got a better idea of the earthquake's psychic damage. We were in the paint store, buying an oil stain to seal the steps, when we felt a rolling aftershock. Having missed the big one, I had your typical Southern Californian, pre-big-one response: "Oh, gee, the earth is moving." Then I looked up and noticed that everyone else was fleeing the building. It occurred to me to run too, but then I remembered that I was on crutches.

"I suppose those windows might work," the architect said skeptically. He tended to be suspicious of job elements beyond his control.

The wood floors were a good example. My friend Debbie had finally gotten financing for her Santa Monica dream house and was busy refurbishing her nest. She'd cornered the market on cheap labor. "I found the most amazing floor guy," Debbie raved, as if she had found the man of her dreams. (Actually, I hoped he was better than some of the men of her dreams. In particular, the ex-boyfriend who recently founded *Modern Goddess,* a magazine targeted to men who wanted to be enslaved by women. Debbie was speechless when he sent her the first issue, filled with articles like "How to Find a Mistress" and "Some of America's Best Dominatrixes." "Didn't you realize?" I asked. "I thought he was just being considerate when he brought me coffee in bed," Debbie said. "He did buy me a pair of black thigh-high boots with spiked heels. But I didn't think anything of it. They were really expensive. I never had such nice boots." I asked how the relationship ended. "I broke up with him," she said. "Ah," I said gleefully. "So you hurt him?")

Debbie assured me that the floor guy was a treasure. "He refinished the whole upstairs and put new bleached oak planks downstairs for under five thousand dollars. Eighteen thousand square feet, can you believe it?" She drove over and picked me up so that I could see for myself. I sat patiently in her Honda while she dashed into the drugstore to pick up a prescription (ten minutes—wouldn't you know it?—there was a line), dropped some clothes at the dry cleaner (twenty minutes—they lost her blouse), and had a key duplicated (ten minutes). But her floors were worth the wait. "His name is Símon," Debbie said, handing me his card. "He's from Peru. Oh, and I better warn you. He loves to talk."

No problem. I was starved for conversation.

Símon was a lanky chain-smoker with the regal bearing and aquiline profile of an Inca prince. "I broke my leg when I was eighteen, so I know what you're going through," he said cheerfully when he saw my crutches. I endured the inevitable X-ray-by-X-ray account of his fracture, which was followed by the tragic saga of his aunt's hip replacement—how her doctor botched it, why she couldn't sue, how she'll never be able to walk again. (Thanks for sharing that.)

In the time it took him to measure, I learned that he came to Los Angeles when he was seventeen because there was nothing to do in Lima at night. He used to be an aerospace engineer, but he also had a law degree. He turned to floors because they paid better. "Would you believe it? The exam for my floor license was harder than the bar," Símon said. "Those questions about carpet pile were really tough." He pulled up a corner of the carpet and ascertained there were fir boards underneath.

"I don't want to promise until the carpets come up and I can see if they're really terrible," Símon said. "But assuming I don't have to do a lot of repairs, you're probably looking at twelve hundred and fifty dollars." Wood floors were what I wanted most. I was ecstatic to hear the low bid.

Not Brandon. "You should have called the guy who did my floors," he said suspiciously. "He did a really careful job." Brandon's floor guy gave me a phone quote of $3,000. "He must be really popular," Brandon said. But we resolved to give Símon the job.

At our next meeting, our architect handed us a revised line-item budget. According to Brandon, who assured us he excelled at estimating, the job would cost $21,000, plus 20 percent for the contractor. He explained that our bottom line had gone up because of the earthquake. We now had to put in a shear wall, a plywood panel that would be bolted to the foundation to keep the house from collapsing in another quake.

What the Architect Guessed	
Cosmetic repair of the master bathroom	$ 4,000
Remodel great room with cathedral ceilings	$ 6,000
Cosmetic repair of the kitchen	$ 1,550
Repaint exterior and interior of house	$ 2,500
Floors (Símon's bid, plus $250 contingency)	$ 1,500
Rebuild back and side steps	$ 1,400
Bike shed	$ 500
New windows	$ 2,550
Fireplace surround for focal point	$ 1,000
Line-item budget costs	$21,000
Contractor's profit and overhead at 20%	$ 4,200
Total estimated budget costs	$ 25,200

"I can live with the increase," Brandon said. "But if the twenty thousand is germane, then something has to go."

We told him not to worry. "Though we will not get angry with you for taking us seriously," Duke added. We decided to postpone any budget cuts until after the contractors had finished bidding.

"You still need to talk to someone about the chimney and someone about the heat," Brandon reminded me.

The heat had been a problem for years. We have four gas wall heaters, but only the one in our bedroom worked. The living room heater was beyond repair, the one in Duke's office only stayed lit for two minutes, and the heater in my office had been murdered by a vengeful heating thug whom I'd summoned one winter when all the heaters were down. The heating thug made what seemed to me to be a reasonable offer to fix the heaters (granted, I was chilly). He didn't have enough thermonuclear thingamajigs in his truck to do the whole job, so he fixed the one in the bedroom and promised to return in the morning to do the rest. In the interim, Duke came home, looked at the bill, made a phone call to the appliance supply store, and announced we were being charged four times the going thermonuclear-thingamajig rate. He called the thug and threatened to report him to the Better Business Bureau.

The thug knocked off a hundred bucks, but we paid dearly. He arrived the next morning in a vile mood, told me that my husband was an asshole, and dismantled my office heater, all the while cursing and muttering. I called my sister and told her that if she didn't hear from me in an hour, she should call 911. (I later made Duke swear that the next time he bullied a repairman, he'd stick around to defend me.) I survived, but my office heater developed a suspicious disease soon after our check cleared, and the thug never returned to complete the job.

Prodded by Brandon, I summoned up my courage and another heating contractor, Señor Warmth, whose life-size image was stenciled on all the company trucks. The dispatcher promised that Señor Warmth would be there at four. He arrived at six, looked at the bedroom heater, and scowled. "Lady, if that thing was to blow in the night, you'd go right away," he said coldly. The only thing that could save me from destruction was to let him put in a forced-air heating system for only $5,000.

Brandon wasn't about to waste precious construction dollars on heat. "I've got wall heaters in my house, and they work just fine," he said. He maintained that we could get new wall heaters at the Home Depot for $300 a pop. Señor Warmth refused to give me a price on installing the cheaper option.

"I'm telling you they're going to blow," Warmth said.

The Beaver saved us, albeit indirectly. His giant saw overtaxed some elderly wiring and shorted out a light socket. Naturally, it happened at night, when electricians charge double their hourly rate, but for once we got lucky: One of our sane neighbors is an electrician. Jeffrey fixed the circuit for $75 and promised to install the new wall heaters for an equally low rate.

That left just the fireplace, which smoked when it was lit. Brandon recommended a company called Chim Chim Cheree. I was reluctant to do business with an establishment named after a Mary Poppins song, but I called anyway. I was put on hold for half an hour while the strains of "Supercalifragilisticexpialidocious" drove me slowly insane. Eventually, a chimney consultant (everyone in California is either a counselor or a consultant) took my name and address and promised to send out a sweep in the traditional tuxedo and top hat the following day. The sweep never showed, and I called to complain. I was put on hold for two choruses of "Just a Spoonful of Sugar Helps the Medicine Go Down."

"Things have been a little crazy since the earthquake," said the consultant. I realized the streets of Los Angeles were lined with toppled unreinforced masonry chimneys. (My friend Blanche, the pug breeder, had lost hers, but she reported a bright side to the quake. "The pugs come right away when they're called," she told me. This is a first for pugs.) I tried to be patient.

"I'll send someone out tomorrow," the chimney consultant promised.

But tomorrow the sweep never came.

Next, I called an outfit named Fiddler on the Roof. Again, I was put on hold, but this time the music was "Anatevka." Again, a harried secretary took my name and address and set up an appointment. Again the sweep never came.

"Breathing too much soot obviously doesn't help the brain," said the Beaver.

Sweep Number Three, Fred, didn't have a cutesy name, which I took to be a good sign. He swore he'd be at the house at four. At two, he left a message on my machine. "I came to your house, but you weren't there."

This was impossible as I still couldn't drive. Fred offered to return the following day at three. I never left the house, but at two I got a plaintive call. "I came, why weren't you there?"

"You must be coming to the wrong house."

"No, I'm coming to the right house."

"Did it have a red door? Was there a heavyset man sawing in the backyard?"

"No, there wasn't a red door. And no one was home."

"Then you came to the wrong house." It was either that or he was phoning from a parallel universe. I went over the directions carefully. Fred promised he'd be there Saturday at noon.

I waited and waited, but he never came. My friend Marjorie came by at one and offered to take me to tea. I was reluctant to go, so certain was I that this sweep wouldn't let me down, but my husband insisted on helping me into her car.

"Mike Ovitz will come to the house sooner," Duke said.

"There are so many people in the service profession," Brandon said. "If someone stands you up three times, you shouldn't use him."

I assured him that if God had walked through the door in a chimney-sweep suit, I wouldn't have given him the job.

"Keep trying," the architect ordered. In the meantime, he got our building permit, finished the working drawings, and solemnly presented us with his final bill.

"My contractual obligation is finished," Brandon said, closing his notebook. I looked at my mate with alarm. When we had originally hired Brandon, he'd given us a two-part contract. The first covered Design, Planning, and Building Permit Documents; the second, Overseeing Bid-

ding and Construction. We'd only signed up for Part One, but the idea of proceeding without Brandon was unthinkable. I couldn't tie my shoes yet, let alone supervise construction. "We'd love for you to supervise our job," I said.

I expected a "thank-you" or an "oh good," but instead the architect spent twenty minutes explaining that he couldn't supervise because it violated his architectural oath. He could only oversee. I ultimately realized that he drew a distinction between the words *supervise* and *oversee*. "Fine," I said. "Oversee the job. Whatever you want to call it, we need your help."

"It's a big decision," Brandon said. "I don't want to push myself on you. When I leave, you two should think it over."

"Honey, we should think about it," Duke said, laughing. After Brandon left we thought about it for a second.

"We'd be crazy not to," I said.

"Either pay him now or pay a shrink later," Duke agreed.

Brandon was still protesting the next evening, when I called to say that we'd made our decision. "Are you sure you don't want to act as your own contractor?"

"It's like being your own brain surgeon as far as I'm concerned," Duke said.

"I'll fax you the second part of the contract," said Brandon. "It's all ready to go."

CHAPTER NINE

A S SOON AS the construction documents were ready for bidding, I called Walt, my Dream Contractor. He'd already given me a wealth of sensible (and free!) advice, and I'd been looking forward to an effortless construction under his benevolent auspices. I was crushed to be the recipient of one last tip. "You can't afford me," said Walt, who was booked solid for the next six months with earthquake repairs.

"Let's work it out a little backwards, let's say it took a month," Walt continued, hastily assuring me that it would take at least two. "It's nine thousand to get us on the job, then you have supervision, that's another five thousand, so you're looking at fourteen thousand and nothing's been done. All we did was sign papers. That leaves only six thousand for what's left. We could maybe buy some lumber. You could build a big frame."

He threw out a final pointer: "Find some decent carpenter and have him live with you for as long as it takes. You'll be at this guy's mercy, and I don't know if it will be up to code, but you can try."

As fond as I was of the Beaver, this wasn't something I cared to try.

Brandon had once lost an impressive addition to his portfolio because his client decided to postpone building until he could afford a first-class contractor. Brandon had no intention of letting it happen again. "There are three types of contractors," he said briskly, at our next meeting. He held up a finger. "Walt is the first type; he's very good at what he does, but he's expensive. His niche is remodeling two-, three-, or four-hun-

dred-thousand-dollar homes for people in Beverly Hills. Twenty thousand dollars is just not in his range."

Only in construction can you feel like a piker for spending a mere $20,000.

Brandon held up two fingers. "The second type is usually a young guy, in his early thirties. He basically worked for years as a framing contractor, then got paired up with a general contractor, who taught him a few tricks, and now he wants to go on his own. But he's still learning. General contracting is more than being able to put up a building and call people on the telephone. You have to know how to present yourself, how to be on time. A lot of these guys have cellular phones, but they don't know how to use them except to call 976 numbers."

This didn't seem like a terrific recommendation, but Brandon insisted it was the *third* kind of contractor who caused all the trouble. He held up three fingers.

"There's something wrong with Type Threes, but you don't know it. These guys get divorced on your job or they have a heart attack and you're screwed. Sometimes it's a personality defect, sometimes just happenstance. You just can't tell where these guys are in their drinking cycle."

You also can't tell where they are in their immigration schedule. Take Carlos, the Israeli émigré who remodeled our front bathroom a few years back. No sooner had Carlos removed our toilet and the sink than his brother and sister-in-law from Tel Aviv arrived in Los Angeles. Carlos disappeared for large chunks of time to help them find a dentist, a lawyer, an apartment, a job. I tried to be understanding, even as a three-week job tiling the shower, installing a new sink, and drywalling the ceiling stretched to six. In exchange, Carlos did a conscientious job. So the glass shower-door enclosure never quite closed and the new linoleum floor cracked within a month. I got even. I sold Carlos my husband's old car, possibly the worst car ever made.

Duke had bought the Toyota Supra secondhand from a Persian on the boardwalk who was leaving the country the next day. It was clear to me that the car had been in a fatal wreck and the bloodstains had been removed by cutting strategic pieces out of the upholstery, but Duke was loath to admit he got a bad deal, even when the engine fell apart the second week and had to be replaced. The lemon had numerous defects; a collapsed passenger seat, a speedometer that was stuck at a hundred miles an hour, and the continuing presence of smoke in the air-conditioning vents. When Duke finally bought a new car, the dealer wouldn't even take it in trade. But on the last day of the job, Carlos mentioned that his brother needed a car. His eyes lit up when I showed him the Toyota. "How much?" he said.

"My husband wants eight hundred dollars," I said. I thought my husband was out of his mind.

"Would he take seven fifty?" Carlos asked.

He would or I'd kill him. A few weeks later, Carlos drove over to have Duke sign the transfer of title. The demon car had a flashy new paint job, and the radio actually worked without spewing smoke. "Aren't you sorry you sold it?" the contractor asked.

I nodded noncommittally, and we parted on good terms. Still, I thought it was tempting fate to call him again. The car had surely blown up by now.

Brandon earnestly explained that it violated his architectural oath to recommend a contractor. In the next breath, he suggested that we call Mickey Marvin, his former boss, a Type One contractor who had gotten burned out doing big projects and was concentrating on remodels. "I've already talked to Mickey about this job, and he's interested in bidding," said Brandon. "This is the kind of job he likes."

We asked why Brandon had stopped working for him. "Mickey's also an architect," he said. "For a while I was allowed to design what I wanted to design, but as he got burned out in contracting he wanted to do more and more of the architectural functions. We've never worked together since I left his office."

This didn't strike me as a good sign.

To reach Mickey was an exercise in modern communication technology. His voice mail instructed me to press 1 for his pager, press 2 for his car phone, and press 3 for his car fax. I half expected an Internet address, like "Mickey@jobsite.com." I pressed 4 and left a message. Two minutes later, Mickey called from his Jaguar (I know this because his first words were "I'm calling from my Jaguar"). He was stuck in a traffic jam on La Cienega Boulevard, where traffic from the collapsed stretch of the Santa Monica Freeway was being rerouted, but he promised to come over as fast as he could. Two hours later I trudged to the door on one crutch and beheld a clone of Bobby Ewing on *Dallas*. He was decked out in Wrangler jeans pressed with a knife crease, a teal Polo shirt, and pristine Nikes with matching teal trim. I gaped. I had never seen a contractor with a hundred-dollar haircut.

Clara and Sophie bounded over and sniffed him. Mickey bent down and gave them each a perfunctory pat, then gingerly picked off the stray pug hairs. "I'm allergic to dogs," he said.

That didn't strike me as a good sign either.

He handed me a slick résumé. "What can I tell you," said Mickey with the kind of over-the-top enthusiasm I associate with infomercial pitchmen. "I'm the son of a son of a builder. I've done shopping centers, apartment buildings, model homes. I do whatever the market demands. I've won extensive awards."

"That's nice," I said politely. I couldn't get over how cute he was. He looked like he belonged on a golf course or on the cover of a brochure for Club Med. Anywhere but a construction site.

"I'm a licensed Realtor, general contractor, and architect."

"That's nice," I said again. I led him around the house, gesticulating with my crutch. He asked searching questions like did I want the insides of my closets painted (sure, why not?) and were the doorknobs going to stay the same? I'd never thought about the doorknobs. It occurred to me that there's a point at which attention to detail becomes ridiculous.

On his way out, I asked for references. "Who do you want?" Mickey asked. "A city councilman? The chief of staff at the medical center? The president of the Rotary Club? I know them all."

I have never understood what the Rotary Club is, so I wasn't impressed. "Why don't you just give me some people whose homes you've done?"

He promised he'd fax them from his car.

To further facilitate our selection of a contractor, Brandon gave us a printed outline with step-by-step instructions seemingly designed for clients with absolutely no common sense. My favorites were "the chemistry between the two of you should be positive" and "If a contractor has no completed work for you to look at, or if his references have bad things to say about the contractor, then think twice about this candidate."

"What if I saw him on *America's Most Wanted*?" I twitted Brandon.

He laughed nervously. "If he comes in and has a scarlet letter branded on his forehead, you should probably skip him," he said. "You should also watch out for the third-generation builders. Those guys talk out of both sides of their mouth."

"Wasn't Mickey third-generation?"

Brandon put his serious face back on and said, "Mickey's an exception. Whoever you choose, you should meet all the contractors personally."

I burst out laughing. "What do you think I'm going to do? Call a stranger up on the phone and say, 'Hi, do you want to make twenty thousand dollars? I'll fax you the drawings?'"

"I don't always know who I'm dealing with," said Brandon.

I felt guilty for giving him a hard time because his suggestions were sensible, if obvious. For instance: "Recruit referrals from friends and neighbors who have had a successful relationship with a contractor." I called Marjorie, who knows everything, and asked who built her addition. "Call Hal," she said. "Hal's terrific." I would have hired him on the spot. Marjorie had previously recommended our housekeeper, who is so honest, intelligent, and calming a presence that she could be the next Dalai Lama.

Hal looked and walked like Walter Brennan playing Grandpappy Amos on *The Real McCoys*. He had a shock of thick gray hair that boyishly flopped over his earnest bovine eyes. His jeans were sagging and faded, and his flannel plaid shirt barely concealed a T-shirt that read: I'M A PRO-FESSIONAL, DON'T TRY THIS AT HOME. Sophie and Clara threw themselves at his feet like devotees saluting their guru.

"It's pug-a-rama," Hal laughed. He bent down and scratched each pug behind her ears. Clara was transfixed and plunked herself down on his shoe. (Marjorie had told me that her dogs, Ralph and Daisy, were in heaven during the entire remodel.)

Any remaining doubts were eliminated when he stopped for a moment to admire the antique coal scuttle beside the fireplace. It had belonged to my grandmother, Rosy, who used to fill it with small bottles of Coca-Cola when I came to visit. She gave it to me right before she died, and it's probably the possession I would save first in a fire. "Imagine a time when they took the trouble to make a container for coal look so good," Hal said thoughtfully.

Brandon had advised us to interview between three and five contractors. Duke recalled Salvador the Shady, a recovering cocaine addict who had done some work on the house when Duke first bought it and was preparing it for rental. "I sort of broke every rule," my husband confessed. "I gave him a big check and let him go buy stuff. I'd give him a couple thousand, he'd do a chunk, then I'd give him some more. What saved me is that halfway through the job his wife saw the house and she decided she'd like to live in it. So he did a really good job, thinking he was going to live there. Then at the last minute she decided not to move."

Ironically, we ran into Salvador the Shady that weekend at the Venice Art Walk. He looked like the freeway killer. "Don't even think of it," I whispered to Duke.

A few nights later, we went to a screening at Sony Pictures. Marjorie's husband, David, had just completed a short film called *Performance Anxiety*. The film was clever and funny—it went on to win the critics' prize at Cannes—but the evening was memorable on two other counts. First, the People's Choice Awards were at Sony that night too, and all the handicapped spaces were blocked off by long limousines and the chauffeurs refused to move (only in L.A.!). I'd just graduated to a cane and was proud that I managed to hike all the way across the parking lot. Second, we ran into Peter, a talented builder who had moved to New York. We asked him to recommend a contractor.

Enter Zachary Hoffman, a hotshot architect/builder, at least in his own mind. I'd already met Zachary at a party the year before when I was trolling for architects. I asked him to look at our house and he'd turned me down flat. "I only do selective projects that interest me a lot," he'd said haughtily, adding that he was into real estate development. Marjorie confided that Zachary had lost a lot of money when the real estate market crashed and he was eager for work.

Zach showed up in a Stetson, Armani wire-rim glasses, and designer jeans. He knelt down and studied the pugs as if they were Rodin sculptures. "Didn't these dogs originally come from China?" he asked. "Weren't they a meat breed?"

This is a part of the pug's noble, thousand-year history that I prefer not to dwell on. My husband believes that pugs were saved from the pot by their utter ridiculousness and desire to please humans. "It's the opposite of singing for your supper," Duke says. "It's singing not to be supper."

Zach followed me through the house, taking careful notes and dropping tantalizing hints about what he could have done if he'd been our architect. *He* could have put up a two-story addition for under a hundred grand. *He* could have landscaped the sides of the house so we wouldn't need obscure glass to block out the neighbors. *He* could have designed a great room without a massive beam. "You had your chance," I said. "You turned me down."

"Funny how things work out," Zach said amiably. He admitted that the economy had pushed him into remodels and building, but he gave it a positive spin. "The recession is making things less of a crapshoot. It used to be like Las Vegas—buy a property, fix it up, refinance, get your money back, buy another. Now it's more like blue-chip stocks. You can buy something and know it will appreciate twenty percent."

All in all, he seemed competent and smart, though the pugs cut him dead. We gave the final set of drawings to our neighbor Jeffrey, who'd expressed interest in bidding when he fixed our electricity. I believe hiring a neighbor is about as misguided as dating one and was relieved when Jeffrey bowed out. "I'm swamped with all this earthquake stuff," he said, "but thanks for thinking of me."

Two weeks later, the candidates were ready. Brandon had warned that the bids might come in a little higher than his estimated cost, and he reminded us that he would make any changes for free. Still, it was hard to remain poker-faced when Mickey handed us a bid for $31,000 for work that Brandon reckoned would be $18,000. "I'd take twenty-five hundred off to have the house vacant," Mickey added helpfully.

Brandon began to toy with his ex-boss, like a cat torturing prey. "How long will this job take in your estimation with them living here?" he asked, as if we weren't sitting right there.

"With them living here, approximately three months," Mickey said. "Without them, probably two months."

"When you say not living here, you mean the whole house is empty?" Brandon asked.

"Right. It would be a free-fire zone for my builders." Free-fire zone is not an image I like to associate with my house.

Moving out would increase our budget, but it would also save our sanity. "It's something to think about," Duke said. "But what would make it more worth thinking about is if you were willing to put in a penalty clause that said we would only have to get a place for X number of months, so that if we moved out and the job ran over, we wouldn't be getting the worst of both sides of the deal."

"I couldn't contain myself to eight weeks," Mickey said. "I'd put the clause in for ten weeks at least."

"Economically, then, we're not saving very much," Duke said.

"It's important to know that there's a certain amount of aggravation that goes with having a house torn up," said Brandon, who later told us with equal conviction that he could set up the job so it wouldn't be intrusive.

Brandon asked about the payment schedule. "You pay nothing on signing," Mickey said. "As we go through portions of the work, I will submit a bill. In a reasonable amount of time I expect a check. If you disagree, you withhold payment. If I don't receive a check, then I stop the job. I let you owe me a lot of money. It keeps me very interested, but then again, I can make your lives miserable if I feel like it. It's my ace in the hole."

That's not the kind of ace I like someone else to hold.

"He seemed like someone who'd be selling swampland in Florida except he thought power tools were a neat thing to own," Duke said when Mickey left.

I asked Brandon if he was alarmed that the bid was so high. "Wait and see what the others come in at," he advised.

Zach came in even higher: $35,000. We were nonplussed, but Brandon forged on, determined to whittle it down. "I made a list of fixtures that will be supplied by the owners," he said. "Tell me if there's anything like that in the bid, and we'll take it out." (Brandon still suffered under the delusion that taking it out of his budget made it free.)

Zach subtracted fifty bucks for lights and a couple hundred for tile. "It's smart that you're buying your fixtures," he said. "One thing a contractor spends a lot of time doing on the job is driving around town, chasing after sixpenny nails, lighting fixtures, plumbing supplies. It also saves you architecture fees because if the architect has to sit down and specify all the materials and pick out all the colors, it takes time."

Funny, Brandon never said a word about lowering his fees.

Duke asked about a discount for moving out. Zach shook his head. "We just work around the clients. We had someone who lived in the upper front apartment of a triplex and rented out the other two. We had to take out his whole staircase to put in a new deck. He didn't have a way to go up and down, but we worked around him. We had a new staircase built and framed, and we set it up so he could get out."

"So we could probably stay," said Duke.

I rolled my eyes. I'd already earned the Good Sport of the Year award touring Malaysia with a broken hip. I had no intention of proving myself further.

Clara and Sophie scurried to the door to greet Hal. "They sure are cute," he said as they leapt at his face like koi surfacing for supper. Clara, an emotional slut, sat in his lap for the course of the meeting.

Whereas Mickey and Zach presented official-looking computer-generated proposals, Hal handed us a handwritten scrap of paper. His bottom line was $25,000, but that didn't include paint. "We're meeting the painter over here on Friday," he said. "That's a separate bid. We'll just tack that on."

"How much more do you think that will be?" I asked.

Hal shrugged. "You know, I really can't say."

Brandon lit into Hal like a senator vetting a Supreme Court nominee. It was like watching a live demonstration of a Type A versus a Type B personality. "You know, I plugged your license number in to the State of California automatic license-checking phone machine, and it came back different," Brandon said smugly. "It kind of startled me." He waved a piece of paper in Hal's face.

"Well, I'll be damned," the contractor said, slapping his thighs. He'd accidentally transposed two of the numbers on his letterhead. "I'm sure glad that you pointed that out."

We were impressed by Hal's graciousness. "How much of the work will you do yourself?" Duke asked.

"Everything but the painting and the tile. It will mainly be myself and Dexter, he's my son-in-law. He'll do the plumbing and the electrical. We'll get some laborers for the demo and the insulation, but that's about it."

"So our house is going to be in your hands?" Duke said, smiling.

"Unfortunately," Hal said, with a little shrug. "I'm getting tired."

Brandon interrupted: "Is there an allowance for dry rot?"

"If it just means sistering some studs on, well, that's no problem. I'm not going to be picky. If it's something we can fix without a major thing, then that's the way to do it."

"What do you expect from architects and clients?"

"Truthfully, things go pretty smoothly. If you don't like something that's going on, just tell me. I don't tend to complain a lot, so I tend to sometimes not say something, just absorb it, but I'll try not to do that."

Brandon couldn't resist a parting shot: "Do you have references they can check?"

A few days later, Hal brought his painting associate, Charley, over to bid. My husband has a theory about painters: "They're all alcoholics." ("Nobody starts out their life wanting to be a painter," Duke explained. "Parents don't stand over you, saying: 'Someday, if you study hard, you'll be a painter. It takes no skill, no strength, it's a crummy job breathing fumes and scraping paint.'") The salmon-nosed, perpetually scowling Charley certainly fit the bill.

At eight in the morning, he was quaffing tequila-laced mocha java out of a Starbucks commuter mug, muttering about the postearthquake traffic on the Santa Monica Freeway. I couldn't tell if he hated me or the house or just the world in general, but as we walked from room to room, he grew increasingly hostile.

He pursed his lips and frowned. "I'm not moving these totskys," he warned me.

"What's a totsky?"

Charley gesticulated like a traffic cop, indicating the troupe of Burmese marionettes hanging from the ceiling, a Baccarat crystal menagerie on the windowsill, and the floor-to-ceiling shelves crammed with books. "Totskys," he said disgustedly.

"Do you mean, *tchotchkes?*"

"Right. Totskys."

"Tchotchkes," I said sternly, hearing my grandmother's chuckle resounding in my brain. "It's Yiddish."

"Whatever," he muttered. "This shit better be out of my way."

That evening, I told Duke that we couldn't hire as a painter someone who put valuable folk art in the same league with matadors painted on black velvet and plastic figurines of kitties performing their toilettes. My husband said that it wasn't necessary to feel affection for a worker (this from someone who has virtually no contact with them). A couple of days later, Charley faxed over a bid for $12,000.

"We could hire Michelangelo for that," Duke said.

This made Hal the high bidder, at $37,000. "It's a little higher than I would have hoped, but it's a hard house to paint," Hal said. "It needs a lot of prep, and I know Charley will do a good job."

For $12,000, I'd do a good job too. I've painted dozens of dollhouses. At that very minute, I was working on a miniature San Francisco Victorian-style antique shop for my sister, with intricate gingerbread moldings in five colors. Besides, when I first moved in with Duke, I painted five rooms of our big house. I spent the first month of our live-in relationship with a scarf around my head, dodging drips. (Why is it that nail polish chips in a day and latex paint remains on the nails for months?) True to form, Duke would pop his head in and thoughtfully point out the spots that I had missed. Then after I'd spent days doing two coats and all the trim, he'd come in like a conquering hero and roll the ceiling.

I reviewed the other bids. Mickey and Zach had respectively allotted $4,000 and $5,000 for paint. Brandon told me that comparing line-item budgets was like comparing apples and oranges. "When contractors prepare these bids, they use a system that's individual and unique," Brandon said. "You don't know how they figure. The drywall for the bathroom can be buried in the drywall cost for the living room." Never one to cling to

principal long, he then suggested that if we plugged Zach's painting bid into Hal's bid, we'd wind up with a figure that was only $300 less than Mickey's bid.

"But we don't want Mickey," I said. "We want Hal." I'd checked his references after our meeting.

"Hal's wonderful," exclaimed the Hollywood screenwriter. "We totally adored him. He can do everything, and he's a really nice person on top of it."

"Hal's terrific," gushed the Santa Monica environmental lawyer. "He's done a million things in our house. The only thing I can say is that sometimes he forgets to ask for his money."

That didn't strike me as an unpleasant quality in a contractor, though in time I would change my mind.

"I hear what you're saying," Brandon said. "With personality and fit you'd rate Mickey last, with Zach second, and Hal first. But before you can commit, you need him to redo that painting bid."

"I'm not worried about the paint because frankly, I think we can find ways around it," Duke said. I knew that he was recalling Pedro and Martín, the day laborers who had tagged our fence. We'd only paid them $900 to paint the exterior, and it didn't turn out half bad (though it did require countless trips to the cash machine, because we had to give them cash at the end of each day).

As Brandon scribbled nervously in his notebook, I called Hal and told him that he had the job.

CHAPTER TEN

H AL ASSURED US that he knew plenty of painters, but ten days passed without him bringing one around. Exasperated by the delay, Brandon contacted Joseph, a painter he knew from his daughter's play group. "Joseph's in his prealcoholic phase," said Brandon, who agreed with Duke's hypothesis.

Whatever his degree of sobriety, Joseph had a remarkably irritating phone-machine message, recorded by his three-year-old daughter: "Daddy's not here to paint," she peeped, "but if you're in a hurry I can come over with my crayons." (What are parents trying to prove when they put a toddler on their machine? That their offspring can speak?) In person, he was a bland, chinless, prematurely balding fellow dressed entirely in beige. His credentials included painting the Getty Museum and rescuing a large seaside hotel from a "too too Cape Cod" color scheme.

"We don't need the Getty paint job," Duke would say later.

"My specialty is matching colors," said the colorless Joseph. "I have a rack of tints in my truck."

As long as I had an expert on the premises, I solicited his advice on the miniature antique shop. It had lots of gingerbread trim, and I was having trouble figuring out which colors went where. Joseph advised teal as a base, terra-cotta for the architectural details, and cream for trim. "You might also use lavender as a punch color," he said. We had a lovely chat about technique ("Just slop the base coat on with a big brush"), and he even lent me a catalog that sold discount brushes. I would have hired him just so my dollhouses would benefit from his expertise.

Alas, Joseph faxed over a $7,500 bid.

I was determined not to turn our house into a financial Bermuda Triangle. My father had warned me that if we sunk too much cash into the property, we'd be stuck with it forever. "People with half a million dollars to spend aren't going to want to buy in Venice," Dad said sagely. Property values hadn't been enhanced by recent news reports that police had to close the boardwalk one Sunday due to gang warfare. Even longtime residents were growing disenchanted with the carnival-like atmosphere and omnipresent drug dealing. "I don't want my daughter growing up to be a hair wrapper," sighed Blanca, a mother of two who owns the bungalow down the street. (Hair wrappers are entrepreneurial hippies who wind impossible-to-remove colorful threads in your hair in exchange for a small contribution.)

Duke and I summoned Brandon for a cost-cutting session. We waited for him to apologize for his outrageous estimate, but Brandon was unrepentant. "I've told you all along that the architect doesn't control the costs," he said, "the contractor does."

"Do they teach you that phrase in school?" I inquired.

Brandon blushed. "Actually, they do." Duke and I later imagined a language tape series for architects. Lesson Two would be "Anything I told you would just be a guess." Lesson Three: "Don't listen to the client, just draw a lot of grass."

"The great room cost more than twice what you thought," Duke said. "What would account for such a huge difference?"

Brandon began picking his cuticles. "It was the shear panel. But that wasn't my fault. That was on account of the earthquake."

"You said it would only add a thousand dollars," said Duke.

Brandon progressed from picking to chewing. "That was my happy-day talk," he said. He suggested that we get down to the business of cutting things from our list.

"But the list has no bearing on reality," I complained.

THE ARCHITECT VERSUS REALITY

IMPROVEMENT	BRANDON'S ESTIMATE	HAL'S PRICE
Remodel big room with cathedral ceilings	$ 6,000	$15,037
Fireplace surround	$ 1,000	$ 1,250
Remove paneling in dining room; drywall	none	$ 1,480
Cosmetic repair of kitchen	$ 1,550	$ 2,473
Change windows	$ 2,550	$ 1,605
Cosmetic repair of master bath	$ 4,000	$ 2,168
Repaint interior and exterior	$ 2,500	$12,000
Bike shed	$ 500	$ 900

"Well, I wish I were better at estimating. I'd be a contractor," he sighed. "My wife told me I was an idiot. I should add thirty percent to whatever I think it is so I wouldn't be so far off. But when I remodeled my house I did it within a thousand dollars, and I've done it before and been really close."

That was as much of an apology as we were going to get.

Brandon's initial idea of cost cutting was to remove the portions of the job that wouldn't enhance his portfolio: the bathroom, the bike shed, the paint job. But the bathroom was a wreck, the house desperately needed paint, and we'd have to put the bikes in the great room if we didn't build a shed.

"Then put off doing the floors," said Brandon.

I had my heart set on the floors.

Duke suggested that we whittle away a few costly design elements that wouldn't detract from the overall picture.

"We could go to a textured drywall treatment instead of a smooth finish," Brandon said sadly. He gave me a look that would have broken my heart if I weren't footing the bill.

"Not cottage-cheese ceilings?" I wailed.

"In that vein, but more of a stippled look."

We kept the smooth walls, but we sacrificed the faux hips (I didn't know what they were, so I doubted I'd miss them), the decorative steel struts (ditto), insulation for the back of the house, and a few kitchen cabinets. Brandon proposed that we go with a mantel made of prefabricated cornices, instead of a custom-made fireplace surround. He sketched out a fireplace that looked elegant on paper and was $800 cheaper. "Good idea," I said, but I would hate myself later.

By the end of the meeting, our bottom line was $23,000. But that didn't include paint.

As luck would have it, the next day, when I opened the mailbox, in addition to the usual discount coupons for Thai take-out, notifications that we'd been preapproved for yet another Visa card, and charity solicitations bearing a celebrity's return address (does anyone really believe that Ed Asner is writing them a personal note?) I found a flyer for Jiffy Paint, a new painting and maintenance company. On the cover was a photo of a group of Korean and Hispanic men in white shorts and sneakers. In the center was a giant trophy. The caption read: TEAM SPIRIT: THE JIFFY PAINT SOCCER TEAM. According to the brochure, highly skilled painters were ready and eager to take on all of my interior or exterior painting needs.

I called for my free estimate. "What you want?" asked the receptionist in a sing-song accent.

I lapsed into pidgin English. "House paint," I said. "In and out."

"Thankyouverymuch," she trilled, running the words together. "Mr. Nuke come. Bye bye."

She hung up before I could give particulars like my name and address. Against my better judgment, I called back.

"What you want?" she trilled again.

It took fifteen minutes to convey my address because the only letters she knew in the English alphabet were *T* and *B*, neither of which are the name of our street. I started to give directions, but she hung up again. Incredibly, the next day Mr. Nuke appeared. He was a scrappy Korean with a big smile and a small vocabulary. I walked him through the house and he kept bowing and chirping, "I understand, I understand," though I would have bet my life that he did not.

Afterward, he pulled out a giant calculator and sat down at my dining room table. "Twenty-nine hundred," he said, bowing low.

"Wow," I exclaimed, bowing lower. "Do you have references?"

"Many many references," Mr. Nuke said, beaming. "I have book in car. Many many nice things they write. I want show you very very much, but I park at beach." I suggested that he bring his car around to our parking lot and show me the book.

"Thankyouverymuch," he piped. Five minutes later Mr. Nuke reappeared. "Very very sorry," he said. "Book not there. Maybe in other truck. I fax."

"Thankyouverymuch," I said.

His references seemed fine. "He usually bids significantly less," said a Hermosa Beach landlady who'd had him paint a dozen units. "They've made some minor mistakes, but they always come back and fix them." What kinds of mistakes? I wondered. "In one place, they left some drips on the kitchen floor. Oh, and they forgot to put on the switchplates."

I could live with that. "Do they understand English?"

"Not always," she said.

The Monterey Park restaurateur was more enthusiastic. "Nuke did a very nice job on the outside of my building," she said. "He washed all the windows, which was not mentioned in the contract. And after the job was done, he even bought me a bouquet."

"Sounds perfect," said Duke. "Let's hire him."

Brandon was aghast. "You do have a tendency to get what you pay for," he warned me. He told me about a cut-rate outfit that he'd hired to paint some apartments he owned. "They forgot to paint the inside of the kitchen cabinets. They missed twenty or thirty corners."

I reminded him that he'd estimated our paint job would be $2,500. "And this is the closest bid."

Our architect has all the principles of a Magic Eight Ball. At first, he may say, "My reply is no," but give him a nudge and another message, "Signs point to yes," swims to the surface. "That doesn't mean I haven't had expensive painters who did a horrible job," Brandon added hastily. Whenever he went into Eight Ball mode, I had to remind myself that the architect could not have been more diligent on the job. In the case of the painter, Brandon not only called the Better Business Bureau to make sure there were no outstanding complaints, but he double-checked the bid with Mr. Nuke.

Hal sheepishly asked for Mr. Nuke's card. "I've been looking for a cheap painter to do my house," the contractor confessed. "I'll try him out on yours."

Just when it looked like our budget was under control, Clara started running away. Our house was fenced in on three and a half sides; the remaining seventy feet was enclosed by a three-foot wall. This had been sufficient to contain the other pugs, but the evil little baby is made of flubber.

We first realized she could jump the wall months earlier, when I came home from lunch with a friend and noticed that the back door was open and Clara was gone. Duke was on the computer intently writing hate mail to his Internet enemy, Ronzo the Clown. I peered over his shoulder and read: "Ronzo@netcom: I have only one question. Do you take off the red nose and floppy shoes when you sit down at the terminal?"

"Where's the dog?" I asked.

"She's around," Duke said absently. Ronzo had recommended that the United States do away with the secret ballot, and Duke was busy putting him in his place: "Don't the big fuzzy buttons on the front of your costume block the view of the monitor?" he typed frantically. (Not for the first time, it occurred to me that the Internet has replaced the neighborhood tavern. But at least if you get in a brawl, nobody gets hurt.)

I searched the house in vain. The dim-witted Sophie yipped at my heels joyously. She longed to be an only pug.

"I don't think I can ever forgive you for this," I muttered to Duke as I ran down to the boardwalk to post signs.

Clara turned up a few hours later, at the crack house down the street. Duke paid a reward, and the little fugitive came home, smelling smoky. She didn't venture out again until I returned from the hospital, when she began to wander off routinely, in search of a more mobile owner.

I called the Beaver and asked how much it would cost to fence her in. He guessed around $800. "The dog is working for *me* now," he smirked. "I put a little transmitter in her head. When I push a button she disappears."

Duke tried unsuccessfully to get a lower bid from an Israeli he found building a fence down the street. But the Beaver remained low bidder. It was comforting to have him back in the yard. "Think of the value of this fence when all the trees are gone," he told me.

I hate it when workers give me guilt for giving them jobs. "Would you feel better if I got chain link?"

"No, it's ugly," the Beaver said. "And chain link doesn't increase in value."

The Magic Eight Ball suggested as long as the Beaver was here we take the bike shed out of the budget.

"We still have to pay for it," I warned him. But I was glad to give the Beaver the job. (The most amusing exchange of the entire construction process came when the Beaver, stretching on tiptoe to shingle the top of the shed, lamented: "When we evolved from our common ancestors we had longer arms. What was the evolutionary pressure to have shorter arms when a long arm would be more useful?" Hal chuckled and retorted: "It was the fashion lobby. There wasn't much we could wear with longer arms.")

Brandon, Hal, Duke, and I sat down for a final budget-cutting session. "We don't really need to spend nine hundred dollars on liability insurance," my husband said.

"Wait," I said. "What if someone gets hurt?"

"I've got workmen's comp," said Hal. "Liability is in case something goes wrong structurally, like if we took out a beam and the roof fell down. We're going to try real hard not to have that happen."

"Would you put it back up if it did?" I asked.

"We can talk about it," the contractor said. We decided to take the risk.

Somehow, we lowered our cost to $22,000, not including the paint and the floors. Brandon presented Hal with an arcane, Byzantine contract that specified among other things that the trash be hauled away once a week and that he was allowed to use only one of our parking spaces. "It's in everyone's best interest that all the instructions that go on in the contract get done," Brandon said.

"I agree," said Hal.

(The construction gods snickered.)

Brandon proclaimed that his niche was organization and weathering the storms of construction: Therefore, he would serve as chief administrator. *He* would approve all payments. *He* would handle the change orders. Again, Hal nodded solemnly, though he winked at me.

(The construction gods giggled.)

"What's a change order?" I asked.

"It's the method that architects and contractors use to track the changes on the job," Brandon explained. "It's the place where the competitive bidding process becomes circumvented and contractors make all their money. They think, 'I've got the job, I can do anything I want.' "

"We won't change our minds," Duke said.

(The construction gods were rolling on the floor . . .)

The contractor presented us with a one-paragraph handwritten contract. After our architect's officiousness, we found it rather charming.

"Do you have an idea of your schedule of payments?" asked Brandon.

Hal languidly put his hands behind his head and stretched. "I hadn't really thought about it, but we can work something out as we go along. It's generally pretty easy. I usually ask for money about the end of every week."

Brandon's dharma is control. "I find the payment schedule to be very important," he said curtly. "Would it be possible to set up a preliminary payment schedule? And could you send that to me for review?"

"I don't see why not," Hal said amiably. He estimated that our job would take two months. He could begin in four weeks' time.

"How would you handle it if we stayed?" Duke asked.

Hal explained that he would block off the front of the house, do the major demolition and construction in the front of the house, and then do the back bathroom and the kitchen later. "If you weren't here, we'd work in all the house."

"Would it be faster?" Duke asked.

"Not really," Hal said. "Though you'd still have to find someplace to put all this stuff."

"We can throw it all in a self-storage bin," Duke said.

I kicked him under the table. "We're not throwing a baby grand into a storage bin."

Life's too short to do certain things: pump my own gas, work at a job that I hate, take a bus tour of Mexico, reconcile a checkbook to the penny, and live in a construction zone. What would I actually be missing? The chance to be woken at 7:00 A.M. by hordes of chain-smoking day laborers? The opportunity to learn how much I loathed my husband by being crammed together in a dust-laden corner of a house with open wounds? I'd never met anyone who'd done it once and said they would do it again.

"How long did they say it would take?" asked my brother, Bobby. He chortled when he heard two months. "They said ours would take four, and it wound up taking seven." He and his wife and three kids lived in construction while they added a third floor. "I remember it as being like a war zone," Bobby said. "They sectioned off a part of the house. We had clear vinyl instead of a roof for six of the seven months. And *we* were building up and the house was big enough. We still had sixteen hundred square feet and it didn't impact the kitchen or the dining room."

If you counted painting and floor refinishing, work was going to be done in every room of our house. "It was dirty and dusty, but we didn't have much of a choice," Bobby concluded. "Where were we going to go?"

I had it all figured out. Venice Beach is filled with cheap apartments. Months before, anticipating we would need a place to live, I chatted up Gomez, the best of the neighborhood landlords. He was an expert on all facets of the building process, having recently completed construction on his version of the Trump Tower, Casa Gomez, an ultramodern glass-and-steel fortress conveniently located across the street from our house. Obsessive-compulsive to the ninth power and unable to let go of any unit he

owned, Gomez thought nothing of giving me tours of his apartments while his tenants were away at work.

As soon as we got a start date, I asked what was available. To my delight, only three of the four units of his flagship had been rented (to minimize wear and tear, Gomez had selected the neatest tenants imaginable: a gay doctor, a gay lawyer, and a gay designer); Gomez was using the fourth, a quasi-legal one-bedroom, as a crash pad. "I wouldn't mind moving my weights out," he said. "If it's just for a couple months."

It was a pleasant, sunlit, airy unit with champagne carpets, alpine white walls, and ample closet space. There was no kitchen to speak of, just a wet bar with a small refrigerator and two cupboards, but Gomez promised he'd put in a stove. My plan was to put most of our things in storage and set the apartment up like a hotel suite—my ideal living space. I'd use the bedroom as an office, and we'd sleep in the giant living room.

It wasn't cheap, but Gomez was willing to take the pugs.

"This would never happen in New York," my agent, Loretta, marveled. "The idea of finding a place across the street. It's unbelievable. I'd have to kill someone and use their place. I'd have to change their locks and say they were a victim."

My husband proposed an alternative. "All we really need is an office for you," he said. I pointed out that it wasn't easy to rent pug-friendly commercial space close to home for only two months. Ever one to rise to a challenge, Duke came home from a bike ride and informed me that there was space in the Charlie Chaplin building, a beautiful old brick structure on the boardwalk that is apocryphally said to have been Chaplin's summer home (it's around the corner from Isadora Duncan's apocryphal summer home). The leasing agent showed me a cozy suite with ocean views and a roof deck for the pugs.

I was almost willing to sleep in rubble, just for the chance to write there, but it cost twice as much as Gomez's apartment. "Everything is negotiable," my husband reminded me. He was half right. The office manager didn't bite, but Gomez dropped his price a couple hundred dollars. "Just as a favor to you," my landlord told me later. "I never negotiate."

That settled, I went to Box City and wrote a large check for cartons, labels, and tape. I love packing because it means that you're going somewhere. I waited until Duke was gone to take the supplies out of the trunk. He would have had me foraging in Dumpsters behind grocery stores, but I prefer to put my possessions in sturdy boxes without suspicious grease stains.

"Real men go to liquor stores," he said later.

Yes, but real men don't pack.

I found this out the hard way, when we first moved in together. We had to vacate two apartments, and the plan was to empty Duke's first. The morning he was supposed to move, I went over to the Sty in the Sky assuming that he could use some last-minute help. I discovered a giant pile of moldy dishes in the sink, eight years of periodicals scattered on the floor, sticky jars filled with strange Chinese condiments, and no boxes.

Duke was drinking Estate Java and fiddling with a computer program to cast the I Ching that he had written by himself in Basic. When I asked when he planned to move, he said, "I'm gathering my forces."

The Force, me, put all his clothes, dishes, records, and books in supermarket bags and damp boxes that I had rescued from the Dumpster while he continued to work on the pseudo random-number aspect of the program. Hours later, after I'd bundled most of his possessions, Duke went onto the boardwalk, hired two burly drunks, and we all pushed his belongings up the street on an old rolling desk chair. What was my reward? Duke told me that he wasn't sure he wanted to live with me and sent me back to my apartment.

The next morning, I arrived at the house with the first wave of my neatly labeled boxes, the now dear departed Bess and Stella, and a set of matching towels, which effectively ended any further discussion. Duke bit the bullet, borrowed a truck, and moved the rest of my belongings down to the beach.

The house has been accumulating clutter ever since.

The upside of packing up an entire house two months after hip-replacement surgery is that you're willing to get rid of anything to keep from bending a lot. Infirmity puts you in touch with what is or isn't really important. It no longer seemed imperative to save the dozens of canvas tote bags I'd picked up at conventions and threw in a closet; the silver-plated chafing dish that I got as a wedding present when I married my first husband, the sheepskin coat my parents bought me when I left for college, or a red leather miniskirt in size 2 that fit me for about twelve minutes when I was twenty-five.

My sister kept me company, via long distance, each day as I packed. (I reckoned that if I packed five boxes a day for the entire month of April, the house would be empty when construction began on the second of May.) "Moving gives you a chance to purge, to get rid of crap you don't need," Laurie said. "When I moved from New York to Chicago, the company paid, and so the movers packed me. I didn't get a chance to purge, and it was awful. Movers have rules that they don't tell you about. They went through my apartment and stripped the place bare. If you left garbage in the trash can, they packed it. On the other hand, I had been collecting matchbooks for fifteen years. They threw them out because they're not allowed to pack flammable things."

Duke suggested a garage sale—my idea of hell whether I'm on the giving or receiving end. He likes garage sales because "you get to investigate someone else's life, and once in a while get a nice deal." While I've met women who have found treasures like a set of Louis Vuitton luggage (including pet carrier!) for $50, all I ever find are burnt-out electric rollers with hairs still on them, Belva Plain paperbacks, and stained polyester sundresses. I imagined myself sitting outside all weekend while strangers picked through my belongings and offered me $5 for a coffee table I once bought for $500.

I shook my head.

"I think bargain, you think parasites," Duke joked. He sprawled on the sofa watching a sumo wrestling tournament while I culled the bookshelves.

The books had been breeding unchecked for many years. We are both avid readers. My ambition is to someday own a home with an oak-paneled library with floor-to-ceiling shelves and one of those rolling ladders. In fact, the first thing I did when I became a home owner instead of a renter was build bookcases. We have since purchased at least a dozen more tall freestanding units, yet there still wasn't a flat surface not covered with reading material.

A book collection is a cross between a Rorschach test and *This Is Your Life*. It marks your life clearly like rings on a tree. Some parts are easy to prune: anything by John Grisham, Scott Turow, or Judith Krantz. The self-help books that misguided me through years of dating. The guides on how to grow house plants when you have a purple thumb. (My solution: Don't bother!) At first, I had too much Jewish guilt to part with my extensive World War II/Nazi collection, but Duke gave me motivation.

"Hitler sells," he said, carting the Nazis off to Recyclopedia, a nearby used bookstore.

I hung on to a complete paperback set of Agatha Christie mysteries, which got me through my parents' divorce, my extensive collection of Royal Family biographies (though I did decide that I could make do with just three life stories of the Queen Mum), and my dollhouse research materials.

Twenty large cartons later, I crossed the Maginot Line between my books and my husband's—where tomes like *Reading Your Future in the*

Cards gave way to *Life Among the Paiutes*. Or as my sister put it, the line between the readable and the unbelievable. "I'm a major reader," Laurie insisted. "But I've never been tempted to pick up a book on Duke's shelves." Among his favorites: *Quaternary Extinctions, Plagues and People, The History of the Negro Rising in Surinam, Cows, Pigs, Wars and Witches,* and *Procopius: The Secret History.*

"How about *Life in the Argentine Republic in the Days of the Tyrants*?" I asked.

My husband considered it briefly. "It's not in such good shape to sell, and it might be useful someday," he said, handing it to me to pack (as opposed to kneeling down and putting it in the box himself). He smiled as I pushed another carton of books into the living room. "I'm really getting this stuff taken care of," he said. "And you know what? Your operation is hardly slowing us down at all."

Laurie sympathized. "Kenny made me transfer stuff from freezer to freezer. We have one frozen eggplant lasagna for ten people that predates me. I don't know where he got it. This is the third house it's lived in. The next time he goes out of town, I'm going to throw it out. It takes up half the freezer."

The stack of boxes grew higher and higher. Duke looked at them, the way pugs look at cats, as if they're not really there. I would say, "Honey, are you going to pack a few things?" and he would say, "I'm building up my momentum." And the next day, I'd buy more boxes and pack some more.

"I wouldn't call myself a pack rat," Duke argued. "I don't compulsively keep things. Things just accumulate." I would beg to differ, since I was the one who boxed up three copies of every issue of every alternative newspaper that he had worked on in the last ten years. He did reluctantly part with his white *Saturday Night Fever* suit and a serape. Things that I gave away that he doesn't know about include: mementos of old love affairs and a shimmering teal Dacron blazer made in Macedonia, traditional home of fine men's couture, which he had purchased on sale at a discount outlet. Duke had come home really excited. "I paid nine dollars," he bragged.

"Very good," I said. "To look at it anyone would think you paid eleven." (To my absolute horror, a photograph of him wearing this jacket later appeared in full color on the front page of the metro section of the *L.A. Times*.)

The final score: I packed ninety boxes. Duke packed two.

He did do the heavy lifting. Three Sundays in a row, he and his friend

David loaded the detritus of our lives into a pickup and carted it off to our storage bin. By the third weekend, my husband's enthusiasm for hauling had waned and we had yet to move the furniture to the apartment. Duke's plan was to have his father, a veteran of bypass surgery, come down from Santa Barbara with his pickup truck to assist him.

I thought not. Our future landlord was behaving like we were moving into the Sistine Chapel. "I don't want the walls to get marred when you move in," Gomez warned on Monday.

Tuesday he fretted, "You're not going to be doing a lot of cooking. I don't want the stove to get caked with grease."

Wednesday he was worried about his water bill. "You don't take a lot of showers, do you?"

I half expected him to make me promise that we would never use the toilet.

My husband's family motto may be "Do It Yourself," but the Latin on my family crest is "Hire Someone." Thursday I called a mover and discovered that I could avoid a lot of stress for under a hundred dollars. Thus it came to pass that Friday morning, five minutes after Duke left for work, a colossal van pulled up and Mr. Immense and Mr. Mammoth, two buffed-up ex-linebackers, stepped out.

"Where's your husband?" asked Immense, hoisting a bedside table under each arm.

"He doesn't know we're moving," I said. "It's a surprise."

"Wish someone would surprise me," Mammoth said, balancing the Sony Trinitron on the palm of his hand.

Two hours later, with a minimum of aggravation, we were relocated. Before they left, I asked the guys to move the sofa bed and my doll-houses—a New York City tenement and an English Tudor—from the living room to the bedroom. The items were too big to move, and Hal had promised that they'd be safe in the back room. As for the antique baby grand, Hal suggested we leave it in the living room, shrouded in tarps. "I'll make sure nothing happens to it," he promised. It seemed easier than watching my landlord have a nervous breakdown as he watched the balky instrument be hoisted up the flight of stairs.

Fortunately, the persnickety Gomez arrived too late to supervise the movers. As it was, he hovered nervously while I unpacked. He pulled the headboard two inches away from the wall. He rearranged my file cabinet so the drawers wouldn't open within four inches of a light switch. Again, he made me swear that I wouldn't hang any pictures. "That book shelf isn't the best choice aesthetically," he complained, pointing to a low, wide unit that I put in the kitchen to use in lieu of cupboards. "Something taller would be a better choice."

"For two months, I'll be unaesthetic," I said, hustling him out so I could make a nest.

Hours passed swiftly. I made the bed. I put out towels. I stacked milk crates in the closet to hold Duke's shirts and socks (he'd given his old bureau to Goodwill). I lined the kitchen drawers with paper towels. After two months of feeling powerless, I was elated to be walking without a cane and in charge. Besides, men have no concept of nesting. They think all you have to do is set up the stereo. If my husband were there, he would have spent hours moving the record player around or finding the optimum place to put the television set.

"Men just plop down and expect it all to be there," Laurie agreed. "They think if they hook up an electrical appliance, that's a major chore. That's all Kenny did, but that's all I heard about for days. How long it took to set up the stereo. Does he think it took a short time to wrap every single spice jar in newspaper?"

Duke looked pleased when he came into the apartment and saw our familiar furniture cozily arranged into a new nest for him. "I think we handled this very well," he said, settling himself comfortably onto the sofa with magazine, snack, soda, and pug.

An hour later he triumphantly hooked up the stereo. "There," he said. "Now it feels like home."

CHAPTER ELEVEN

O N THE first Monday in May, after nine months of planning, construction was set to begin. The early-morning clouds were drifting in as they do every day in May at the beach. I couldn't have been more ecstatic if I were in a taxi en route to the airport about to depart for three months in Bali. Obviously, I had tumbled down the rabbit hole, into Remodel Land, where everything is topsy-turvy. Why else would I be so eager to give a virtual stranger a key to my house and a thousand-dollar check?

Our contractor had initially wanted thrice that, but Brandon, master of the Rigid Payment Schedule, had turned him down flat. "I don't like putting too much money in the start-up contract," the architect said. "Lots of contractors love to get lots of money up front, and then they're in the driver's seat."

Hal accepted the rebuke with a terse little smile. "The first week I'm going to be writing a lot of checks, and I'm going to have to get a Dumpster and stuff like that," he said, easing up against a corner of the wall to scratch his back. He resembled a Norman Rockwell illustration of a homespun grandpa. It seemed disrespectful to deny him money. But Brandon remained firm.

At 8:30 sharp Hal pulled up in his baby blue Chevy four-by-four and shambled through the back gate. "Good morning," I cried merrily, thrusting his check at him as if I were a doting uncle, rewarding my favorite nephew on his wedding day. It wasn't until Hal pocketed it that I noticed two of his fingers were in a splint. "Are you okay?"

Hal yawned. "I drove a nail through my hand. It's no big deal. But I think we better start the job tomorrow because I have to go to the doctor."

It wasn't what I'd call a good omen.

And there was worse to come.

The week before, on my way home from Box City, I'd driven past a vacant lot stacked with firewood. I noticed a sign stapled to an adjacent telephone pole: FOR A GOOD SWEEP, CALL BUD! I reached for my cellular phone. The fireplace was the only remaining wild card in our construction budget. For weeks, I'd been trying to get a sweep to give me an estimate, but I was batting zero-for-six.

Bud assured me that he could correct any problem, and he gave me his word that he'd be at my house at noon the following day—"unless it rains," he cautioned. "I don't sweep in the rain."

It hardly ever rains in May, but the next day it drizzled. To my astonishment, Bud showed up anyway. He looked like a toasted marshmallow, short and tubby with a sooty bald spot and a clinging aroma of burnt embers. He waddled in, dragging the tools of his trade: six-foot sweepers that looked like bottle brushes for the world's largest baby, a vacuum the size of a Honda Civic, and a filthy sheet, which he carefully taped to the opening of the fireplace. "Is it messy?" I asked. (Remodeling Law Number Three: Everything is messy.)

"I haven't made a mess yet unless something happens today," said Bud.

I complimented him on his professionalism, even though the only sweep I had any familiarity with was Dick Van Dyke in *Mary Poppins*.

"Those other sweeps are flakes," Bud said, "but it helps me because I'm not a flake." He used to be a machinist at Hughes Aircraft, and then a union leader, but he got laid off and went to locksmith school. Then one fateful weekend eight years ago he helped his brother do his chimney and he found his calling. "Sweeping pulls in the money better," he said, wobbling up the ladder to the roof.

He lowered a light down the chimney and whistled. "Oh man, this is wrecked. You've got a cardboard damper down here. All this damage you see is from not having no rain cap for the water. In the old days you didn't used to need it, but this is hurt something awful."

"But you can fix it, right?" After all, on the phone he had said that he could correct any problem.

Bud wobbled down, shaking his head. Our chimney was terminally ill; it needed to be completely rebuilt, a job that was beyond his ken. "I have an associate that can rebuild chimneys from the bottom up. I need to consult with him." Bud wouldn't take any money for his examination. "I'm not dishonest like those other sweeps," he said.

The next morning, I got a call from Bud's associate, Monroe, a mason. He said he was having the year of his life repairing earthquake damage but promised to try and squeeze us in later in the week, "as a favor to Bud."

Tuesday morning, right on time, Hal eased himself out of his four-by-four. Five minutes later his wild-eyed partner and son-in-law, Dexter, pulled up in a psychedelically painted van. With him were José and Ludwin, day laborers from Oaxaca whom Dexter had found in front of the building-supply store on Eleventh Street where pick-up laborers traditionally gather.

"Good morning," said Dexter, tall, slim, and remarkably dapper in a khaki jumpsuit and hip boots. I gave him the Best Dressed Award on the spot. "From my Devo days," he said smiling. Dexter, a drummer on the dark side of thirty, is only doing construction until he lands a recording deal.

"Good morning," I said, adding hastily, *"Buenos días."*

The work crew pushed past me swinging hammers and pry bars.

"Get rid of everything," Hal ordered. (*"Deshaga todo,"* he told José.) An instant later I heard a thunderous clap, and a mushroom cloud of plaster and dust arose. My contact lenses became unbearable, and I retreated to our clean, peaceful apartment.

Four hours later I popped in to see what was going on. The platoon were picnicking on the front lawn, polishing off the first of what would be thousands of Big Macs and unpeeling the first of what would be tens of thousands of fast-food wrappers, which they discarded wherever they happened to be. (An entire herd of cattle died for our house.)

Inside, it looked like downtown Beirut in the Green Line days. If I'd had any doubts about moving out, they vanished instantly. No human being could live in such chaos. A single guy, maybe. The living room had been hacked apart like a carcass picked clean by a pack of carrion birds. It was exhilarating to see the offensive components of my house cut out like malignant tumors. Gone were the cheap plywood paneling, the moldy vinyl shower surround, and the cheesy acoustical tiles that always reminded me of the Fort Garrison elementary school. I wondered who invented acoustical tile? Probably the same person who invented cottage-cheese ceilings.

"It was probably a big achievement," said Dexter, the only garrulous member of the crew. "It was cheap and easy to put up. It's better than most things they had to cover the ceiling with at that time."

If demolition made it impossible for us to change our minds, it also provided immediate feedback on the wisdom of our decision. The wall between the living room and sunporch had been hacked away, except for a little strip at the top ("We leave the ceiling joists to support the hips until the house is better framed," Hal explained). The front of the attic had vanished, and I could see fifteen feet up to the rafters. For a moment, I stood there marveling at what we had wrought. I was overwhelmed with pride and wonder.

Then I walked through the house and noticed where the debris had ended up.

It was my understanding that the back bedroom would be sealed during the major demolition. In accordance, we'd moved the dollhouses and the sofa bed into the room for safekeeping. But not only had Hal and his men failed to seal the room, they were using it as a trash can. I watched in horror as José unceremoniously tossed an armful of plywood siding at the foot of the uncovered sofa.

"No!" I shrieked. "*¡No puede dejarla!*" (You can't leave it there!) My language skills are heightened by stress.

I picked my way through a plaster hail storm to lodge a complaint with the contractor. He flinched as if I were causing him pain and made little circles in the rubble with his toe. "It costs six hundred dollars a week to rent a Dumpster," he said sadly, "and I'd rather not do that if I don't have to."

At first, I felt guilty for complaining. Then I remembered a technique called the Broken Record, which I learned in an assertiveness training course. You're supposed to repeat your point in the face of all objections. "I don't want the trash in the bedroom," I said again.

"Well, I'll see what I can do," Hal said, grimacing. Then he switched on his assertiveness training tool—an ear-splitting electric saw that sounded like the offspring of a dentist's drill and a car alarm. I fled to the apartment.

The next time I checked on the job site (it was too painful to think of that war zone as my home) the trash in the bedroom was waist-high.

I called my husband at work and asked what to do. Perhaps it was not wise to seek advice from a man who has never washed a coffee cup in his life. He, too, acted as if I were being unreasonable. "Honey, construction sites aren't operating rooms," Duke said, helpfully adding, "Can I put you on hold for a minute?"

Brandon had instructed me to bring any problems to him, so I put in a frantic call. The architect had already visited the job site (it was impossible to keep him away), and he agreed that the house was trashed. But he didn't see what all the fuss was about.

"As soon as Hal began to use the back door as a staging area all the dust and dirt went everywhere," he explained, as if I couldn't figure that out.

"I thought he was going to rent a Dumpster."

"Well, I guess he decided to save some money. Now he says at the end of the week a guy's going to come and haul the trash away. It's cheaper for them to generate all the trash they're going to take."

It still didn't make sense, but I didn't push it. "At least make them cover the furniture," I said with a sigh.

"That's reasonable," said Brandon, as if my previous objection was not.

It's unbelievable how rapidly four men can wreak havoc. They were like an unleashed force of nature, a hurricane or a tornado, only not as neat. Within forty-eight hours the baby grand piano, covered with blankets, was the only thing standing intact in the living room (it reminded me of the opening scene in the movie *The Piano*, where the piano is abandoned on the beach). The back garden was trampled, and I had to wade through a sea of refuse to squeeze through the back door. Any rooms that weren't being worked on were overflowing with menacing-looking tools and machinery.

And it wasn't just business dirt. The guys left entire meals strewn around the house. (Sophie and Clara regarded the job site with the same kind of wonder with which Heinrich Schliemann viewed old Troy. Clara would trot into the office and emerge with a five-day-old burrito fragment in her mouth. Sophie burrowed under the trash pile and scored a cupcake.) The toilet was rarely flushed. For eight years, I'd insisted that people smoke outside. But not only didn't the workers ask if they could smoke, they put cigarettes out on the floor, on the wall, wherever. It was like watching my house be gang-banged.

Still, the destruction was riveting in its sheer awfulness. It's exhilarating to see a concept become reality (though I must say I preferred the creative process in miniature, where if a project becomes too messy, you can always stick it in a closet or a drawer). The stripped-down roof had a certain majesty that was quite beautiful to behold. It reminded me of a thatched *palapa* in Mexico. Each day brought a souvenir of the previous occupants: scraps of gray flocked wallpaper, an original brick mantel, and high on the rafters, the charred evidence of a fire. Dexter, who once lived on our street, recalled that there'd been a fire in 1975.

And speaking of conflagrations, midway through the demolition Monroe, the mason, arrived to inspect the fireplace. "Nice old house," he grinned. He saw the charred rafters and added, "Nice old fire." I got the feeling I wasn't exactly in a position of strength.

"You're lucky the house didn't burn down with the fireplace this bad," Monroe continued. He told me that the firebox had to be six inches deeper.

"But it's been this way for eighty-two years."

"Originally when they built it, I'm sure it worked fine," he agreed. "There was enough air flow over the existing buildings to precipitate enough draft to make it work. But the buildings got much higher, and the upward draft to draw a fire through a flue is suppressed by the buildings next door."

I stared blankly.

"The building next door stifled the fireplace. It cuts off the prevailing wind."

Not to worry; Monroe could fix it, though he warned, "Whatever I do has to be legal." (In building jargon "legal" is a synonym for the price of a small car.) "The key thing is to build it out further. And you'll have to learn to build a fire that functions well under the circumstances. On a cold winter night with a big draft there's enough wind to build anything. But if there's no wind, you'll have to limit the size. Smokey the Bear says, build a fire to the circumstances."

Smokey the Bear would also probably caution against plopping an unreinforced masonry chimney down on sand less than ten miles from the Newport-Inglewood fault. But a journey through the crawl space under our house—which looked like a big sandbox, or kitty litter box depending on how close you got to the sand—revealed that there was no concrete foundation supporting our chimney.

I summoned Brandon. He bicycled over on his shiny red mountain bike. He reminded me of a performing bear.

"What does this mean?" I asked. (Silly question. It meant what all problems in construction mean: more money.)

"We're going to have to pour a concrete pad," Brandon said. "I'll write up a change order." (*Change order* is also synonymous with more money.)

I recited what was becoming my mantra: "How much?"

"Let me work up a price for the concrete," Hal said.

"I'll run up a price and get back to you," Monroe said. A few days later he informed me that it would cost $4,000 to do the job. "I know it's expensive. But there's nothing like real brick."

There's nothing like bankruptcy either.

"You know, there's another option," Brandon said thoughtfully. "We could take the old chimney out and put in a prefab steel-can system."

He could have been speaking Swahili. "You mean those cheap tacky gas logs that they have in model homes?" Why not Video Fireplace, a videotape of a burning log?

"No, you can burn real wood in these. They have five or six inches of sheet-metal planking around refractory masonry and an integrated ash lip. There's a band of steel around the whole thing. If the fireplace gets detailed correctly, it will look very nice."

It didn't sound very nice. "How much?"

"My mother's cost a thousand." Brandon turned to Hal. "If you can run up a price on installation too, that would be terrific."

"It shouldn't cost more than a thousand to install," said Hal. (When he wanted to do something, he gave prices on the spot. When he didn't, he stalled.)

The next day, Hal knocked on my apartment door. "Here's the literature for the fireplace," he said, handing me a brochure with a picture of a black metal fireplace complete with a roaring blaze and tacky glass doors (mandatory by law in California, but Brandon assured me we could remove them after we passed inspection). Inside, the hero fireplace was photographed wearing various mantels: marble, plaster, stone, and brass.

"I don't think this counts as literature," I said lightly. But maybe it did. The text extolled cryptic but apparently vital features that I heretofore didn't know existed: High Dome Transition Design, Realistic Masonry-Look Refractory, Quiet-Mount Doors, and Polished-Glass Grills. To remodel is to wrap your ego around a whole new crop of status symbols that can be appreciated only by another remodeler. Mercedes, Rolex, and Louis Vuitton give way to Armstrong, Anderson, and Kohler.

"How ugly are these things in real life?" I asked. Hal was a craftsman. I trusted his taste.

"It's not the same as real brick," Hal conceded, "but it's not hideous and it's a lot cheaper."

I wanted to see it in person, so Duke and I went over to a fireplace boutique in Santa Monica. (When you're remodeling, you discover specialty stores five minutes from your house that you never noticed before and will never notice again. I think they appear just for your job, like Brigadoon.) The fireplace in question was a simple metal box with a metal pipe that went up the chimney. The fireplace could be hidden with tile, marble, stone, or granite. It cost only $1,000. Only $850 with our contractor's discount.

Duke suggested that we check the Home Depot, the vast homeowner's inferno where feverish do-it-yourselfers give up the better part of their Saturday afternoons to troll the wide aisles pushing a baby forklift. They were running a parking-lot special on a flush hearth circulating fireplace. Only $350.

"Why don't we get this one?" Duke asked.

"Let me see the literature." The airbrushed picture showed the fireplace modeling a heavily veined marble mantel with brass trim. It reminded me of a fireplace you see in one of those closed-gate real estate developments named after the builder's wife—Melody Woods! What really turned me off was that the selling points had been explained in a way that made them completely undesirable. Durable refractory lining looks like real firebrick! Glass doors enhance appearance!

"I don't think so."

"It's exactly the same," Duke argued. "Let's get the cheap one."

Call me an alarmist, but there are certain words I don't like to hear together: cheap fireplace, discount brakes, cut-rate surgery . . .

I pulled out my cellular phone and called Brandon.

"You don't want that one," he said. "It's like the Chevy of fireplaces. Maybe a Pontiac. The other is a Buick."

"A Buick doesn't seem that much better than a Chevy," I said.

"Would you like it better if I said it was the Cadillac?"

I'm ashamed to admit that I would.

Luckily, the discount hearth was too big to put in the car, so we postponed buying it. Brandon called around and located a cheaper fireplace boutique in Woodland Hills that sold the Buick for only $650. We agreed to buy it. But the next day, when the architect appeared on the job site brandishing a change order in triplicate for me and Hal to sign, I noticed that the fireplace he had specified cost $860. It was a fancier model.

"It's three inches higher and two inches deeper, and the chain folds into a recess in the fire screen, so you don't cut down the firebox," Brandon explained. "It's only three hundred more, so I took the liberty of changing it."

I took the liberty of changing it back. (When you're remodeling, you've got to constantly resist other people's insinuations that you're a tightwad.) "Does the fireplace company have you on the take?" I asked half jokingly.

Brandon blushed. "The company supports architects very well. They give me design kits, four-color brochures, and a number I can call for assistance. I'd prefer a house in the Bahamas."

So would I. But it didn't look like we'd be vacationing for a long time.

Even before the fireplace debacle, it became obvious that we were going to need a contingency fund.

"These guys are notoriously poor businessmen," my brother, Bobby, warned me. "The contractor gives you a price, and once he gets involved he sees that it's not the way it's supposed to be. Everywhere he turns, he miscalculated. And he expects you to pay the difference. My lawyer told me to expect to pay at least twenty percent more than they said. But I didn't budget for that. I figured it was going to be the way they said. Boy, did I get screwed."

Our accountant had suggested that we apply for a home-equity credit line, which would allow us to write checks as we needed them. The interest was tax-deductible, and several of the local banks were running special no-fee promotions. Once again, Duke made the high-profile calls to the banks and obtained the applications. Once again, I got saddled with the paperwork. This time, though, I had all the pertinent information on hand from refinancing and I'd gotten over my aversion to borrowing money, so the task was a tedious breeze.

Bank Number One rejected us right away because, under the question "Home improvements to be made?" I had written: "Remove wall." The loan was being promoted as a way to finance home improvements, but bank policy ruled out structural changes. Go figure. I became alarmed. If this was standard operating procedure, we were in trouble. A few days later, Bank Number Two (which hadn't asked about our home improvements) notified us that we'd been tentatively approved. There was just one formality. They wanted to send a drive-by appraiser to look at the property.

I offered to bring them a copy of the appraisal that was done when we refinanced.

"It wouldn't be too much trouble?" asked the loan counselor.

"Oh, no trouble at all," I fibbed. In fact, I had to make fifteen calls to Barry the Beverly Hills Loan Broker to request a copy of the appraisal, which I had requested when we'd closed escrow but had never received. Barry didn't return my calls. I finally sent him an urgent fax saying that we were being audited. He called and said that he didn't have our file anymore; it was at a warehouse in Simi Valley that didn't have a computerized filing system. It took a week and a half to unearth our paperwork. But it seemed better than letting a new appraiser near our property.

My husband thought I was overreacting. When Bank Number Three, his company credit union, conditionally approved our application pending an appraisal, Duke told the appraiser that he could go to the job site anytime he wanted. "The house is always open," said Duke, and I wondered about his common sense. (I was reminded of the time we went through Customs after a South American holiday. The Customs officer asked if we'd been on vacation. "Sort of," Duke replied and the officer immediately searched his bag.)

As luck would have it, the credit union appraiser showed up on the same day Hal and his crew removed the front wall of our house to work on the shear wall. José and Ludwin were on the roof, dismantling our brick chimney with their bare hands. Ludwin threw a brick to José, who tossed it to Dexter, who threw it into the garden. It created an unfortunate impression.

"The appraiser called," Duke confessed that night at dinner. "He said it didn't look like there was much of a house."

I prayed that Bank Number Two would be satisfied with the old appraisal. They still hadn't gotten back to me with confirmation. But the expenses marched on.

"Don't worry," said Duke, who didn't have to write the four-figure checks every Friday and watch our bank balance dwindle. (He gets panicky writing checks for over $23, so I got stuck with the job.)

Our intrepid architect had devised a rigid payment schedule whereby I paid Hal 10 percent of the job each Friday if he had performed a given task to Brandon's satisfaction. The first payday arrived and the demolition was virtually complete except for the window seat that Hal liked to sit on, the carpets (Hal wanted to leave them in place until the end of the job to protect the floors), and the kitchen counter. "We can always pull it out later, it only takes a second," Hal said. (Our contractor had an aversion to finishing a task, but we didn't know it at the time.)

Friday afternoon Brandon bicycled over with a stack of lien releases for Hal to sign in triplicate and a change order authorizing the contractor to pour a concrete foundation.

"Why do we need a concrete foundation if we're putting in a light-weight metal chimney?" I wondered.

Brandon began his ritual dance of obfuscation. "I was hoping to set the post for the ridge beam onto the foundation for the chimney, but in reality there was no foundation."

"Didn't you notice that it wasn't there?"

"I never went under the house," Brandon said. "Theoretically, it was supposed to be there."

Hal guessed the cost to pour the foundation would be "only a couple hundred, maybe less."

Rule Number Four: It's never, ever less.

Hal tried to cheer me up. "There wasn't any big problem with dry rot and termites," he said. "We found a couple pieces of dry rot in the bathroom, but it's no big deal." I smiled and handed him a check.

I was gratified to see Frank, the trash hauler, pull up in a flatbed the size of Rhode Island. (In fact, the way to any contractor's heart is through his vehicle. Yell "Nice truck!" on a job site and everyone whirls around.) He and his men (who looked like grown-up versions of Pig Pen, the slob in the cartoon strip "Peanuts") dragged the garbage through the kitchen, across the uncovered white-vinyl floor, which was only a year old.

"That will clean up just fine," Hal assured me.

Fool that I was, I believed him.

CHAPTER TWELVE

THE PACE of renovation is inherently unsettling. The first week the army marches in and trashes your largest financial investment, rendering it uninhabitable, possibly forever. Unless you are a whiz with a router, which I am not, when you visit what used to be a sanctuary and discover that it's open on one side like a dollhouse, and every neighbor, tourist, surfer, schizophrenic, and drunk who passes by is peering in, you have to wonder: What am I going to do if they don't put this back together again?

And you realize you're at their mercy.

At this point of maximum chaos and vulnerability the invaders switch gears. Instead of blitzkrieg in Poland you get trench warfare at Verdun. For the next few weeks there was no significant progress, unless I counted the intricate web of two-by-fours that went up at glacial speed along the walls and the newly raised ceiling. The only thing that came quickly were Fridays, when I had to write another gigantic check.

The exposed house made me feel incredibly insecure, like I was lying on the gynecologist's table with my feet in the stirrups in front of a crowd of critical strangers (I was not surprised to learn that the house is a metaphor for the body in dream language). My usual tolerance for disorder is about three minutes at most, and I grew frantic for the wounds to be closed. Yet every time I dropped by, it seemed that Dexter was on the phone lining up the evening's music gig, Hal was foraging for a tape measure (tape measures are cousins to pens—you either have twelve or you have none), and Jaime, the courtly framing carpenter who had joined the team after demolition, was slicing yet another length of lumber with the shrieking saw.

On the rare occasions when my husband, whose tolerance for chaos is about three years, visited, the saw was instantly switched off, and it was all good fellowship, like Hail Caesar. But my arrival was invariably heralded by a disharmonious screech. This kept me from objecting to the immense heap of lumber in our bedroom and the mound of rubbish in the front yard that grew and grew and grew. ("You've got a perception of a construction site that's really too neat," chided Brandon, whose gigantic sign advertising his services could be seen above the rubble.)

According to our architect, who oversaw the job like a playground monitor in elementary school, the guys were doing the rough framing. "It's when they put the structure up," he explained. "The joists, the posts, the wood frames, the studs, the headers. All the stuff that goes on before the drywall that you never see."

"Oh," I sighed, "the boring stuff."

"They call it rough because no one gives a shit how it looks," said Brandon, who bicycled over every day to check the size of the lumber in the studs. "Did you know that two-by-fours are really one-and-a-half-by-

three-and-a-half and a six-by-fourteen is really a five-and-a-half-by-thirteen-and-a-quarter?"

Of course I didn't. I just knew that Hal and Dexter spent interminable hours crawling under the house and hardly any time on activities with real decorating potential such as installing the kitchen counter or the bathroom vanity.

The architect explained that they had run into a structural jam. "What happened was that the original house was balloon-framed," said Brandon. "You had studs going every thirty inches on center down below your floor, and what Hal is doing is bringing the whole cripple wall up to code with two-by-fours, sixteen feet off center."

I tried to decipher that.

"A cripple wall is a little short wall that continues down to the foundation," said Hal, who was as clear as Brandon was obtuse. He had to fix the cripple wall so he could attach the plywood shear wall, or as he laconically put it, "There wasn't enough of it as there needs to be now, and what there was was shot, so we replaced it. It's a fairly important part of the house, but you can't see it."

If I can't see it, I'm not interested. Hindsight being twenty-twenty, I should have been more grateful. Hal didn't present us with a bill for rebuilding the subfloor, but he brooded about his failure to do so for the rest of the job. "It was extra work and he thought it would be cheaper and I think it made him angry," Brandon confided. Perhaps it wasn't our subfloor. Perhaps Hal was in the throes of a tragic love affair. I'll never know. But the sunny, twinkly-eyed contractor we had hired seemed to have been replaced by his gloomy twin.

At the start of the job, my husband had made a little speech. "The whole secret is not making lots of changes," Duke said. "That's what winds up costing you, all those little changes."

I was reminded of the little speech he makes before we go on vacation: "The whole secret is to take a small suitcase." Then he buys a dozen batik shirts or a stone sculpture, which we have to lug back in a bag purchased on the spot. We now have disposable suitcases from all the world's cultures.

I promised to keep my whims in check. But it's impossible to wind up paying what you thought you were going to pay. Construction is an uncontrollable collision of fantasy and reality. The architect draws a nice picture, but the contractor has to contend with the problematic three-dimensional world. Remodeling is like pulling a loose thread on a cheap sweater—the job keeps unraveling.

"All we were trying to do was expand our breakfast room so we could put a table in it," my friend Rusty said. "The project started out being under ten grand, but then when we were jacking up the floor to even out the sagging floor joists, we ended up pinching all the kitchen cabinets so none of the drawers opened. So we had to buy new, seven-thousand-dollar cabinets. When we took out the old cabinets, we found that whoever put them in subbed together the wiring using lamp cords. So all the wiring had to be replaced. In the course of doing that, we broke a pipe, and the plumber came and said that we better fix the feeder lines in the basement so we'd have good water pressure. And as long as the walls were open, he said that we should put in copper pipes."

If you somehow manage to evade the Law of Unforeseen Consequences—and we were frankly amazed that Hal didn't uncover a cracked foundation, mildew, earthquake-damaged footings, or leaking sewage—it's impossible to resist the As Long As They're Here syndrome. In any residence there are thousands of glitches that could use a little tweaking. Generally, you let all the glitches slide because it's a nuisance to find a repairman or to do without water, electricity, or a kitchen while the repair is being made. But with remodeling comes opportunity. Your house is filled with supermen who can clearly do anything. It seems ridiculous not to put a new linoleum floor in the laundry room or install the Mano de Salamanca door knocker that we bought five years ago in Spain and never figured out how to screw into the door. After all, when would we be in this position again? (Never, I hoped.)

Duke went into the living room after the chimney had been removed. He noticed the late-afternoon sun streaming through the gaping hole in the roof and had an expensive epiphany.

"Honey, you know what would look great?" he asked. "Skylights."

"We can't afford them," I said flatly. We were still awaiting approval on our home-equity line.

"But it would really make the room sing," Duke said. (For what we had already invested the room should sing the "Hallelujah Chorus.")

Our architect took Duke's suggestion and ran with it. "If the budget considerations hadn't been what they were, I'd have suggested skylights," Brandon said. "Le Corbusier said, 'Architecture is the masterly, correct, and magnificent play of forms of light.' "

Brandon was never more efficient than when he was separating us from our money. In a nanosecond he figured out that according to local energy codes, we could add ten square feet of glass. And wouldn't you know it? The Buick of skylight companies—our architect was on the take there too—had just the model we needed. "It's a continuous translucent double-glazed self-flashing dome," Brandon said, as if he were saying "Chanel suit."

While I was struggling to decode this, the architect further clouded my mind with another of the countless lose/lose decisions that mark the remodeling process. Did I want the 14 ¼″ x 22 ¼″ model for $54? Or the 14 ¼″ x 46 ¼″ model for $75? Whichever we picked, he suggested we put in two.

It was like spinning a roulette wheel marked with all zeros, double zeros, octuple zeros. The house always won.

"Let's go for the big ones," said my husband, Diamond Jim, who remained blissfully unaware of our bank balance.

"Whatever size we get, let's make it a size where we don't have to cut any rafters," Hal said tersely. He seemed to be annoyed about something, probably the subfloor. His charge for the skylights was steep: $350 per light.

"Too much," I said promptly. Hal, who hates haggling as much as I do, offered to cut it down to $300.

"I'll have to get back to you on that."

"If I was undergoing a remodel like this, if I had to go borrow that thousand dollars from my mother, I would feel confident that it would be worthwhile," said Brandon.

"You're not looking at thousands of dollars in medical bills," I snapped. Even with insurance, a new hip and four months of physical therapy is not cheap.

"I know, I know," Brandon said. "And I'm not a writer whose income goes up and down."

Even though this statement was true, I had a knee-jerk reaction to prove that it was not. Remodeling defies the principles of modern commerce. You shell out great sums of money to people over whom you have no authority or power, yet these same people are constantly insinuating that you're cheap. (It reminded me of medicine, another area where you shell out great sums of money to people over whom you have no authority or power, who make you feel guilty for questioning a bill.) Construction workers are the blue-collar version of the snooty salespeople at Gucci who make $8 an hour but look down on you if you balk at a $400 alligator wallet.

Fortunately, I was immune to shame. When I moved into our sunny, clean, quiet apartment, I had a revelation: I didn't really like our house. This was something that had never occurred to me in the eight years that I had lived there. I felt like a woman in a toxic relationship who suspects something is bothering her but doesn't know what it is until her boyfriend goes out of town. Suddenly she realizes: It's him.

I knew I was in trouble the very first morning in the apartment. The pugs began yapping at 7:00 A.M., and instead of being able to roll out of bed, open the door, and throw them out into the fenced-in yard, I had to get dressed, hustle them downstairs without incident, walk down to the boardwalk, and make small talk with a guy wearing only a skimpy bathing suit and a boa constrictor named Fred. And I still didn't wish I was back in the house. I wasn't even nostalgic that night after dinner, when I had to wash all the dishes by hand because we had no dishwasher—and Duke had made his messiest dish, eggplant spaghetti, which involved the chopping of a lot of ingredients and a red sauce that splattered.

Renovation is like dating. It goes a lot smoother when you don't give a damn.

If I had cared desperately, then Hal or Dexter probably would have needed a quadruple bypass midway through the job or developed a heroin addiction or taken an impromptu vacation. Instead, they appeared like clockwork every morning at eight-thirty, clutching Styrofoam cups of coffee and Egg McMuffins. The contractor and the architect would have had an ongoing power struggle. Instead, they got along fine. In fact, stopping by the job site was like crashing an Iron John convention.

"I remember being a kid and running all over the scaffolding at the houses of people doing work," Brandon recalled one afternoon. "I thought, 'This is fun, I'll do that when I grow up.' "

Hal chuckled. "We always played in the sand pile. There was always sand on every construction site."

"There used to be gravel pits by this one school I went to. We used to run off the top right into the sand, like snow banks," Dexter said.

What could I possibly contribute to this discussion? Memories of my days in summer camp? Fortunately, Sophie trotted in with a rancid sparerib that she'd uncovered in the laundry room and I had to wrestle it away. (The pugs rechristened the job site the French Fry Mine.)

Dexter started doing construction when he was in college. "I'd get jobs with other musicians whose dads did this for a living," he confided as he was mitering joists. "They'd bring me on, give me fifty a day. I got a job with some guys I was recording with, they built houses as well."

The only connection I could make between rock music and construction was the ability to withstand deafening noises. I suggested that if he sampled the swoosh of the compressor, the hellish whine of the saw, and the thump, thump, thump of the pneumatic nail gun, he'd have a surefire hit.

"If I put them in with really pleasant sounds, I'd come up with something really dynamic," Dexter agreed. "Kind of like sitting in your house listening to a pretty piece of classical music and a big DC-3 flies over."

Kind of.

Perhaps the greatest perk of apathy was that each weekend when Duke and I made the Home Owner Stations of the Cross—Lighting World, Tile Palace, the Snooty Faucet Shoppe, Home Depot, IKEA—I was able to exercise restraint. Fixing a home is much like planning a wedding; it's tempting to throw a lot of cash into the mix to make sure you get the one of your dreams. There's no such thing as a simple choice: For every decision there are a million options and each has the potential to break you financially or make your house look cheesy. I know brides who have agonized over the right seating cards, nut baskets, and garters. But home owners have to wade through a far more vast pool of particulars.

Brandon gave me a shopping list, and every weekend Duke and I embarked on a scavenger hunt. Item Number One was a shower valve, the spigot thing the water comes out of, and the controlling faucets (though curiously not the metal gizmo that goes around the drain—that you have to buy separately). We started at a designer-quality bath furnishings showroom where faucets with names like posh hotels—Park Lane! Mayfair! Regent!—are individually mounted on Lucite plaques as if they were stags' heads. I admired Gothic Moderne Suite, a pair of old-fashioned faucets with little white disks on the handles that said "hot" and "cold" and a matching wall spout. Of course there were no price tags. If you have to ask, you can't afford it. "You're looking at six hundred and fifty-four dollars and ninety cents," the bath counselor begrudgingly informed me.

I was dumbstruck. "Is it platinum?"

"Polished chrome with ultra brass," she said haughtily. "Perhaps you'd like to see something a little more basic." (Unspoken but clear was the accusation "since you're a skinflint with no taste.") The basic model was a phallic protuberance that looked like something you'd find at a kinky sex store. Not only was it hideous, it was $343 and we'd have to wait ten weeks for delivery.

I'd never stopped to contemplate the value of a shower valve, but I knew it wasn't that. There are certain items that I believe human beings should be given gratis just for being on this earth: pillows, garbage cans, step stools, and definitely shower valves.

On our way out, we passed the decorative-hardware department. I stopped to admire simple red enamel draw pulls for our kitchen cabinets. We needed fifteen. How much could they possibly be? I took a number. Twenty minutes later, the decorative-hardware counselor informed me they were $12 apiece, and we'd only have to wait sixteen weeks for delivery. "I have something a little nicer, if you're interested," she said.

I felt like a philistine, but I passed.

We returned to the Home Depot. Duke pushed a cart the size of a pickup truck over to the shower-valve aisle, where to my consternation the units were displayed seven feet over my head. I supposed that was how I was going to view them in the shower, but I got the feeling they were hiding something. The reasonably priced models, "builder's grade," they called them, were amazingly ugly. The manufacturers probably brought in a special design team and had them work overtime to come up with something that hideous.

After a brief debate about the advantages of a two-faucet system versus a futuristic gear-shift apparatus, we chose a plain $89 unit, blessedly without faux crystal handles.

"You're not going to put *that* single-control thermostatic faucet unit in your house," said Davey, the aghast balding sage of the plumbing-supplies department. Without any prompting, Davey revealed that he used to be a plumber. He launched into a litany of worst-case scenarios—$500 repair bills, cold showers, molting tile—that could happen to us if we chose this brand. Instead, he recommended we buy a competing model that cost only $10 more.

"He's probably a shill," Duke said, but we bought it anyway, out of admiration for the marketing ploy.

We didn't know it at the time, but we'd committed a remodeling faux pas of enormous consequence. We didn't check to see if there was a matching set of sink faucets to install in whatever vanity we opted to buy. This lack of foresight meant that we violated the fifth rule of remodeling: Everything Must Match.

"No one will notice," said Duke, who has never read *Elle Decor* or *Metropolitan Home*. Just one issue would disabuse him of the belief that people are reasonable and practical. He would no longer be able to state with such conviction that most people prefer linoleum to tile because when you drop dishes on linoleum, they don't always break.

In a way, it was good that we made the mistake. Much in the same way it's good when your new car gets its first parking-lot ding. The faster you give up perfectionist standards, the better off you are. One afternoon three weeks into the job, I went over to the house to pick up the mail and beheld the centerpiece of the great room—the Big Beam!—looming above my head. It was a massive expanse of fir: six inches wide, fourteen inches deep, twenty feet long, and 555 pounds. It took Hal, Dexter, Jaime, and two diminutive Oaxaceños five hours to put it in. I suppose I should have watched, but in my experience, it's never a positive experience to watch a man install something.

"Do you like it?" asked Hal.

"Does it matter?" I replied. Secretly, I felt the beam was too big (Nadia Comaneci, who lives in the neighborhood, could perform her winning routine on it), too low, and off-center. But I kept my mouth shut. I figured I'd get used to it. (And indeed I did.)

"I like the beam," said Duke, who has the male affinity for largeness. "It gives the room focus."

In any case, the room looked a lot better. And "better," unlike "perfect," is a goal you can achieve without losing your sanity.

On the other hand, the more improvements you add, the worse the remaining things look. In the back bathroom we were changing the vanity, the floor, the walls, and the light fixtures. "What do you want to do about the tub?" asked Hal. The tub had always looked fine to me, but the contractor pointed out a faint brown stain around the drain and asked, "Has that always been there?" Who knew? It was Duke's bathroom. The contractor was also troubled by the thick coat of caulking at the edge of the tub. He warned, "I don't know if that will clean up." Certainly not the way *he* cleaned, I thought.

I asked how much a new tub would cost. "Only two hundred dollars for a cast-iron one," Hal said. Fortunately the room was too small to accommodate a Japanese soaking tub or a round sunken Euro-tub with a whirlpool. (The prefix "Euro" in Constructionese means something that costs three times as much as you expected to pay.)

"Only two hundred dollars," said Duke. "Let's go for it." Actually, the cast-iron tub was only $279, but we bought it anyway and had it delivered.

The next Friday, Duke came home from work early. He wanted to go swimming in the ocean, but I dragged him to the weekly payday meeting. I had a funny feeling that I'd need moral support.

Sure enough, Brandon gave us a disapproving look and squared his shoulders. "We have some new business that just came up," he said sternly. "You know Hal has been doing a lot of extra work that he hasn't been paid for, and you really can't take advantage of him doing things for free."

"Excuse me," I said. I'd just handed the contractor a check for $3,000. "What are you talking about?"

"It's the bathtub," said Hal, in that incredibly hurt way men have of bringing up an offhand remark you made six months before that they've been holding against you ever since. "No plumber would install it for nothing."

"Hal and I were talking, and he thinks a hundred and fifty dollars is a fair price to install the bathtub," said Brandon. "You know you have to be careful not to make any assumptions that he will do things."

"Don't patronize me," I snapped. "I asked how much it cost, and he said two hundred dollars. What was I supposed to do? Read his mind?"

The Magic Eight Ball came up with a different message: "My sources say no." Brandon smiled uneasily. "I'm sorry if you think I was patronizing."

I would have given Hal the $200 dollars just to keep him happy, but my husband, the official bad cop, intervened.

"The thing is that if you had told us a new bathtub was three hundred and fifty dollars, we wouldn't have bought it," Duke said. "So can you make a small adjustment in the price?"

"How about a hundred dollars," Hal said resentfully.

"Perfect," Duke said.

"Outlook good," said the Magic Eight Ball.

That afternoon, the bank called and said our equity-line loan had been approved. We now had what we thought was a comfortable contingency fund. We okayed the skylights. We sprung for recessed lights too. We thought we might even have enough cash left over to buy some furniture. Maybe even to go on vacation.

We were wrong, of course.

CHAPTER
THIRTEEN

ALKOMMEN TILL IKEA!" said a booming loudspeaker voice accompanied by merry accordion music. "Welcome to IKEA, the home furnishing store from Sweden!" I squeezed Duke's hand delightedly as we glided up a precipitous escalator and entered the home-owner equivalent of Disneyland.

There are more than a hundred of these gigantic yellow-and-blue monoliths (the colors of the Swedish flag) around the globe, in picturesque places like Vienna, Lausanne, and Jeddah. We have come to the unscenic Carson branch. It is a thirty-minute drive on the decidedly bleak, traffic-clogged San Diego Freeway, past half a dozen Denny's and the lot where the tethered Goodyear blimp sleeps. Since our remodel began, we have been making this pilgrimage to little Sweden almost every Saturday.

At first I thought that the Scandinavian theme park was just an advertising gimmick like Häagen Dazs (it's American) or the Express Campaigne, the phony French clothing store that is really operated by the Limited. But IKEA was actually founded in 1944 by seventeen-year-old Ingvar Kamprad, who grew up on a farm called Elmtaryd in the parish of Agunnard, in South Sweden—hence the strange name and the presence of Swedish meatballs and lingonberries on the café menu. Kamprad's dream was to give the average person a chance to fill their homes with good-looking, inexpensive furniture and a chance to test their skill putting together the furniture, which comes unassembled, along with nonverbal, iconic instructions (when you're selling to speakers of twenty languages this is essential) and a special wrench.

According to Jenny, my Swedish correspondent on the Internet, almost every home in Sweden has something from IKEA. Once a year they send their catalog to every household in the land. Even to King Carl XVI, to whom IKEA is an official purveyor of home goods. (Did he have to assemble his throne with a special golden wrench?) The success isn't surprising. Whereas most remodeling emporiums make you feel like a miser—"What, you don't want to spend six hundred dollars on a faux antique brass Victorian doorknob?"—IKEA gives you the sense that you can afford anything.

The store is laid out like a fun house, with a path marked by yellow arrows that customers must follow from entrance to exit. God help you if you try to swim against the tide of raging consumers. Instead of mirrors that make you short, they've got sofas, dining rooms, home-office supplies, and light fixtures, artfully arranged in cozy model rooms. Each item has a snappy Scandinavian sobriquet to anthropomorphize it and an *"otroliga priser!"* ("impossible price!"). Duke and I walked about five yards, past Drott, a $29 white lacquer bookcase (we have seven) and Hova, a $149 beech armchair upholstered in nubby cotton, before we spy a potential purchase—Rasmus, a $79 lacquer desk, and his buddy, Preben, a matching file cabinet, whose *"enkel att montera"* (easy assembly) would later prove to be infernally difficult.

"Rasmus would look good in my office," Duke said wistfully. "What do you think, the black finish or the white, or maybe oak."

"Black," I said firmly. "But we'd better measure first." All around us shoppers were having the same conversation in all the languages of Los Angeles: Spanish, Korean, Japanese, Mandarin, Cantonese, Armenian, Samoan, and Farsi.

We dutifully plodded through the marketplace, past Rugs and Carpets, where Duke picked up Basnäs, a $29.95 yellow-and-green dhurrie, even though we had no idea of what our color scheme would be or where it would go. Past Bed and Bath, where I grabbed Mariana, a $49 all-cotton duvet cover with matching pillow shams. We self-righteously bypassed the tableware section, filled with cutlery seemingly designed for gigantic Swedes. (We once purchased Lampa, a set of flatware, but I couldn't get my hand around the spoon.)

"Remember that article by Oliver Sachs in *The New Yorker* about the autistic woman who designs slaughterhouses to keep cattle reassured?" Duke asked. "This kind of reminds me of that."

My friend Debbie lasted five minutes in IKEA before she began hyperventilating. "Once I got in and realized I couldn't get out, I totally panicked," Debbie said. "This guy in a red T-shirt came over and asked if I needed any help, and I started crying and said, 'Yes, get me out of here!' He said I had to follow the yellow arrow, which took me through every floor of the store."

My husband had his traditional plate of Swedish meatballs and lin-gonberries to keep his strength up and then we continued along the path until we arrived at our destination: the bath shop. We had ostensibly come to buy Ego, a black Art Deco–inspired bathroom vanity and sink that we had been admiring for months. Not that our contractor is close to doing something tangible, like installing a vanity—he's yet to install our sky-lights, and the fireplace is sitting in a box in the bedroom—but Brandon has warned us that it is best to order all our items early, just in case we have to wait.

Actually, you never have to wait at IKEA, where part of the charm is instant gratification. A cheerful associate in a red T-shirt handed us a slip for our vanity and sink (total price: $240) and instructed us to go to the self-serve warehouse to pick it up. This swift transaction struck me as miraculous. A couple of years ago, before the coming of IKEA, we spent three months combing the designer-quality bath furnishings showrooms and home owner warehouses for a simple non-wood-veneered vanity that was under a thousand dollars. We eventually concluded that vanities were the black hole of American design and settled for a pedestal sink.

Duke loaded our bulging shopping cart onto a handy conveyor belt, which guided us down the stairs toward the checkout. Before we could get there, we passed the drawer-pull department and saw red enamel knobs similar to the ones for $12 apiece that we admired at the designer quality bath furnishings showroom. These knobs, Factum, cost only $8 for a card of six, so we tossed them into the cart too.

It only took a moment to pay for all our merchandise with our yellow-and-blue IKEA card (which we will be paying off until the millennium). All those impossibly small prices added up to an impossibly large sum. Then we went outside and reality struck. A look of horror came over my face, and every other wife's face in the parking lot: The feeding frenzy was over; now we had to cram the purchases into the car. Of course, IKEA of-fers home delivery, but it's the only thing in the store that's not cheap.

"It's not going to fit," I said. "We're going to have to have it deliv-ered." Of course, IKEA sells roof racks, but they don't work on my Audi sedan.

"I'll make it fit," Duke vowed.

All around us, couples were having the same conversation in all the languages of L.A. The guy in the next car was trying to stuff a queen-size mattress into a Toyota Camry, swearing in Taiwanese. His wife was telling him that it won't fit in Cantonese.

Duke miraculously managed to stuff Ego into the trunk, but the door wouldn't close with Rasmus wedged in the backseat. "Let's just pay for home delivery," I said again, but Duke pouted.

"If I have to pay for delivery, I don't want it."

A curbside attendant, who'd seen every variety of human wishful thinking when it came to the geometry of these packages, hurried over to save the sale. "I can shrink-wrap it," he said, producing a roll of industrial strength Handi Wrap. He hoisted the desk onto the roof of my car. Then he wrapped the plastic round and round it, passing the roll through the open doors, securing it to the roof. We got in and closed the doors, holding the bandage in place. "Good luck," he called as Duke drove off, a tail of Handi Wrap flapping in the breeze.

The next day, Sunday, was warm and sunny, but Duke couldn't play beach volleyball. There was more shopping to do. Shopping during remodeling is different from shopping in real life. Normally, you have a certain amount of money and you're keenly aware of how it's being spent, or else you see something that you can't live without and you buy it. But when you're remodeling, cash becomes as unreal as Monopoly script. We didn't earn the money, we borrowed it to fix up the house, so we felt obligated to spend it. Plus we absolutely *had* to buy certain items, whether we liked them or not.

Light fixtures, for example, are strangely uncompelling. I don't think twice about spending a couple hundred dollars for a dress that I might wear six times, but I balk at forking over the same amount for a lamp or a ceiling fixture that I'm going to see and use every day. I routinely yearn for new towels and sheets, yet I've driven past House O' Lamps and Lamp City a thousand times and never felt the urge to stop and browse. But now I was a customer, like it or not.

Lights fall into three categories: (1) Wondrous and Expensive, (2) Heart-Stoppingly Hideous (which, for mysterious reasons, are heart-stoppingly pricey too), and (3) Dull. Lamps of the first category either resemble Calder mobiles, defy gravity, and/or feature exquisite twinkly little halogen lights that hang from invisible wires and look a lot like Tinkerbell. They cast maybe one watt of light (the cuter the lamp, the less likely you are to be able to read by it). I recently accompanied Debbie to a lighting boutique, where she purchased a $250 Italian reading lamp that looked like it belonged on the bridge of the starship *Enterprise*. I would love to own such an electric sculpture, but you can't own just one, because it puts your other lights to shame.

This brings me to Category Two. I have yet to enter a light store without being staggered by bad taste. I suspect there is an antidesign council somewhere in a trailer park that comes up with these atrocious yet ubiquitous fixtures: chandeliers of cascading Plexiglas that look like they belong in the lobby of a Las Vegas casino. Tiffany-inspired pendant lamps with a theme like "kitchen spices" rendered in ersatz stained glass. Even, in this age of political correctness, a torchiere featuring an illuminated black jockey (who buys these, white supremacists?). The other day I toured a million-dollar model home at the top of a mountain in Pacific Palisades. No expense had been spared. Yet hanging in the foyer was a ghastly brass chandelier that looked like an elongated upside-down tulip. So go figure.

When I began looking for fixtures, I became hyperconscious of the lights around me (when you're looking for a roof, the whole world's a roof). My friend Marcella is a lamp fanatic, with a penchant for whimsical kitsch like a lamp made out of a Chinese hand-carved duck with a fish in its mouth, an illuminated two-headed African-statue lamp, and a cat lamp that doubles as a planter. I asked her to explain the appeal of this junk. "Lamps give you a chance to have funny weird objects around the house that are functional," Marcella said. "My favorite is my chicken lamp because the top comes off and you can hide things."

I don't need a lamp to be a stash or an objet d'art, which is why our house is filled with Category Three: dull, with an industrial twist. All I want a lamp to do is shed light, preferably as much as possible. I like my rooms to be blinding, like the beach in the midday summer sun. Gomez, our landlord, created this effect by installing recessed lighting—"can lights," he called them. I asked Brandon what it would take to install a

few. "All it takes is a change order," he said predictably. "How many switches do you want? One or two? Or one for the middle and two?"

I have never thought about switches in my life.

"Do you want to turn them all on at once?" Brandon probed.

You bet.

"You think the switch only has one position anyway," my husband said laughing.

When I was growing up, my father was forever admonishing me to turn off lights, because of the electric bill. My former husband continued this harangue, and it drove me nuts. At the age of thirty, I divorced him and lived alone for the first time. I reveled in the freedom to leave the lights on in every room of the house until the day my electric bill came. I was afraid to open it for two weeks. From all the warnings, I expected it to be around a thousand dollars, but to my astonishment, it was only thirty bucks. I never worried about a light again. Duke, to his everlasting credit, has never chided me, though he quietly turns the lights off behind me.

Hal agreed to supply the eyeball trim for the can lights at $75 a pop. But we still had to supply track lights, a bathroom sconce, two bathroom fixtures, and an outdoor light. The latter only comes in three equally inappropriate styles, which are sold everywhere—traditional shiny brass coach lamps (who has a coach?), spotlights that look like they belong in concentration camps, and, in a nod to Southern California's position on the Pacific Rim, green bronze Japanese pagodas.

We had already craned our necks in Lamps Plus, Lamp City, Lamp Village, House O' Lamps, and a dozen other similarly idiotically named establishments before we pulled into the Lighting Palace, which was having a monster sale on track lights (track lights, like sheets, are always on sale). The owner was having an animated conversation on the phone in Farsi, so we looked around and found a new kind of outdoor light, one that looked like a Deco cocktail shaker. Duke spent a half hour deliberating as to whether he could put a photo cell in it, but the owner never acknowledged we were in the store. Los Angeles shopkeepers think that it's a clever sales ploy to ignore you. (Recently, while I was in Chicago visiting my sister, I walked into a store and a friendly clerk said, "May I help you?" I thought she was being sarcastic.)

Eventually, Floyd, a tanned, fit youth who would rather be playing beach volleyball too, emerged from the back and deigned to sell us the tracks and the cocktail shaker. "What kind of bullets do you want on the tracks?" he asked. (Did a *woman* name them bullets? I think not.) He gave us a choice of phallic projectiles. "Whatever is easiest to change the bulbs in," I said. They were going on a fifteen-foot ceiling.

"Oh, then you need Mr. Long Man," Floyd said, referring to a long pole with a gripper at the end, which was obviously not named by a female either. It cost an additional $30.

Duke fondled Mr. Long Man lovingly. "I don't think we need him," he said. What are we going to do when the bulbs burn out, bring in a cherry picker?

Floyd showed us a $75 decorative sconce with a halogen bulb that would be perfect in the bathroom. We broke down and bought that too because the salesman offered us a special discount. It turned out to only be 10 percent off, so we postponed buying the matching ceiling fixture. On the way out, Duke pointed out a $200 ceiling fan that he thought would look nice in the bedroom, and a $400 cobalt blue Jetson-like chandelier with twinkling halogen lights. A light went off in Duke's brain. "As long as they're doing the electricity, why don't we have Hal move the junction box in the dining room so we can put that over the table?"

"Let's think about it," I said, pulling him away.

Our next stop was Ceramic City, to select tile for our bath and fireplace. For weeks I'd been bugging Hal for the measurements. "There's no hurry," he said, but suddenly his tile guy got an opening in his schedule. "When's the tile going to be in?" he asked impatiently.

"When you give me the measurements," I said.

Duke and I headed east on Washington Boulevard, away from the clean sea air, past miles and miles of ugly houses. In Baltimore, where I grew up, it is common to find interesting-looking row houses or clapboard two-story Victorians in working-class neighborhoods, but in Los Angeles even upscale neighborhoods boast remarkably bad-looking constructions: teensy stucco boxes painted chartreuse or mauve or flesh; strange combinations of styles like Polynesian Tudor or Mediterranean Cape Cod, and Dingbats, two-story apartment buildings built over a parking garage that have names like the Sand Castle or the Sun Spot.

Ceramic City looks like a cross between a lobby in a prehip Miami hotel and my Grandmother Flora's bathroom (my grandmother was the first person I know to install a maroon toilet and matching sink). It is run by an Israeli family who promised the prices are the lowest in town. Certain ethnic groups seem to gravitate toward certain home-owner specialties. The Iranians seem to have cornered the light-fixtures market, the Koreans, paint, and Israelis have a lock on tile as well as carpet-cleaning concessions.

Here they have an interesting bait-and-switch technique, which goes like this. First, they mail out a million coupons, promising to clean five rooms of carpet for a ridiculous price like $19.99. To get them to honor this offer requires an advanced degree in assertiveness training. David or Avi shows up—just off the plane from Haifa. He inspects your rugs, sighs plaintively, and begins to mutter in Hebrew. He warns you that unless you sign up for the preconditioning treatment, the special spot remover, and the Teflon coating (only $85!) your carpets will fall apart. Should you fail to succumb, he asks to borrow your phone. He and his boss have an animated discussion in Hebrew. The boss asks to speak to you and offers you a special price for everything because "you seem like a nice Jewish girl." Over the years, I discovered the secret phrase for demurral: "My husband won't let me pay more." Avi shampoos your rugs, albeit not very well, accepts his $19.95 check, and bolts out the door to attempt to browbeat the next sucker.

As soon as we entered the Ceramic City showroom, I was beguiled by the exquisite patterns and bright colors. Some women have a weakness for kitchen appliances or curtains with puffy chintz valances; I adore tile. For the first time since our remodel began, I yearned to be a millionaire so I could transform our beach bungalow into a miniature Alhambra. With an unlimited budget, I could cover the kitchen counter with darling Portuguese tiles hand-painted with whimsical fruits and vegetables. I could turn our bathroom into a replica of an ancient Greco-Roman bath complete with Etruscan-inspired mosaic floor.

My reverie was interrupted by our tile counselor, Shoshanna, who was dazzling in a luminescent turquoise silk blouse, a shocking pink-and-fuschia paisley sarong skirt, and most impressive, four-inch royal blue spike heels. I felt like a rube in my jeans and sneakers. Since my hip surgery, I'd been high heel–impaired, which only made me feel more inadequate.

"What are you doing? Kitchen? Bathroom? Entry?" she asked briskly as I stared worshipfully at a display of deep green glazed terra-cotta tiles with a border of hand-painted fish.

"How much are the adorable little fish?"

"Nine dollars," she said.

Thinking square feet, I did the calculations. "Four hundred and eighty dollars."

"No," said Shoshanna, "nine dollars *a tile.*"

"You're joking?" But of course, she was not.

"I can give you a very good price on marble," said Shoshanna, leading me over to a shimmering pink-veined slab that looked like it belonged in a honeymoon suite in the Poconos around a heart-shaped tub.

I shook my head. "Too shiny."

Shoshanna stayed at my heels like a border collie, herding me past a display of reproductions of tiles that paved twelfth- and thirteenth-century abbeys and cathedrals, past imported Brazilian petroglyphs, to a display of classic white hexagons, with red, green, black, and blue diamond inserts. The hexagons cost only $8 a square foot, only $6 with a contractor's discount (Hal had given me his license number). Three hundred and sixty didn't seem unreasonable.

"Look, honey," Duke called out from behind a rack of Italian tiles painted with sweet little suns, moons, and stars. He waved me over to a display of very similar hexagon tiles. These hexagons have black diamond inserts and are on sale for only $3.25 a square foot. Shoshanna flinched.

"You could buy that," she said, though her implication was clear: If we have any standards, we will not. "That tile is thinner. It's builder's grade."

"Does it come with red diamonds?" I asked.

"The special price is just for black diamonds," she said. "But I tell you what you can do. Buy some red ones separately, and scatter them around. The red ones are a little more expensive, but you don't need that many."

"Sounds perfect," I said.

I wanted to put the hexagons on the floor and the walls, but Shoshanna cringed. "It's just for the floor," she said, as if I were breaking an ancient tile law. She gave me permission to buy white tiles for the shower, black quarter round trim, and fifteen black tiles for a checkerboard border at the top.

"Fine," I said weakly. "Now for the fireplace."

The fireplace surround had gone through numerous incarnations as our dreams gave way to economic reality. Plan A was inspired by a honeymoon trip to Spain, where I fell in love with the brightly colored geometric tile patterns that reminded me of a Mondrian painting. Duke, who has a genius for complicating the simple, had taken pictures, and he suggested that Brandon knock off an intricate four-color design.

Then, on a scouting expedition to a fancier showroom, the Elite Tile Palace, Duke became infatuated with tumble-stone marble tile that looked like granite. The four-color mosaic gave way to a subtle checkerboard with the pink-and-gray marble squares. It would have looked marvelous. But the tumbled marble cost *only* $30 a square foot.

Back at Ceramic City, Shoshanna watched with ill-concealed frustration as we rejected faux bricks, granite, pastel glazes, earth tones, Italian terra-cotta, ersatz Delft, porcelain pavers, and daisy-laden mosaic panels with a banner that read MI CASA ES SU CASA. (I already have a similar plaque that I had made in Guadalajara to discourage houseguests. It says, MI CASA NO ES SU CASA.) After half an hour of deliberation, we agreed on what appeared to be pale pink hexagon Mexican pavers with matching two-inch diamond inserts, and a terra-cotta border. My only concern was that some of the pavers looked kind of orange, a color I detest. "Are you sure these will be pink?" I asked.

"Of course," she lied.

Shoshanna suggested we throw in a few diamonds hand-painted with merry designs. I spent a joyous twenty minutes choosing *tulipans* (tulips), *golondrinas* (swallows), and *mariposas* (butterflies) before she revealed that each two-inch diamond cost $3. They were made in Puebla, a town we'd driven through recently. "Honey," Duke said excitedly. "You know what we could do . . ."

"We can't drive to Mexico now," I said firmly.

Shoshanna presented us with a bill for $900. "Too much," said my husband, who has even tried to get a discount at the Brooks Brothers factory outlet. (The clerk shook his head sadly and said, "At Brooks Brothers, we do not bargain.") My stomach began to churn, and I retreated to a remote corner of the store and began studying a panel of Idaho quartzite. I would like to live in a fixed-price world.

"This is a very low price," Shoshanna said. As a basis for comparison, she showed my husband an invoice from the only person in the history of the store who had ever paid full price. Duke later surmised it was a collector's item.

"That's a very interesting document," he told her, "but we don't want to pay full price."

Shoshanna consulted with her brothers, two former paratroopers, in rapid-fire Hebrew and returned. "Do you want me to show you something cheaper?"

Duke shook his head. "No, I want you to make an adjustment on this price."

I hadn't felt so uneasy since Duke sold our ten-year-old stove. We had placed a classified ad in the *Recycler,* a local paper composed only of classified ads, asking $60. Seth, an affable landlord from Manhattan Beach, called, made an appointment to see it, and agreed to buy it. Duke was disconnecting it when two more buyers arrived. I thought we should give it to Seth, but to my horror, my husband said, "Let's have a Dutch auction," a process in which bidders make decreasing offers. Duke started the bidding at $250, and to my stupefaction Seth bought it for $110. Duke wanted to charge him an extra ten bucks for the hood, but I threatened to kill him.

Shoshanna slunk back to her calculator and, after much muttering, knocked another hundred off the bill. I gave her a deposit, and she gave me the evil eye. "The tile will be in at the end of the week," she said.

As the Magic Eight Ball says, Don't count on it.

CHAPTER FOURTEEN

IT WAS Week Four, but it felt like Week Forty. Monday morning brought Inspector Percy Chang, from the City of Los Angeles Building Department, for our structural-integrity inspection. Brandon had warned me not to be alarmed if we didn't pass. "Hal's doing his best," said the architect, who had bicycled over to perform a preinspection inspection. "But they always find something wrong, just because they're inspectors."

I knew the type. "He's like a copy editor."

"Building inspectors have rights like the police," said Brandon, who confessed he'd been busted for bootlegging apartments before. "They come whenever they feel like it, and they get to inspect everything—the electrical, the drywall nails, the framing—and if it's not all right, they make you do it over. Contractors play this game where they leave something for them to find."

Writers do the same thing with copy editors.

"I guess building's a lot like writing, only dirtier," said Brandon. As he bicycled away, he called out a final warning. "Make sure he signs the card. I don't want to cover up the framing and have them come back and ask, 'Do you have permission to cover?' "

I wasn't worried. Our contractor had a strong incentive to make sure things went smoothly. He was broke—again! Brandon's intricate and draconian payment schedule tied Hal's weekly payments to progress benchmarks like "finishing the rough framing" and "passing the inspection." In theory, this was sensible, but in fact the contractor was ten days behind because of the fireplace and the nefarious cripple wall. For a moment, I assumed that we didn't have to pay him for work not accomplished, but it turned out that wasn't the case.

"Contractually, you're not obligated, but you don't want to make him mad," said Brandon, who rivaled Neville Chamberlain as a master of appeasement. He suggested a prorated partial payment, which he claimed was based on the percentage of the job completed but was actually influenced by other factors such as whether Hal's landlady had cashed his rent check. I wasted several hours each week listening to Hal and Brandon make a case for the amount that each week's check should be for.

One Friday, when Hal wasn't ready for the rough-framing inspection, Brandon recommended that we give him half his payment as a token of good faith because the crown molding was on the job site.

"But then I won't have enough to pay my men," Hal had wailed plaintively, rolling his eyes and raising his shoulders up to his ears so he looked even more like an old codger than usual. In a piteous voice, he asked if we could also pay him for the skylights. Guilt notwithstanding, I didn't see why we should. Holes were cut in the roof, some wooden frames were in, but the skylights were lying on the bedroom floor along with the fireplace and the new bathtub. According to Brandon, we weren't supposed to pay for change orders until the work was done. But Hal was phobic about finishing things. There were half a dozen things in the house that he could have finished that he did not.

"The skylights will be in by the end of the day," Hal promised.

I wrote the bigger check. But when I went to the house for the inspection, the skylights were still lying on the bedroom floor. And Hal was still short of cash. "Can you write me a check after the inspection?" he whispered, when Brandon was out of earshot. "I've got to run to the bank to cover some checks."

I expected the inspector to be a weathered, overweight, nit-picking bureaucrat, but Percy Chang was a soft-spoken former marathon runner in his late twenties who had been recruited by the Building Department when he was a senior at USC. Percy had a passion for his job that a development executive at Fox would envy.

"I've been everywhere from a flea-bitten house in Watts to the Playboy Mansion. I've done Norman Lear, Ed Asner, and John Candy too, when he was alive," Percy said proudly. He grew even more animated when he realized that he'd heard me on the radio. "How come there's no show for home owners?" he complained, adding that he would be the perfect host.

A sample of his material: "Psychologists are the hardest people to inspect. They're the most paranoid. Couples are the easiest. They seem to be stable. I guess the contractor holds them together, because they have a common enemy."

I forced a laugh as he crawled under the house to examine the bolts on the shear wall. Percy dusted the sand off his knife-creased jeans, scraped the cat dung off his shoes, and sighed.

"Well, if the house falls now, it will fall in one piece," he said. He signed the official house report card approving the rough framing—"not too much wrong that they can do to framing"—but suggested that we add kicker panels under the house to keep the walls from tilting in an earthquake. ("I honestly believe they're going overboard on this earthquake stuff," Brandon would protest later.)

"How much?" I asked Hal. Ever since the bathtub altercation, I'd been zealous about asking the price of everything. It made Hal uncomfortable to talk about money (though he didn't have trouble begging for it). He thought of himself as an artist who was above material transactions—until payday.

"I'll have to work something up," Hal said evasively. (We never did get that price.)

"While you're at it you should change the galvanized pipes to copper," said the inspector, explaining that copper ones didn't corrode.

"How much?" I said again.

"Oh," Percy said airily, "between one and six thousand."

"I'll think it over," I lied.

I walked the inspector to his car. A rheumy-eyed youth in a yellow knit cap, a multicolored, blindingly loud dashiki, and dreadlocks blowing in the breeze was moving into the Roach Motel with his roommate, Beth, a wholesome young blonde who seemed pleasant enough but was bound to have a fatal flaw because the landlord attracted lowlives like a bug light attracts mosquitoes. (Beth's flaws turned out to be alcohol and men.) "So she made a few unfortunate life choices," said my ever-tolerant mate.

"Hey, mon!" hailed Rasta Man, and Percy shuddered. He pointedly told me that *he* lived in San Pedro, in a decent neighborhood near the docks (near the docks is never a good sign), and suggested that I move there too.

"How did you get talked into this place?" Percy asked.

"I married it," I said with a sigh.

The longer I was out of our house, the more I dreaded our return. I was content in our apartment, where a sophisticated security system shielded me from common Venice annoyances such as the record seventeen "gang-related" murders that had occurred in a nearby neighborhood since the beginning of the year. I didn't even feel threatened when I received yet another letter from yet another film-location manager warning me of yet another spectacular special effect that would take place down the block.

"Dear Resident," read the latest missal. "We will be filming scenes for an upcoming Movie of the Week. Filming will take place between 8:00 P.M. to 3:00 A.M. and will involve mostly exterior dialogue, a foot chase, and some gunfire." (How do you distinguish fake gunfire from the real thing, I wondered.)

Gunfire was tame. A few months before, a film crew blew up a bus a block from our home for the Keanu Reeves action hit *Speed*. Venetians, immune to the bizarre, blithely went about their business as the crew prepped the bus for demolition (there was even a stand-in bus, which watched the hero bus with ill-concealed envy). It was perhaps the only time in history when the opening gambit at the local dry cleaners was not "Are my clothes ready?" but rather "Have they blown up the bus yet?"

So grateful was I to be in my cozy fortress, I didn't even mind Gomez, who in another situation might be the landlord from hell. Shortly after we moved in, Gomez decided to move the kitchen cupboards in the unit above us. I was sitting in my office trying to write when I heard relentless pounding and the unmistakable screech of a Saws-all. I went upstairs to complain. "I have to do the noisy stuff before I can do the quiet stuff," said Gomez, proudly showing off a new saw that could cut through concrete, metal, and wood. My landlord agreed to do some manual stuff while I was working, but in exchange he wanted me to keep him apprised of my actions. "Let me know when you're going out," he said. "Even if it's for five minutes, so I can make this cut."

Gomez routinely shut off the water for hours at a time—"Just got to cut out this pipe," he explained—though he considerately brought me a bucket of water so the apartment would remain clean enough to pass his frequent pop inspections. Gomez had unfailing instincts for sloth. No sooner had I spilled a drop of Diet Coke on the impossible-to-keep-clean champagne carpet than he arrived to measure the height of the bathroom lights. But I remained sanguine, even when he buzzed me on the intercom to point out that I had left the porch light on. I did balk when Clara strayed into the unit he was working on, in search of a burrito, and Gomez cautioned, "Watch the carpets. She has sawdust on her paws."

"Her paws are the size of dimes," I replied evenly.

Around this time, my husband accused me of being negative about our house. "We're spending all this money," Duke said. "It would be good if you had something positive to say."

When I look at Duke I'm frequently reminded of a majestic male duck.

His plumage is beautiful, but when the going gets tough he is frequently found paddling peacefully on the pond, quacking loudly and happily, before abruptly disappearing from sight in a brief flash of orange webbed feet.

It was easy for my husband to be upbeat. He left for the office just as the workers were arriving. His day was not interrupted by entreaties to make tedious decisions such as "Do you want the batten boards to extend to the bottom of the house?" He didn't have to endure the objections of our parking tenants whose spaces were routinely blocked by the workers' trucks. (Brandon's intricate contract expressly forbade more than one truck from parking in our driveway, but the architect warned me that it was in my best interest to let it slide.) Duke didn't have to make a fuss when the contractor seemingly installed the wrong window in the great room. (To my relief, we finally had windows again.)

"It's just missing a grid that snaps into place," Hal explained. "The window guy forgot to order it. It'll be here in a week." (It wasn't.)

Duke returned home after the aggravation was over and admired the day's progress: a greenhouse window in the kitchen; a pair of double-hung wooden windows with obscured glass in the dining room that blocked the view of the Roach Motel. Then my husband made complex suggestions such as, "Honey, why don't we bury stereo wires in the drywall?" and saddled the beleaguered job boss—me—with the details of implementation: drive ten miles to a stereo store, pick out the perfect kind of speaker wire (a skill that is governed by the Y chromosome), try to guess where Duke wanted the speakers.

"How much?" I asked Hal again and again. I saw the contractor more often than I saw my friends, yet we never grew close. There was still an undercurrent of annoyance on the job site that I couldn't explain.

"I get the feeling that Hal underbid it," was Brandon's guess.

I got the feeling that Brandon was driving the easygoing contractor nuts with his change orders to sign in triplicate, lien releases to be filled in by any pickup laborer who set foot on the premises, to say nothing of the endless meetings, but Hal smilingly maintained that he enjoyed the organization. Then again, Hal smilingly maintained that nothing was bothering him either.

I feel remorseful complaining because our contractor, while sulky, took great pride in his work and never cut corners. After he installed the new windows, he took out the old ones on his own and reframed them just because he didn't think they looked right. When I logged on to America Online's Home Owner bulletin board, I didn't have a juicy contractor horror story to share, unlike Striker210, who wrote, "How would you like to see your contractor on *The Ricki Lake Show* when he was supposed to be at your house?" Or Shadow12n1, who came home unexpectedly to discover her lingerie drawer open and her burly contractor prancing around in her black lace teddy. "The police said that I had to pay him the remainder of what I owed," she reported. "And I couldn't deduct the price of the lingerie."

Still, it's difficult to relish a relationship that is predicated on you writing checks for more money than you made last year to someone who is inwardly seething because you didn't give him more.

Jaime, the courtly finishing carpenter, contended that hostility was normal. "It's the hardest thing about my job," he said. "People hate me. I see it in their faces. They don't want me there. It's intrusive, coming into their lives every day. But I can't help it. That's what I do, I build."

He had a little trick. "When they're living there, I take the wife aside and hand her a large hammer. I say, 'Here, go for the wall, get your aggressions out. At first, they're timid. They say, 'I can't, I can't.' But then they get into it. I had one wife, she demolished the whole wall for me."

Alas, there was nothing left for me to destroy and I had no desire to participate in the task at hand—installing insulation. What is it, anyway? Who needs it? Was it there before? I didn't care. Some home improvements are dearer to the heart than others. I did care that the continuous dome skylights were lying on the floor two weeks after we'd paid for them. "I need ventilation for the insulation," Hal said. The following week, he didn't want them to be marred by the drywall.

"You'll enjoy the process more when it becomes more like fixing a dollhouse," Duke assured me.

I wasn't assured. With dollhouses, you have total control over your environment, which in fact is largely the appeal of the hobby. In the full-scale world, I was powerless. I'm a person who detests houseguests (my sister once threatened to buy me a welcome mat that said GO AWAY). It was bad enough that relative strangers had keys to my home (which they casually left in a pot in the backyard so more strangers could let themselves in and toss half-eaten Chicken McNuggets under the kitchen sink). But the workers also gave grand tours to any vagrant, beachgoer, or string-bikini-clad nymphet on Rollerblades who expressed curiosity. Ian, the penis-enlarger entrepreneur, stopped me on the boardwalk one morning to critique the job.

"You should have added a second story as long as you were tearing the place apart," he said.

"Thank you for your input," I said, gritting my teeth.

When you undergo a renovation you essentially announce to the neighborhood that you have cash to burn. This wasn't something that I cared to advertise in Venice.

Another morning, in the front yard, I encountered a particularly irritating neighbor whom Duke refers to as "the Cockroach" because he lives underground in a hole under the trash bins and skitters away if you look at him. He was burrowing through the trash heap selecting choice lengths of redwood siding.

"What are you doing?" I asked.

"The guys said I could take the spare wood," the Cockroach said. "Do you have a problem with that?"

Actually, I had several problems, but it was not in my best interest to undermine Hal's authority. Construction is a game of pacification. You pay the bills, but the contractor holds the cards because he can stop your job. It's like being held hostage.

"There's a guy next door, Rufus, with dreadlocks," Hal said another day. "He keeps telling me that he can do drywall. I have no objection if he helps us, but I don't know what your relationship is with him."

"Relationship?" I stammered. "We have no relationship." (Judging from the number of people who pulled up to his apartment, knocked on the door, accepted a small envelope passed through a window, then sped away, I'd be willing to bet that this wasn't a person I wanted to know.)

"He seems okay," Hal said, and I felt ashamed for being intolerant.

"I don't like the idea as a matter of course," Brandon said, and I smiled gratefully. "It's too incestuous. If there's a problem, a guy next door could do a lot of damage."

With gritted teeth, I told the Cockroach to continue, but I asked Hal not to give away materials again without permission.

"It might as well go to use," Hal said. "It's just going to get hauled away."

When? Come the millennium?

According to Brandon's labyrinthine contract, our trash was to be hauled away weekly. Six weeks into the job, the leaning tower of scrap wood, plumbing parts, and discarded pizza was 62 inches high, 109 inches long, and 52 inches wide and featured items like empty cans of Mighty Dog ("I don't know where that came from," Hal said), a tub of drywall mud with Egg McMuffins floating in it, most of a jade plant that Jaime had recklessly pruned when he installed the front windows, and a flourishing colony of ants that would later stubbornly resist a wide range of anti-ant technology. Still, the contractor balked at hauling the garbage away.

"It will cost me two hundred dollars," Hal said, digging a little hole in the dirt with his toe, "and I'd rather not pay that."

I'd rather not pay for lots of things, but *I* didn't have a choice.

One evening, Duke returned from the job site looking gloomy. "Our refrigerator has died," he said. "The compressor is shot."

"It can't be," I said. We'd bought the big Amana only four years ago, and we regarded it with an inordinate amount of pride.

"I guess he missed his friend the stove," said Duke, speaking of the beat-up stove he'd sold for $110.

We summoned a refrigerator specialist—curiously, the only appliance repairmen who don't charge extra for coming at night. Twenty-two-year-old Dimitri had recently arrived from St. Petersburg and gone straight to refrigeration school. (For some reason, three of the refrigerator-repair places that we called were staffed by Russian émigrés, perhaps because they're used to the cold.) Dimitri agreed that the compressor was shot. "We could give it one try to see if we can get it started," he said, but a jump failed to bring the Amana back to life.

Naturally, Dimitri said it would cost $400 to install a new, bigger compressor. An appliance repair is invariably a couple hundred dollars less than a new one, which brings you right to the point where you have to think twice about dumping it. The decision is not so much economic but rather depends on how attached you are to the particular machine.

"For a hundred dollars more we can get a new one," said Duke, who felt personally betrayed by the refrigerator. My husband may be frugal, but he has an uncharacteristic lack of faith in appliance repair. Last year, when he had the flu, he lay on the couch for a week, moaning like he had the Ebola virus. Then our Sony Trinitron died.

"The television is broken," Duke groaned.

"Go back to sleep," I said. "I'll call the repairman in the morning."

"We have to get a new one."

"Why? This is the first thing that's gone wrong with it in ten years."

"It's the beginning of the end," Duke said ominously.

I was sentimental about that Sony Trinitron, even though I'd turned it on myself perhaps a maximum of twelve times in the entire time I'd owned it. My former husband, Richard, was a television addict. He kept three televisions going day and night because he liked the noise. When I left him, I couldn't bear the thought of owning a television, so I gave all the sets to him. My father considered this a crime against nature. I was living in Baltimore at the time. We went to Rosh Hashanah services, and afterward Dad looked at me gravely. "It breaks my heart, thinking of you all alone without a television," he said, handing me a check. "I want you to go buy yourself a big color set with a remote control."

I didn't want a big color television set, but I bravely ventured forth to the appliance store. They had fifty sets going nonstop, and I began hyperventilating. It reminded me of my bad marriage. I bolted out of the store, only to return later with a friend, who made the purchase for me. He drove the set back to my apartment and asked where I wanted him to put it. "In the closet," I said. There it remained, in its box, for three years. When I began dating Duke he set it up and has enjoyed it ever since. I was loath to replace it.

But while I was flipping through the phone book looking for a repairman, Duke roused himself from his torpor, combed through the Sunday paper for a sale (televisions, like sheets and track lights, are always on sale), and got dressed for the first time in a week. He came into my office and announced that we had twenty minutes to get to Circuit City before they closed. My husband remained on his feet long enough to purchase a new Trinitron, drag it home, and set it up, before collapsing on the sofa clutching his brand new clicker.

Duke asked Dimitri in Russian what brand of refrigerator he recommended.

"Hwirlpool is the best," said Dimitri.

Ten minutes later we pulled into the parking lot at Adrays, a local discount chain staffed by cutthroats on commission whom I suspect were too aggressive to make it in the used-car business. The instant I entered the store I got a headache. Perhaps I was anticipating the inevitable fullcourt press to convince me to buy an extended warranty. Or perhaps it's just that I don't like appliance stores. So many big-ticket items, so little I want to buy. With refrigerators, all you seem to get if you spend more money are incomprehensible options such as tempered glass shelves (what are *they*?), humidity control (so the hair on the peaches won't frizz?), and see-through doors. (So people can see our half-eaten apples, numerous containers of yogurt, and sticky bottles of Thai fish sauce?)

"The see-through door does solve the old enigma about whether the light is on when the door is closed," Duke noted.

Actually, the only difference between a $600 model and a $1,000 one are a few extra drawers that say, "Fruit," "Meat," "Deli," or "Crisper." (What is a crisp, anyway?)

"Often I put the wrong thing in just to see what will happen," my sister told me. "It doesn't seem to make any difference."

The only option I found remotely tempting was the ice-maker/cold-water dispenser on the door. It would add $300 to the price tag, plus plumbing charges. Frankly, it's not that hard to fill an ice tray with water.

"Ice and water that comes out of the refrigerator never seems safe," said Laurie, who has one. "It seems like it's going through some dangerous tubes."

Duke located a big white Hwirlpool that was on sale for $500 dollars, probably because it doesn't have an egg module.

"Does it come in black or stainless steel?" I asked.

"For this price, you can only get white, almond, and harvest gold," said the salesman. "I've got a black Amana for two hundred more. If you want chrome, that will run you around fifteen hundred, plus the decorator steel trim panel, the toe plate, and the louvered grill." (I find it a little scary that you can buy outfits for appliances.)

"White's fine," Duke said.

"No it's not," I said. The week before we had purchased an adorable chrome-and-black Magic Chef stove.

"Where is it written that appliances have to match?" Duke asked loudly. All the women in the appliance department stopped and stared as if he were out of his mind.

The salesman suggested that we switch the color of our new stove from chrome to white, since it hadn't been delivered yet. My husband protested that the stove looked better in chrome, which was true, but I silenced him with a glance. Somewhere in the back of my mind, I'd stopped thinking dream house and begun to think resale value.

"Do you need anything else?" asked the salesman. "We're having a special on Maytags. No payment for a year."

"No, thank you," I said firmly. We have a pair of large old Maytags in the laundry room. They take up a lot of space, but they work just fine.

"Wait," said Duke. "If we get a stack washer and dryer, we can reclaim the laundry room. Hal can take the old sink out and build the stack unit right in the corner."

"God knows what that will cost," I groaned.

But my husband knows how to win an argument with me. "You'll need a place to work on your dollhouses."

He had a point. I used to have a little workshop set up in a corner of the sunporch. But the sunporch was now part of the great room, and I couldn't imagine doing my miniature painting and wallpapering and shingling in there. I reasoned that in a year's time when the bill came, we'd have money in the bank again.

The salesman happily wrote up the order. "How about a new dishwasher?" he asked. At the rate we were going, he had a chance of winning Salesman of the Month.

"Why not?" I said recklessly, though I felt like I'd been kidnapped by the appliance aliens. "Our dishwasher is a wreck."

"I'm personally attached to that dishwasher," said Duke. He got it in lieu of rent from one of his tenants, a construction worker, who found it in a building he was demolishing. The dishwasher, which we named Manuel after the incompetent waiter in the television show *Fawlty Towers,* sat under a tarp in the yard for years until we moved in and Duke triumphantly hooked it up. "Manuel has never let us down," Duke said.

"We'll think about the dishwasher," I said. The salesman spent another twenty minutes trying to convince us to spring for an expensive three-year extended warranty just in case all our brand-new appliances broke down. We managed to resist.

"What are we doing?" Duke asked on the drive home.

I shrugged helplessly. We were out of control.

CHAPTER FIFTEEN

REMODELING IS the manifestation of a million decisions. At the beginning, the choices come at a slow, steady pace. Paint the beam or stain it? Single or double-paned glass? Eyeball or floodlight? Half inch or quarter inch between tiles for grout? But as the job moves from incomprehensible structural underpinnings to accoutrements that make you comfortable and that you can actually see, the decisions come rapid-fire, like an automatic pitching machine gone amok.

Eight o'clock Wednesday morning, I was washing my hair when the telephone rang. Duke was fast asleep and didn't stir. I hurried out of the shower and grabbed the phone.

"Sorry to bother you," said Hal, "but Dexter's putting the gas line in the fireplace, and he needs to know where you want the key. It's not in the plans."

"I need five minutes," I said apologetically, as if that were unreasonable. I threw on my clothes, grabbed the pugs, and dashed over to our house, which to my relief was looking less like Baghdad after the bombings and more like the morning after a wild party where the main event was a flour fight. The air was noxious with drywall dust, the carpets (which still hadn't been removed) were streaked with crusty white goo. Clara and Sophie trotted in for their morning nacho hunt and instantly turned white as if they'd been dusted with powdered sugar. It reminded me of the scene in *A Hundred and One Dalmatians* when the Dalmatian parents tell their pups to roll in soot to hide them from Cruella, the Dalmatian pelt-hunting villainess.

In the instant before my contact lenses began scratching it was possible to discern that the great room was worthy of a "before and after" spread in *Metropolitan Home*. The drywalling had been under way for a

164

week, and the fifteen-foot vaulted ceilings were covered with sleek gray gypsum board studded with nails. Hal was smoothing a gray joint compound in the cracks. "Shouldn't you wear a mask?" I asked, wheezing.

"Nah," he said. "You get used to it." Hal solicited my opinion on an idea he had for a difficult-to-reach niche. "Instead of putting drywall there, we could leave the old paneling exposed," he said. "Kind of pay homage to the old house." The paneling was circa 1950—not an era worth honoring. I opted for drywall.

I waded through a sea of discarded nails, siding scraps, Sheetrock remnants, and tubs of topping compound to the hole in the wall that housed the prefab fireplace. "Have you given any thought to where you want the gas key?" asked Dexter, natty as always in a miraculously pristine yellow jumpsuit and red rubber hip boots.

I had never heard of a gas key. Constructionese is a language largely made up of names for gizmos that laymen don't know exist. If you don't know the nomenclature, heaven help you.

"It's not really a key," said Dexter, who didn't have one on the premises that I could look at. "It's more like a switch, which turns on the gas to ignite the wood."

"Why can't we just use matches?"

"You do use matches," Dexter said patiently. "The gas just gets the fire started faster." (Or as Brandon put it later, "Anyone who was thrown out of Boy Scouts can look like a champion because they've got the gas turned high. In fact, any idiot can start a fire in three seconds.")

Dexter advocated putting the key inside the firebox so he wouldn't have to go under the house to run a longer gas line.

That struck me as dangerous. I suggested putting it on an outside wall instead.

"I suppose the gas line would reach," he said skeptically.

I was terrified that the wrong choice would blow the house sky high, so I called Brandon, who lived to solve these riddles. He wasn't home.

Fortunately, on the way back to the apartment, I ran into Gomez, my landlord. He was stuffing trash bags into his customized Dumpster, muttering about his lazy tenants who had failed to tamp them down. I hoped that he wouldn't notice the empty box of Milk-Bones in the top bag and trace it to me. Gomez has cut small holes in the lid of the heavy metal Dumpster to keep the homeless ("Drunks and bums we used to call them, before they became fashionable," Gomez says) from digging through his garbage. It keeps scavengers out, but it also keeps out the trash.

"Where's the best place to put a gas key?" I asked.

"Do you know what one looks like?" he asked. I shook my head. Gomez wiped his feet scrupulously for a good five minutes before entering his shrine. I followed him to his pride and joy—a two-bedroom apartment on the third floor with a sea view, parquet floors, and a spacious kitchen with built-in appliances.

"You and Duke should sell the house and move in here," he said. "It's only two thousand a month."

Believe me, I was tempted.

With a practiced hand, Gomez opened the apartment door with his pass key. He gave the place a quick inspection. "How could he have left the bread-maker on? It could explode," he sighed, turning it off. And then, "Those sheets are a little loud for my taste." Finally he led me to an ostentatious, gray marble fireplace. Behind the granite mantel was a round metal plate the size of a half-dollar with a protruding metal doohickey that looked like the thingamajig that opens a can of sardines.

"Always put it on the outside of the wall, around the back where it doesn't show," Gomez said, smugly adding, "That guy on *Home Improvement* has nothing on me." He shuddered when I told him that Dexter recommended putting it in the fireplace. "When you go to turn it off, you'll torch your hand."

I thanked him and hurried out before he decided to visit my apartment, where Duke had accidentally blazed a trail of coffee drops from the kitchen to the bed.

"Don't you want to hear my secret about the placement of light switches?" Gomez called. "You have to ask yourself, 'Where's the handiest place for someone to touch?' "

Duke's car was in the shop, and I'd promised to take him to pick it up. As we were pulling out of the driveway, Brandon darted out of the house. He'd bicycled over to check the spacing on the drywall nails. "Do you want the cupboard over the refrigerator to go out to the door?"

My mind clouded. "I don't know." All I really wanted was caffeine.

"If it does, it means that it won't clear the door exactly and may have to be firred out," Brandon pressed. "Hal's getting ready to build it, and he needs a decision."

Fortunately, Duke was in a hurry. "We can't discuss this now," he said. Brandon accepted the delay. Duke's time, unlike mine, was valuable.

I dropped Duke at the car dealer and hurried back to Ceramic City. Shoshanna was wearing a long, gauzy, mint-green-and-tangerine chiffon skirt (the kind that would later be recalled because they burn up in three seconds), a low-cut halter top, and a necklace with her name spelled out in pavé diamonds. Today her spike heels were the color of mango sorbet, with tiny bows in the back. She clickety-clacked authoritatively across the slate floor and greeted me with startling news: "Your tile is here!" (It was supposed to have arrived two weeks ago.) She shouted an order in Hebrew, and an ancient gentleman appeared pulling a dolly stacked high with cardboard boxes.

"May I see it?"

"It's not necessary, I already checked the order," she said. The geezer was halfway to the parking lot.

"If you don't mind, I'd like to see it."

Shoshanna exhaled sharply, blowing her bangs out of her eyes, then ripped open the boxes with the tips of her fingers, careful not to damage her Barbie-doll pink acrylic nails (average maintenance time: seven hours per month). "See," she said wearily. "Here's the black-and-white tiles for the bathroom. And the Mexican pavers."

The pavers looked kind of orange. "You sure that's the pink color?"

"It's definitely pink," Shoshanna said, holding up a piece of the terracotta border the color of salmon sushi. Her eyes narrowed, and I could see the perfect arc of khaki eyeliner on her lids. (The ability to put eyeliner on without smudging it is a genetic trait. If you have the eyeliner gene, you can apply it on the freeway while going sixty miles per hour.) She blew her bangs again. "I don't know how this happened."

"What's wrong?"

"The border is wrong. The triangles that fit into the hexagons are in the wrong place. You can't use it."

"Then why did you sell it to me?"

"It works on the display," she said. "They must have changed the style."

Shoshanna gave me a choice: Either she could take the tile in the back of the store and saw off the offending triangles, or I could choose a different border.

"Won't it look strange if you slice off the triangles?"

"Not very," she said. "But if you want, you can choose another border. If you don't mind waiting."

She clickety-clacked over to the paver display, which was set up like a vertical book, with pages made out of tile samples. At least three million brain cells fried themselves as I flipped through borders with leaves, borders with flowers, borders with birds, fishes, bugs, even Spanish homilies. They all looked orange to me, but Shoshanna swore they were pink too. Overwhelmed, I pointed to the simplest version. "How much?" (If I had a dollar for every time I asked this question, I would not be in debt today.)

"The same as the one you got."

"Fine," I said. "How fast can you get it?"

"Maybe by the end of the week."

I called Hal to check the schedule. He sounded irritated. "The tile is supposed to be here."

"You said we didn't need it for a couple of weeks."

"The tile guy had an opening in his schedule, and we grabbed it. He's starting tomorrow."

"Can't he start with the bathroom?"

"I suppose," he conceded. "But the tile is supposed to be here." I refrained from pointing out that the drywall was supposed to be finished last week and the fireplace was supposed to be finished last month and the skylights were still lying on the bedroom floor.

"For ten dollars, I can put a rush on it," Shoshanna said helpfully. "You can pick it up tomorrow afternoon."

"Why should I pay for a rush if it's your mistake?" (Duke would be so proud.)

"Okay, we'll pay the rush," she said, fiddling with the calculator. "But you owe another thirty-seven fifty."

"You said the border was the same price."

"It is, per piece," she clarified. "But the old border came in twelve-inch pieces, and these come in six inches, so you need to buy more."

I no longer had the strength to argue, so I wrote a check.

On the way home, I stopped by the paint store. Mr. Nuke and his crew of Jiffy Painters were scheduled to begin work in a week (though at the rate Hal was going it would probably be at least two), and I needed to select colors. I figured it would be relatively easy, since the interior was going to be white, but paint stores operate on the assumption that more is more. French White was too gray, Bone White too beige, White Rum too yellow, and White Suede, kind of pink.

"Don't you have White White?" I asked in growing frustration.

"Of course," said the paint dispatcher. "It's called Swiss Coffee." He handed me a swatch. "Are you thinking of gloss, semigloss, eggshell, low-sheen, or flat?"

I was thinking about running away to Tahiti.

I left with a headache and a hundred paint swatches, and hurried home with the tile.

"Did you get grout?" Dexter asked as he helped me carry it inside.

Nobody said anything about grout.

"You got to have grout. Maybe Hal can pick it up. But first you've got to choose a color. Gunmetal Gray would look good in the bathroom. Or maybe Alpine Blue. Do you know if you want sanded or unsanded grout?"

I thought I was going to lose my mind.

The radio was blaring "Stairway to Heaven"—again (I liked it when I was sixteen, but I never imagined that I'd be listening to it for the rest of my life). Hal was foraging for the piece of two-by-four on which he'd written the measurements for the new refrigerator, the same measurements that I'd given him two hours ago. "You wouldn't happen to remember the dimensions?" he asked. "I hate to call Brandon, you know how he is."

As a matter of fact, I did. I gave him the measurements.

Hal smiled sheepishly. "About the cupboard that goes over the refrigerator," he said. "Brandon was thinking you might like it to go all the way to the door. I can make it bigger, but it will cost a little more."

I was tempted. For weeks I had been drooling over kitchen magazines. These glossy publications could be used by cults to break down a person's will. The editors hold out a promise of an orderly life that keeps you comfortable and well fed. Life isn't worth living unless your kitchen has dozens of ornate cabinets made out of a rare wood such as batwillow.

Acres of black granite counters complete with rolltop "appliance garages" (God forbid the toaster oven shows). A cooking island the size of Maui so that six gourmet chefs who trained at the Cordon Bleu can simultaneously whip up a midnight snack. A blazing fire. A two-hundred-year-old Shaker trestle table that comfortably seats twelve. And don't forget the ceiling racks of copper pots and pans without so much as a hint of grease.

I started to ask Hal how much, but the screech of the saw jolted me back to reality. Our kitchen is barely six-feet-by-nine. The existing cabinets are unrefined and probably made of particleboard. Hal could extend the cupboard he was building to Mars and back, and Martha Stewart still wouldn't be caught dead in our kitchen.

I told him to stick to the plans. "No point in putting Cadillac parts in a Model T."

The decision-making process marched on.

"The hose that came with the faucet in the bathroom has a leak," Hal said. (The criticism was silent but implicit: If only you'd sprung for a $250 model . . .) "If we take out the faucet, will you drive over to the store and exchange it?"

I checked my watch. It was almost four o'clock. The Home Depot is fifteen miles away. Only a fool or a commuter gets on the San Diego Freeway between three-thirty and seven. "I have to work," I said, feeling guilty about my priorities. "Can't you leave the faucet in place and get another hose?"

"I suppose we could do that," Hal said haltingly. I knew my cue. I said the magic words and learned: "Around six bucks."

What's six bucks?

The next morning, I was sound asleep when the phone rang. "Sorry to bother you," Hal said, "but the tile man's here and he needs to know whether the tile should go to the edge of the tub or beyond that."

I threw on my jeans and flip-flops and hustled to the job site. (I suspect the reason that construction workers whistle at attractive females passing by is that the lady of the household is so frazzled she looks like hell.) Hal was having an animated pantomime with Alfonso, the tile man. He spoke about twelve words of English.

"Buenos días," I said breathlessly. Alfonso smiled. (It is helpful to be able to speak Spanish on a job site in Los Angeles. Latinos don't take kindly to being bossed around by a woman in a language that they don't understand. But my Spanish is clumsy enough that he automatically felt superior.)

Alfonso wanted to stop the tile at the edge of the tub, even though the wall ended only a couple of inches away. I shook my head. *"Al fin de la pared,"* I said firmly, ignoring the dubious looks. I'd already checked the tub in the apartment to see what Gomez had done. My landlord had also installed a recessed tiled shelf in the shower to store shampoos and conditioners. In halting Spanish, I explained the concept to Alfonso and added the obligatory, *"Quanto cuesta?"*

"Cien dólares," said Alfonso. A hundred dollars.

"Demasiado caro," I sighed mournfully. A wire shelf that hung over the shower head was only $3. (I've regretted saving that hundred dollars ever since.)

I called the tile store. The tile wasn't in. "Maybe tomorrow," Shoshanna said. But tomorrow it was the same story. And the day after tomorrow as well.

Meanwhile, Hal had another problem. "Do you have a moment?" he asked politely.

Did it matter?

"I went over the books last night and I figured out that I've laid out three hundred dollars more than I've gotten back. So I'd like three thousand dollars this Friday."

"You sure three thousand will cover three hundred?" I jested.

Hal was grim. "I pay these guys six hundred a week, and I only got fifteen hundred last week."

"But that's because you didn't finish everything," I said. The dents in the drywall needed smoothing. The mammoth truss cords that supported the beam were in the backyard. Granted, the prefab fireplace had been moved from the bedroom to the hearth, but the chimney pipe hadn't been connected, the flashing on the roof wasn't installed, and the windows hadn't been trimmed out. For someone who was hurting for cash, he sure was taking his time about giving us a price to prepare the laundry room for the new washer and dryer.

"Did you bring this up with Brandon?"

"You know how he is," Hal sighed. He scratched his back with a piece of two-by-four. "I'm thinking of giving this all up and going to work in a lumberyard somewhere."

"I'll talk to Duke," I promised. I hated to argue about money with Hal because he was fundamentally so honest and decent. And he was doing a beautiful job.

If I didn't get the message, on my way out I ran into Jaime, who was nailing a batten board in place. "If I wasn't working here, I'd be starving," he told me.

I had to feel kind of sorry for people depending on the largesse of a freelance writer.

Brandon wasn't moved by Hal's plight and recommended that we only give him fifteen hundred. "If a contractor can't float three hundred dollars for a week, he's in big trouble," he said. "He's behind because he rebuilt the cripple wall, but he's also behind because he blew it. He figured the job would go shorter than it did, and he still has the labor costs."

"We might as well give him what he wants," said Duke. "What do we prove by holding him up? He won't do it any faster. It's not worth the aggravation."

It was Friday—again. I trudged to the house, checkbook in hand. Brandon was eyeing the drywall for nicks and rough spots. Dexter was on the phone booking a recording studio. Hal was shuffling through the papers on the grand piano looking for the measurements for the washer and dryer. "It should cost three hundred and seventy-five dollars to install them," he said finally. "Assuming we don't run into any problems."

I signed the change order. I had no choice. The washer and dryer were scheduled to be delivered the following week.

I stopped in the bathroom to see how the tile was progressing. Alfonso was quite cheerful. He brought his wife and three young children to the job every morning and they spent the day at the beach, returning at five o'clock tan and sandy. This was a better scenario than what happened to a friend of mine. Her contractor brought his three-year-old son to the job every day, and she wound up doing child care.

Alfonso had floated a mortar bed and was carefully laying the black-and-white hexagons on the floor. It looked marvelous. *"Me gusta mucho,"* I smiled.

"Gracias," said Alfonso. *"Dónde debo poner los azulejos rojos?"* (Where should I put the red tiles?)

"Esparzalos, por favor." (Scatter them, please.) *"Quando este listo, voy a ayudarle."* (When you're ready, I'll help you.)

For a moment, I felt really pleased about the job, and about my Spanish, which I learned by listening to a hundred cassette tapes in my car. Then I walked into the great room. Jaime had spent the day installing the pièce de résistance, the fireplace surround. I recoiled in horror. Instead of the handsome carved-wood mantel that Brandon had promised, I beheld a bunch of flat ticky-tacky picture moldings fitted together. The matching ticky-tacky mantel was only two inches wide. What good is a mantel that you can't put anything on? Our fireplace was supposed to be the focal point of the room, not something you found in an ersatz Victorian fern bar.

"We have a problem," I bellowed, loud enough to be heard above the saw, the nail gun, the radio blaring "No Time" by the Guess Who, even my neighbors' dueling phone-answering machines. Hal and Dexter materialized instantly, in a cloud of plaster dust. I'd yet to lose my temper on the job site, but the response was so satisfying that I resolved to do it more often.

"What's the matter?" asked Dexter.

"The fireplace. It's too small, it's too flat."

"I think if it were bigger, it would look too massive," Dexter said consolingly. "As a border, it's perfect."

"I think it looks okay," Hal agreed. "Though I can see what you're talking about."

"Such a shame, I took such time," said Jaime.

I am uncertain about many elements in the construction process. But I know when something's awful.

"Brandon!" I hollered. The architect, the arbiter of good taste, slunk in. "Do you like this?"

"I'm not surprised it came out flat," he said.

My voice went up a tone. "Do you like this?"

"What I envisioned when we did this was that we weren't going to be able to afford the big fireplace surround that we had wanted. This provides some of the grandeur of a classical fireplace, but because it's premanufactured the prices are cheaper."

My voice went up another tone. "Do you like this?"

Brandon flinched. "Given this parameter, I think it looks okay."

I was practically screaming: "DO YOU LIKE THIS?"

"It's not optimal," he admitted.

"Why don't you just say it doesn't look as good as you thought it would. I can accept that."

"You didn't enjoy it as much as I thought you would," said Brandon.

Hal seemed kind of tickled to see Brandon in the hot seat. "Do you want me to see if they have a bulkier molding?" he asked. "Of course, there's not much we can do without taking it all apart."

This was getting irritating. I said the magic words—again.

"It depends on what we do to it. If we have to buy a lot of new moldings, it could get expensive. There may be parts that have to be made."

"What if we just used a big piece of wood and kept it plain, like the beam?" I asked.

"That would work," said Brandon. "We could build the fireplace up to have the same muscularity." He grabbed a sketch pad and tossed off a neat drawing. He gave Hal a superior grin, like it was all his idea. "We're looking at trying to mimic what goes on in the truss."

"Do you want a one-by-four depth or a one-by-six?" Hal asked.

"One-by-six," I said confidently. The workers looked at me with admiration. I smiled sheepishly. "You finally reached my level of dollhouse expertise."

"Remember that movie *Flight of the Phoenix?*" Hal said. "There were a lot of men in it and a crashed plane in the desert. And the one guy took control and told the rest they were going to rebuild the plane. About halfway through, they found out that he's never built a plane. Models are what he knows. It was a big crisis in confidence."

Brandon wasn't going to relinquish control that easily. "Do you want the header to run past the joint?" he asked.

I was stumped.

"We'll work something out," Hal said, and I smiled gratefully.

CHAPTER SIXTEEN

THE CLOSER the job came to completion, the more fed up I got. It's not that I didn't like what Hal was doing—quite the contrary, his carpentry skills were as refined as his accounting skills were not. "Isn't it beautiful? I love that," he exclaimed one morning, pointing to an old attic vent that he had magically transformed into a clerestory window. "As rough as it was and with as much stuff as was under there, it's amazing how smooth it came out." Overnight, he built a stately new fireplace surround as impressive as the other was tatty. Despite all our change orders, he was only two weeks behind schedule. He never missed a day.

Still, there's a limit to how long you can enjoy an experience that eats up your time, energy, and bank account.

Wednesday morning I walked to the house, intending to go to the paint store. There were four trucks blocking my car. I sighed impatiently. The painters were starting Monday, and I still hadn't picked a color for the outside of the house, a task I took about as seriously as naming a baby. The last time we'd painted the house, I'd sent Duke to the store for white paint. He returned with twenty gallons of a curdled, creamy French Vanilla that he'd got on sale. This time, I was determined to get it right.

But first I had to get out of the driveway.

"I'm sorry," said Hal when I went inside to complain. "The tile man is working out of his truck, Dexter can't park on the street because his car doesn't lock, Jaime is cutting the kitchen counter, and I'm only going to be here for five minutes."

"I understand," I said. "But please keep my space free." I refrained from mentioning that Brandon's contract had specified that only one truck could park in our driveway and there had never been fewer than three.

"I'll do my best," Hal said, sounding piqued.

I drove to a nearby paint store on Lincoln Boulevard—another of the Brigadoon-like shops that I had never noticed until I began to remodel and would never notice again. I brought Clara along. It was a dark, dingy store, somewhat like Cheers, only the regulars here brought their own booze. Surly men in splattered clothes sat around the paint counter and bitched about their indecisive customers. Customers like me, no doubt. Clara sat on a high stool and promiscuously yipped at all the alcoholics. At eight in the morning they weren't so drunk that they couldn't tell that she was a dog, but in another hour, I could tell it would be dicey.

For months I'd been studying *The Painted Ladies,* a book of photographs of fancifully colored Victorian houses in San Francisco. After rejecting a palette of blues (there was already a surplus of blue houses on our block) and grays (too trendy, Brandon said), I had decided on a pale Spanish pink with dark gray or slate blue trim. In Petite Designs, my favorite dollhouse store, it would have been simple. Mini Builders only make one shade, Victorian Pink, and it's ideal. But the full-scale world offered more choices than a baby-naming book. Let's see, did I prefer Pink Sugar, Baby Girl Pink, Sherbet Rose, or Pink Swirl? (I couldn't imagine saying, "Turn left at the Swirl-colored house.") Pink Parasol was too cloying. Cherry Float sounded like a porno star. For trim: Tabby Gray? Lava Flow? Carolina Gull? Gettysburg? I pitied the poor copywriter who had to come up with those names. Reading through the swatches, I could easily chart her mental collapse. Relatively apt names like Peaches-O-Cream gave way to mystery hues like Hob Nob, French Topsail, and Adonis.

"Pink Flamingos looks nice with Turquoise," said the paint dispatcher, over the incessant thump-thump-thump of the mixing machine. He showed me a special brochure with ghastly color combinations that you see only in Southern California. Mauve and Mesa Tan, Cape Cod Blue and Antique Gold, Envy Green and Mango Orange.

"No thanks," I said, staring at the swatches. Pompeii looked too red. Petal Rose, too orange. The problem with all these choices is that they decrease your chance of ever being right. It's like going for a physical and the doctor orders a zillion different tests. He's bound to find something.

"Why don't you buy a few sample quarts and see how they look on the house?" said the paint dispatcher. "It will save you money in the long run."

Dexter watched curiously as I covered the peeling siding with stripes of Dust of Rose, Pink Mums, Nantucket Shell, Dash of Ebony, Lava Flow, and Russian Blue. None of these vaguely resembled the color on the swatches. Shouldn't there be legislation regarding accuracy in paint labeling?

"They'll look better when they dry," Dexter assured me.

Actually, they looked worse.

I returned to the paint store with a jar of my dollhouse paint. A big sign in the store claimed that the fancy paint computer could match anything, even a faint accent on a scarf. In reality, the computer worked like this: The dispatcher held up my jar of paint to a series of color chips and hollered to his buddy, "What do you think? Thistle Dawn?"

"Looks more like Heather Rose."

Neither looked right, but I bought both. I didn't get a chance to test them though, because there were six trucks in my parking lot and I couldn't pull in. I left my car in the alley and stomped inside.

"I'm sorry," Hal said. "But the glazier came by with the window for the bathroom, and the inspector came to look at the drywall and decided to go down to the boardwalk and get something to eat. He should be back any minute."

"What am I supposed to do in the meantime?"

"The tile lady called. The fireplace pavers are in. I need to know how thick the tile's going to be so we can float the mortar bed. Why don't you go pick them up?"

I had work to do, but why should that stop me?

As I cruised down Venice Boulevard, it seemed like every home I passed was painted a hideous shade of pink. Shoshanna was decked out in a Pale Amethyst sundress with Eggplant pumps. (I tried to look apologetic when Clara enthusiastically clawed her Lilac hose.) I grabbed the fireplace tile and a sack of unsanded Gunmetal Gray grout. For a moment, I naïvely believed that our relationship had run its course.

"How is the bathroom tile working out?" asked Shoshanna, when I had one foot out the door.

"The floor is gorgeous," I gushed. It's amazing how even cheap tile brightens up a room.

"Too bad you only have one bathroom," Shoshanna said. "We're having a special on floor tile."

I should have kept on walking. I would have kept on walking. But the linoleum in the other bathroom was cracked. The floor was only sixty-nine inches by forty-eight inches. How much could it possibly cost to put in plain white tile? (The walls in the shower were already tiled.)

"Almost nothing," Shoshanna said, shrugging. "Maybe fifty dollars in materials."

What's $50?

I returned home. Hal was parked in my space.

I tried to look intimidating, but it's not easy to do when you're four-foot-ten. "This is getting tiresome," I said.

He cracked his knuckles one by one. "I guess that I could park on the street," he said. "But it would sure slow things down."

I counted to ten slowly. "Don't bother," I muttered. I handed him the tile and went to find a space in the street.

Hal was waiting in the doorway, looking harried. "You didn't get enough liners."

"You said twenty feet. I got twenty feet."

"There are only ten feet in the box."

I called Shoshanna. She insisted that she had given me twenty feet. It was useless to argue. I ordered more. Shoshanna reluctantly agreed to trust me for the $37.50 (how much had Duke saved?) plus an extra $10 for the rush charge. "The last overnight rush took a week," I complained.

"This time will be different," she lied.

My sister assured me that it violated the laws of the universe to purchase the correct amount of tile. "We had this little hippie guy who loves tile," Laurie said. "He convinced us to do a three-color pattern—rose, gray, and cream—in our front room. He wanted to do the pattern so much that he said he wouldn't charge us for his labor. He didn't realize you could buy tile in a specific quantity, so he ordered big boxes of each color. He was cheap, but we wound up paying through the nose for the materials."

Brandon bicycled over just as I was leaving. "We have a problem with the border in the shower surround," he announced. "The plans call for a black tile every foot, but you didn't get enough black tile."

"Hal told me to get fifteen, I got fifteen."

"Well, you wanted the tile to go to the wall instead of the edge of the tub, so now we need more," Hal said.

Rule Number Six of Remodeling: It's always your fault.

"There's a way around it," Brandon said. "Instead of an alternating black-and-white border we can do a one-to-three ratio and set the black ones on an angle, in a diamond pattern, to mimic what's going on in the floor."

Alfonso, Hal, and I knelt on the floor while Brandon demonstrated how the surrounding tiles should be cut. He was two tiles short, but I remembered that we had a few red tiles left over from when we did the shower surround in the other bathroom. So eager was I to avoid another trip to the tile store that I clambered over a mound of baseboards, pushed aside the tile-cutting machine, and crawled around in the drywall dirt until I located them under the uncovered fax machine. My bad hip was throbbing, but my mood lifted as we played with the pattern until we got it right. Tile is an addictive substance.

"That will work," said Hal.

"*Es bueno,*" Alfonso agreed.

As long as we were on a roll, I asked how much it would cost to tile the other bathroom floor.

"Two hundred and fifty dollars," Hal said. "Same as the other one."

"But it's half the size."

Hal shrugged. "Looks like you got a low price on the other one."

"Are there any extra charges for taking out the toilet and the sink and putting them back?" I asked carefully.

"Nothing," said Hal. "Two hundred and fifty dollars."

"It would really dress up the room," Brandon said.

I decided to think it over, and went outside to test the paint. On paper, Thistle Dawn looked like a lovely desert sunset, but it turned out to be a vertigo-inducing Pepto-Bismol pink. I recalled reading somewhere that police stations paint interrogation rooms that color because it saps people's strength. Or was it that doughnut shops use the color to keep patrons from lingering?

"I like that," Dexter said. "What is it? Antique White?"

"Are you joking or color-blind?"

"Color-blind," Dexter said, "but I can tell hue by the way the color vibrates."

Yeah, right.

That night my husband, who has a genius for complicating a situation, took a picture of the house with a special digitized camera that he has at work. He scanned the image into his computer and handed me a stack of black-and-white pictures. "You can color them in with Magic Markers and see what color you'd like."

Who had time to color?

Duke wasn't enthusiastic about tiling the bathroom floor. "Let's wait," he said. "We can always do it six months down the road."

As if I ever wanted to see another contractor. "If we wait, we'll have to do without a bathroom for at least a week," I argued.

He was in no position to insist because I had yet to generate a change order. It was Duke who had wanted the skylights, Duke who had wanted the light box over the dining room table moved, and most recently, Duke who had wanted a vent for the new range hood. Originally, the latter hadn't seemed like an expensive proposition; in fact, Hal had discovered an old venting pipe in the attic and offered to hook it up free of charge. But no sooner had we bought it than the situation got more complicated. Why was I surprised?

"The pipe in the attic that goes to the outside is an asbestos pipe," Hal informed me.

My heart sank. "Does that mean we have to call in the space-suit people?"

"No, we'll just wrap it up in plastic so nobody sees what it is and bury it under the house. But we're going to have to run a new pipe up and that's not in the original bid."

"How much?" I said wearily.

"One hundred and fifty dollars." It seemed unnecessary, since the new hood came with a filter and a blower that didn't need special ventilation, but my husband was adamant.

"If you really want the tile floor, then get it," Duke conceded. His philosophy on negotiating change orders? "Give the wife what she wants or my life becomes a living hell."

Thursday morning I trotted over to the house to give Hal the okay. I was gratified to see that the carpets had finally been taken up and that old fir floors actually existed underneath. However, the old flea-ridden carpets had been hurled in the front yard, on top of the trash heap, which hadn't been removed in seven weeks.

"How much longer is the trash going to be here?"

Hal pursed his lips. "I don't know what day the trash guy's coming. Maybe Monday, maybe Wednesday. The longer we wait, the more he can take."

"Make it sooner," I said, as if I had a choice. "And you can go ahead and tile the bathroom for two fifty."

Hal gave me the grievously-wounded-mastiff look. "The two fifty is only for the tile. It's another hundred to take out the toilet and the sink."

"What?" I screeched.

Hal wagged his finger in the shame-on-you motion. "You forgot to ask me how much."

It was all I could do to keep from screaming, "Liar liar, pants on fire." I pointed out that I had a witness. Brandon was standing in the bathroom with me when Hal said the $250 covered everything.

"That's bullshit," Hal snapped. "I never said anything. I'm underbidding anyway. If you don't like the price, then don't do it."

Why did I get the feeling that he was in the throes of a toxic love affair?

I was livid. I had gone out of my way to be agreeable. I had kept my mouth shut about the trash, the parking spaces, the constant demands for money. The worst part was that I still wanted the damn tile.

My brother-in-law counseled me to remain firm. "On one job, I said, 'I want to move the fireplace,' " the Shark recalled. "The contractor said, 'No problem.' He never said, 'More money.' Then he gives me a bill at the end of the job. I said to him, 'When I asked can you do that, did it occur to you to say it would cost more money?' He said, 'I figured you knew that.' I said, 'Well, how would I know that?' He said, 'A double-sided fireplace, that costs a thousand dollars.' I said, 'Well, how would I have known that?' " The Shark stood his ground. "I wound up giving him a small percentage of what he wanted," he said.

I am not that strong.

I drove to the paint store—again! This time I was certain. Brandon had lent me a paint wheel with thousands of paint chips that had been given to him by the paint company that catered to architects. He vowed that the colors were true, and after an hour's deliberation, we'd made a decision: Pompeii, with Ashes of Hope as trim. (In retrospect, these names weren't a good sign.) "You're not seriously going to paint a house this color," said the paint dispatcher. "Your neighbors will puke."

"I live in Venice," I said.

"Oh, then it's okay," he said.

But when I striped it on the house, I wanted to puke.

I returned to the apartment and burst into tears.

An hour later, Hal called. "I owe you an apology," he said. "I went over this very carefully in my mind. And you did ask how much it would cost to remove the sink and toilet, and I did say, 'Nothing.' But I was thinking of something Brandon had asked me earlier about how much I'd marked up the subcontractors' bids. And the answer to that was 'Nothing.' And then when you asked me I got defensive and said 'Nothing' again. It didn't occur to me that I'd misinterpreted the question altogether."

"So you'll do the bathroom for two fifty?"

"Well, no," Hal said. "I can't do that."

"It's your call," Duke said.

I gave Hal the extra hundred dollars. (Don't tell the Shark.) But I began to resent the contractor even more than he resented me. Duke and I resolved that we wouldn't ask for another thing. When it turned out that we needed to put in a new linoleum floor in the laundry room, I let the guys from the linoleum store do it. I pitched a fit, and lo and behold the trash got hauled away. But my sense of control was short-lived.

"What do you want to do about the kitchen sink?" Hal asked the next morning.

Jaime had cut a twenty-three-inch hole in the new black-and-white Formica counter. Duke suggested putting our old sink back in, but you can't put a dull stainless-steel sink into a new countertop. So we made yet another pilgrimage to the Home Depot, where I found an adorable $200 porcelain sink. Of course, you can't put an old faucet in an adorable new sink, so a new high-end faucet was added to our list. And of course, we needed a new disposal. And all these improvements were going to make the old light fixture look shabby.

I broke down at the checkout counter. It was like the last day of vacation when it suddenly dawns on you that you have gone through a thick wad of traveler's checks. At the beginning of a remodel, money is everything, but as you go along, it becomes secondary to the vision. You can't have the house looking like a glorious jewel and leave the cracked linoleum or the icky light fixture, so you spend and spend and spend. Then one day it suddenly occurs to you that all that play money you've been throwing around is real—and it's in someone else's bank account.

Alas, trying to control construction costs is like trying to control the cost of a hospital stay. You may not realize that when you sneeze and the nurse hands you a box of tissues, it generates a $5 charge on your bill. But you still have to pay.

By Week Seven, I couldn't walk through the door of my house without hearing about some alarmingly priced extra that had been overlooked.

An electrical outlet for the new, automatic-ignition stove. A door for the laundry room. The clear window in the bathroom needed to be replaced with obscure glass. The old floor plugs had to be abandoned. And it wasn't just Hal and Brandon who generated these changes. Anyone could play.

Brandon waylaid me on the way home from the market. "The inspector said we have to put an access door in the bathroom so there's a way to get to the plumbing in the future."

"It's no big thing," Hal said. "We'll just cut a square hole in the siding and put a removable panel on it."

It sounded simple. "Is that an extra?"

Hal widened his eyes until he looked like Dondi, the comic-strip urchin. "It should be. It's not something we figured on doing."

"How much?"

"Fifty dollars should cover it."

What's $50?

Thursday, Hal presented me with a bill for all the completed extras. It came to $800. It seemed high.

"I gave the tile guy two hundred dollars more because the shower surround got more complex," Hal said. "I hope you don't mind."

I most certainly did mind. "You should have asked us first."

Hal glowered. "I'm adamant on this," he said. "I'm not going to say anything else."

I called Brandon. "Contractors are notorious for coming up with a bill after the fact," he said. "Then there are emotional ramifications. If you don't pay, then they can say, 'Okay, well, we're out of here.' " He advised us to pay Hal and keep him happy. "We're only talking about two hundred dollars," he said.

"Then you pay it," I hissed.

After a pause, another message swam up in the Eight Ball window, "My reply is no."

Brandon continued, "The time he should have brought it up is when we were working on the border. But Hal never says anything, and then he acts hurt. That's his operating style. When he's magnanimous, he does it quietly, so you never know, but he keeps score. And when he wants something he expects you to jump because he's done all these things."

I felt awful. I didn't want Hal to hate me.

"Well, he would have hated you anyway," Brandon said. "You can't fulfill his expectations because he doesn't tell you what they are until you violate them. Might as well piss him off by being careful about how you spend your money."

Brandon promised to back me up at the Friday meeting. Just to be on the safe side, I had Duke come along. Faced with a strong male presence, Hal accepted the decision without a demurrer. I felt like I was a tiny pearl revolver and my husband was a .44 magnum.

After the meeting, Símon, the floor guy from Peru, came back to look at the floors. He too was in a vile mood. He had driven from Newport Beach and gotten stuck in traffic because O. J. Simpson was taking his joyride on the San Diego Freeway. Símon crawled around the floor inspecting the boards, then left without saying a word. That night, after O.J. surrendered, Símon phoned.

"Are you sitting down?" he asked. "I'm going to have to replace a lot of the wood. The new wood is around four hundred dollars. And labor is five hundred. So it will probably cost around twenty-two hundred with all the repairs." I didn't understand how $500 and $400 added up to $2,200, twice the original estimate, but the wood floors were the one improvement I desperately wanted.

"Might as well," I sighed.

"Of course it may not look that terrific," Símon warned me. "The new boards aren't as wide, and so there will be a gap between the new and the old."

"Are you sure you want to do this?"

"Oh yes," he said. "I love a challenge."

I hung up and reached for the calculator.

We had exactly enough money left to finish the job.

CHAPTER SEVENTEEN

DECORATING MAGAZINES would have you believe that remodeling is akin to alchemy. Perhaps this is true if you start out with the typical "before" picture that the editors highlight each month. The two-hundred-year-old, three-story farmhouse on top of a hill with a panoramic view of Lake Champlain that only needed an infusion of a couple hundred thousand dollars to turn it into a palatial retreat. But when you begin with a cramped, tatty, twelve-hundred-square-foot cottage, a budget of $20,000, and a view of eight scummy neighbors' windows, it's an inherently frustrating process. It's like the difference between buying a new car and a used one—you get what you can afford, instead of what you really want. The few improvements that you do manage merely underscore the shabbiness of the things you've overlooked.

I couldn't walk into our bedroom without getting depressed. It was the shoddiest room in the house, yet it was the one most people saw first. Short of breaking through the wall and enlarging it, there wasn't much I could think of to give it a lift. When pressed, all Brandon could come up with was faux beams, but even he admitted it wasn't worth the extra $400. I was thinking of offering the room to *House Beautiful* as a challenge to those top decorators who regularly transform dilapidated mansions into sleek showcase rooms. Let's see what sisal, expensive chintz slipcovers, suede walls, and grottoesque lighting could do for a nine-by-nine hidey hole with six doors (it was like sleeping on the set of *Let's Make a Deal*). All I could think of—and afford—was paint.

"Why don't you do a window treatment with brightly colored valances?" asked Brandon. "Everyone paints a room to make it different."

"Everyone drinks water when they're thirsty," I said. "That doesn't make it a dumb idea."

Admittedly, I was high on the powers of paint, having finally settled on a color for the exterior of the house. I had my friend Billy to thank. He had come to Venice to jog on the beach and dropped by the apartment to borrow our shower. He found me scowling at a deck of paint chips, like it was a tarot hand with the Three of Swords, the Ten of Swords, the Five of Pentacles, and the Tower, indicating trauma, poverty, and violence. I had given up on pink and was ready to paint the house white.

"If you want to sell 'er, paint 'er yeller," Billy said. I'd never heard that saying, but curiously, an hour later, the pawnbroker who lives across the street took note of the Mondrian-like paint squares on the back of the house and said, "You want to sell 'er, paint 'er yeller."

I took it as a sign from God.

I returned to the paint store, where I was welcomed as a valued customer, having already purchased the equivalent in sample quarts that the painters would later buy for the whole house (so much for saving money by having the paint included in the bid). I had them whip up some Golden Goddess, which should have been called Grey Poupon; Panama Hat, which was supposed to be a pale yellow but in fact looked like a symptom of cholera; and Rio Fleece, a vibrant, sunny, gumball yellow, which proved to be just right. For trim, I picked Charcoal, with an International Red door. (I have a thing for red doors; blame it on the formative years that I spent with my mother at Elizabeth Arden.)

"You'll never lose the house," the paint dispatcher jested.

But Duke, Hal, and even Brandon agreed that it was inspired.

Unfortunately, that decision took up so much energy, it pushed me over the edge. After having made umpteen decisions in the course of the remodel, I found myself staring at my closet each morning, unable to figure out what to wear, let alone pick a miracle color to metamorphose a gloomy room. Besides, a long time ago I'd made a fatal mistake, and it haunted me. After I got divorced, I moved into an apartment and went on a painting spree. I covered the bedroom walls with Fire Engine Red, which looked dramatic but kept me up all night. Not only did I lose sleep, I also lost my security deposit.

In desperation, I consulted Richard, one of my favorite editors. He lives in an apartment in Hollywood that is so tarted up that Duke says, "It makes the word *frou-frou* seem too butch." Richard agreed that the paint was the solution. "A bright color will distract from the fact that the room is uninteresting," he said. "Maybe a deep strong salmon with a pale yellow ceiling. Or a hearty eggplant. But don't you dare put deep blues. Your husband will never touch you again."

Duke turned ashen as my color consultant wandered around our house muttering under his breath, "Deep green, or deep peach, with maybe a pale blue ceiling to suggest the sky." After inspecting, and to my everlasting pride, approving my choice for the outside—"Not bad for a straight person," Richard said—he came up with a plan. I was to paint Duke's office, my office, and the bedroom increasingly deep shades of yellow to give the warrenlike rooms the illusion of light. Shuffling through the paint-chip deck with the assurance of a casino dealer—"It's the small hypothalamus, that's what we're good at"—Richard pulled out Wax Bean, Pearblossom, and for the bedroom, Creamcake, colors that I would never have chosen in a million years, which I subsequently noticed in the next issues of *House Beautiful* and *Elle Decor.*

"You can also put in an old chandelier with a big mirror behind it that you can use for sexual pleasure," Richard said. "Give it a kind of a New Orleans je ne sais quoi." His final dictum: "Get rid of all these schlocky light fixtures this instant."

To my utter astonishment, Duke obeyed. We braved the Fourth of July sale at IKEA and picked up Skur, a high-tech ceiling spotlight on sale for $12 (we bought two); Kvissel, a dhurrie rug in the appropriate yellows; Felice, a matching floral duvet cover; and Bert, a set of drawers on wheels. Then Duke dragged me out of Sweden forever. "Life's too short to spend another weekend at IKEA," he said. Had we gone a day later—after Dexter was finished assembling Ego, our inexpensive vanity—I would have known that all the low-priced furniture has an Achilles' heel, which is why it's low-priced. Ego, for example, lacks the whatchamacallit that opens and closes the drain. Instead it has a rubber stopper. It's the contact-lens Bermuda Triangle.

From IKEA we went to the Lighting Palace. We had only planned to buy a track light for over the dining room table, but with Richard's orders resounding in our brains, we purchased a white ceiling fan to go over the bed. We talked about buying a white iron bed and new bedside tables.

Rule Number Seven: To remodel is to render your house unsuitable for all your old furniture.

"There's nothing in the contract that says anything about our installing light fixtures," Hal muttered when he saw the fixtures. I popped the question and learned, "Two hundred dollars should cover it."

I couldn't bear writing another $200 check, but luckily I had a brainstorm. "How much were you going to charge to install the shower-door enclosure?" We hadn't purchased it yet.

After a long pause, Hal said, "Two hundred dollars."

"What if we use that money for fixtures and get a shower curtain?"

"I could do that," Hal agreed.

"The only problem with shower curtains is that if you don't make sure they're closed, the water leaks out and you get dry rot," said Brandon. But we decided to take our chances.

Monday morning, right on schedule, Mr. Nuke appeared with his painting crew. Given his low-ball bid, I expected him to bring a platoon of illegal aliens, but there was just Mr. Hong, a scowling thirty-year-old in white Bermuda shorts and his assistant, Juan, from Acapulco, who spoke no English and no Korean. Brandon hovered nervously as I gave Mr. Nuke a $1,000 deposit. In his heart, our architect was certain that we were making a terrible mistake; we should have gone with his recommendation, Joseph, the $7,500 bidder.

"The paint job is the thing you see, the end product," Brandon warned me. "A good painter can make a lot of mistakes look good."

"We can't afford a seventy-five-hundred-dollar paint job."

"That's my pet peeve as an architect," Brandon said. "My clients don't have enough money for me to spend."

Brandon shifted into hyperfascist mode to make sure the painting came out okay. It was a little problematic, since Nuke and Hong knew only two hundred words of English between them, but Brandon persevered. He asked how many coats the price included. "One coat primer, one coat paint," Mr. Nuke said. How much would it cost if we needed a second coat? "Don't worry," Nuke said. "We guarantee coverage with one coat." Mr. Hong scowled.

Then there were the toe kicks for the baseboards. Brandon had spent hours agonizing over who should come first, the painters or the floor guy. This is the construction equivalent of the chicken-and-the-egg debate. If the floor guy goes first, then the painter has to protect the pristine floors, which means that the painter has to be supercareful, something I have never known a painter to be. But if the painter goes first, then he has to come back after the floors are finished to paint the toe kicks, which must be installed after the floor is finished or else they will get chewed up by the sander. Of course, the return visit costs extra.

The decision, like many in the remodeling game, was made by expediency—the painters were available first. Duke came up with an ingenious, cost-saving solution. "Why can't the painter paint the quarter rounds before they're installed?"

Hal thought for a moment. "We could buy the base shoes and have them here," he said. Of course, if we wanted him to install base shoes in the whole house, not just the great room, it would be one hundred and fifteen extra. We agreed.

"Someone will have to touch up the nail holes," Brandon warned.

"We can do that," Duke said blithely. (Nothing like crawling around on the floor with a creaky hip, painting baseboards.)

Brandon asked Mr. Nuke how much it would cost to paint the pile of quarter-rounds stacked in the backyard.

Mr. Nuke bowed deeply. "Mr. Hong take care of everything." Mr. Hong looked like he wanted to slug his boss. (We would later learn that Mr. Hong despised Mr. Nuke because he always underbids the job and then sticks Mr. Hong, his nephew, with the difference.) Mr. Nuke waved good-bye and sped away in his truck, never to appear again.

I carefully went over the color scheme. The beam and the fireplace were to be whitewashed. The great room was to be Swiss Coffee with an eggshell finish. The kitchen and bathrooms, Swiss Coffee with gloss finish.

"Will there be any problem covering with that?" Brandon fretted.

"No problem," said Hong. "Very good choice." He almost choked when he learned about Richard's yellows. "It's like baby colors," he complained. Then he recited what would be his standard response to any request that I made: "What does your husband think?"

"He likes it," I said. "Don't you?"

"I'm not color consultant, I'm painter," Mr. Hong muttered. He had been a doctor of alternative medicine in Korea, but he got bored reading pulses and turned to paint. "This way you don't have to think so much."

Brandon gave final instructions about taking down the blinds and not painting the hinges or the tracks in the new windows. "I know, I know," Mr. Hong said impatiently. We crossed our fingers and left. When I stopped by a couple of hours later to help Alfonso scatter the decorative fireplace tiles, Mr. Hong was missing. Instead of sanding and priming and puttying holes, he had simply slapped some masking tape on the light switches and split.

To his credit Brandon didn't say, "I told you so," though he was thinking it really loud. He left three messages for Mr. Nuke, but the calls were never returned. "I suppose it's better than getting a number that's been disconnected," Brandon said glumly. He suggested I go to the bank and stop payment on the check.

The bank had already cashed the check. "I've never heard of crooked Koreans," I said.

"Thieves comes in all nationalities," said Brandon.

"Don't worry," said Duke. "*We* checked the references."

We worried anyway. But the next morning, Hong appeared with gallons of paint. Brandon tried to show him who was boss. "I'm really disappointed in you," he said. "It looked like you guys just split with the money."

Hong flushed angrily, and pointed a finger at Dexter and Alfonso. "They weren't ready for paint." Brandon was at a loss for words. Technically, the painter was correct: The contractors were supposed to be off the job site, but instead Alfonso was floating a mortar bed in the small bathroom ("No sense interrupting the job," Hal said), Dexter was installing the vanity, and Hal had left a note on a two-by-four saying that he'd gone to bid on another job. Brandon had given up trying to organize Hal.

"You'll just have to work around them," the architect said. He warned me to keep a close watch on the job.

I tried. But the paint fumes gave me a terrible headache. To Brandon's delight, Mr. Hong was using industrial-strength enamel paint. "It gives a much smoother finish," Brandon said. It also gives off a ferocious chemical odor. Mr. Hong's attitude was more toxic than the air. He viewed me (and all women) as insignificant entities to be ignored. My arrival was met with a terse, "Get out. You're in my way." When I made a request, such as, "Could you please paint all the doors in the bedroom yellow instead of white, so they don't stand out?" the painter scowled and asked, "What does your husband think?"

My husband thought Mr. Hong was a borderline lunatic. "It's the radio," Duke said. "He doesn't have a radio. Everybody else on the job has a radio. Anybody normal who was painting a house would have a radio."

There was no love lost between the contractor and the painter either. First Hal was sulky because the painter refused to move the mound of used bricks from the old chimney that Hal had piled next to the house. "It's not my job," the painter said.

Hal looked so peeved, I offered to help. In the course of bending down and picking up the bricks, I lost my wedding ring. Hal and Dexter helped me rummage through the sand, but we couldn't find it. Fortunately, on my way back to the house I spied it lying on one of the thousands of Big Mac, Taco Bell, and Kentucky Fried Chicken wrappers that were embedded in the garden.

"You sure were calm about that," Hal said admiringly.

Compared to remodeling, a lost wedding ring was low on the stress index.

Mr. Hong was always annoyed about something. One day, it was that the contractors hadn't replaced a dry-rotted board outside the bathroom window. "They expect me to paint that?" he snarled. The next day he was miffed because the door to the crawl space under the house was missing and he had to wait twenty minutes while Hal built a new one before he could paint it. Then there was a further delay while we looked for Clara, who had gone exploring in the crawl space and had been accidentally boarded in.

Hal was vexed that the painter didn't sand the new fireplace surround as smoothly as he would have liked. "If I had realized it was being white-washed, I would have sanded it myself," he said. (There had never been any question of the surround being anything but whitewashed.)

Dexter claimed that when the painter pulled down the kitchen light fixtures he frayed a neutral line, which screwed up all the circuitry in the house. (I didn't have the guts to tell him that it was Duke who had re-moved the light fixture.)

"If you had hired Charley, you would have had the Rolls-Royce of painters," Dexter added, referring to his colleague with the $12,000 bid. "This guy is like a Honda Scooter."

Ten days passed in a passive-aggressive haze. Everyone working on the job was mad at me because when they said they could do X for $5,000, I didn't say, "Oh, please, take ten." By the end of the job, Mr. Hong was seething because the white paint didn't cover the wall as well as he'd like. And the yellows hurt his eyes. "You pick stupid colors," he muttered, tossing his Styrofoam cup of Miso Yasai Ramen into a drywall bucket.

"Are you going to clean that up?" I asked.

"It's the finisher's job," he replied.

I turned the supervision over to Brandon, who had a genius for zero-ing in on the one spot that wasn't quite right and who, moreover, was male. Misogyny notwithstanding, Mr. Hong did a fine job. A new paint job is a wondrously tangible achievement. It doesn't take an expert to know it looks better. For the first time in eight years the house was free of peeling paint. The rooms were cleaner and brighter and infinitely more cheerful. The merry yellow exterior elicited compliments from most of our neighbors (though a disconcertingly high percentage compared it to a bad acid trip). Every moment I spent in the paint store seemed worth it.

Even Brandon was satisfied. "This is a free lunch, and in my experience there is no free lunch," he said. "He's done as good a job as the seventy-five-hundred-dollar painter. In fact, I can't think of what more you would have gotten for another forty-five hundred dollars."

Naturally, we didn't notice the mistakes until after we had paid Mr. Hong and he had dropped over the horizon. Then we discovered gray paint on the sofa, a missing blind, and a couple of radiator covers he had overlooked. But the only serious inconvenience was that Mr. Hong never got around to the strips for the baseboards.

"It's my fault," Brandon said sheepishly, "I forgot." He suggested that we paint them ourselves, rather than hire another painter.

It went the way most jobs in our house do. I got the unwieldy strips lined up neatly on sawhorses and carefully began priming. Duke showed up when I was almost finished with the first coat, told me what I was doing wrong, and drove off to get more brushes. When he finally returned, raving about a fish taco stand that he had discovered, he took over. He paints five times as fast as I do, so the job went quickly.

Mr. Hong was also lax about getting the paint off the windows, but

that was no surprise. The biggest lie in remodeling is "We clean up every-thing." For weeks, Hal had been promising that he'd leave my house spic-and-span. I had grave doubts, which were reinforced the day the stove and refrigerator were delivered. Instead of washing the grimy kitchen floor or even sweeping it, Hal simply had the delivery men shove the appliances in place so the gray sludge and sticky adhesive didn't show.

Brandon attempted to convince Hal of the importance of cleaning up his mess before Símon, the floor guy, arrived and made another one. But the contractor was vague on what he intended to do.

"I guess we'll sweep and vacuum the floors," Hal said. When I mentioned scrubbing, he rolled his eyes. "I suppose we could do the kitchen floor." There was no mention of the bathrooms, which after two months of only male usage looked like the men's room in a truck stop on the I-95. Or the drywall and grease-pencil marks on the windows. Or the tools that were scattered around the house. Or the filthy bedroom blinds, which were lying in a quagmire of drywall mud and dirt.

Hal frowned. "We didn't take the blinds down, the painter did." Brandon pointed out that the house hadn't been sealed off during the demolition and things got dirty. "I suppose if we have time we could take them out and hose them off."

He promised to cart away the wood chips, roofing material, broken windows, empty Coke cans, old doors, nails, odd chunks of wire, wire nuts, hose, stakes, empty Dr Pepper cans, wood studs, tubs of moldy wet pieces of drywall, tile chips, discarded caulk guns, plastic drop cloths embedded with mud, nasty pieces of fiberglass insulation, empty 7-Up cans, rusty plumbing parts with funny-colored liquid dripping out, scrap lumber (none of which was useful because they took the good stuff), carpet scraps, empty Snapple bottles, and linoleum remnants that were part of the landscape of our house. But he never got around to it. When Símon arrived the following Monday to begin the repair work, our yard looked like a landfill.

The remaining furniture in the house had to be moved outside into the debris while Símon did the sanding. (Actually, Símon didn't do the sanding, he didn't lift a finger the entire time, he just smoked cigarettes and barked orders in machine-gun Spanish, and his troops did the rest.) Hal promised that he'd get right on it, but then Símon's squad cut a gaping hole in the living room floor, revealing nothing but sand under the house. Hal suddenly realized it was a perfect opportunity to install the diagonal bracing under the house, and he scooted to the lumberyard to pick up more wood.

"I was wondering how we'd get under there," he said blissfully, as Dexter angled a giant two-by-four through the floor. "This works out perfectly."

"We could just bury him there," Duke said. "It worked for Gacy."

I watched with dismay as Símon's laborers dumped the sofa bed on a pile of fast-food wrappers. They squeezed my New York City tenement dollhouse into the laundry room, but the English Tudor was too large, so they dragged it outside and set it in the sand. Hal swore he'd wrapped it in a tarp, and he was as good as his word.

"What about the piano?" Símon asked.

What about it? Shrouded in tarps, the antique baby grand had remained in the living room through demolition, framing, drywall, and painting. Hal had used it as a desk, but Símon refused to work around it. Nine men, including my husband, were standing in the living room when Símon said, "You'll have to get someone to move it into the kitchen," but no one lifted a finger to help. It took five calls, but I finally located a piano mover who promised to come the next day. It cost $60 to move the piano ten feet.

But what was another $60?

Símon was as charming and garrulous as Mr. Hong was not—probably because he never broke a sweat. The little time he spent on the job, he lounged in his truck listening to World Cup soccer. Occasionally, he could be heard exhorting his *soldados* ("Keep sanding and soon maybe you can have citizenship"). "You have to be firm with the guys, otherwise they walk all over you," said the Inca prince, who confided that he was weary from his labors. "I drop them off, I run do another estimate, I bring them something to eat, I show them how to do something, and then I go do another estimate."

I couldn't fault his system, and neither could Hal or Brandon, because Símon wouldn't let them in the house. With lightning speed, his *ejército* replaced the damaged boards, filled in the termite holes, and dragged their hefty, howling sanding machines through the great room, offices, and bedroom. My heart filled with joy as old paint, drywall crud, and clinging carpet threads disappeared in a cloud of eye-stinging dust, revealing lovely peg-and-groove floors, the home improvement I'd always wanted. By the time the third coat of water-based stain had been applied, the floors were brilliant.

I didn't begrudge Símon a cent because he was the only subcontractor on our job who wasn't resentful. "Contractors act that way to force the client to pay more money," Símon said. "There's always more on a job than you expected to do. Like I forgot to charge you to make all the wood thresholds for the house. But it's crazy to make a big deal about it for fifty dollars."

"What's fifty dollars?" I giggled.

"When I go in, I tell the guys to do everything possible to please the client because the client is boss. If we do the job, the client is happy. The client will refer people. And we have self-respect. My guys, when they go home, they're happy because they did good. If they don't do good, they feel ill. Last night, Pedro called. He was very upset. He said, 'I forgot to put the threshold back on the house in Venice.'"

This seemed apocryphal, since I'd called Símon the night before to ask where the threshold was. But I smiled and thanked him again for doing a wonderful job. He advised me to let the floors harden as long as possible before we moved back.

I was in no hurry. The next day I was sitting alone in the house, admiring my shiny floors, when I heard what sounded like someone either having great sex or being murdered. I noticed a crowd gathering around my front gate and went outside just in time to see a bleeding, naked woman sprint past. Down the block, no less than a dozen LAPD officers had surrounded a small bungalow and were forcing the occupant to lie on the sidewalk, facedown (in Venice, a particularly cruel punishment). The suspect kept trying to lift his head. "Keep your head down or we'll shoot," the officer barked, and a neighbor darted into her apartment building to fetch her video camera. ("Just in case," she said.) Meanwhile, a police helicopter hovered overhead while two cops broke down my neighbor's gate to pursue the bleeding victim.

My neighbors and I watched it unfold in much the same carefree, curious spirit with which we watched the last eclipse. "Love the color scheme of your house," said Kelly, an aspiring opera singer. "How did you ever come up with it?" She was relieved to learn about my numerous trips to the paint store. "Took me three trys to pick a white for my bedroom. I was going to be sick if you picked that out on the first try."

Another neighbor asked a cop if this was a bad neighborhood. The cop shrugged. "In some neighborhoods we don't respond to domestic violence reports. Of course, in some neighborhoods, it's a misdemeanor."

My most anxious moment came when two officers escorted my husband home. Duke had been swimming in the ocean and was stopped when he tried to walk up our street. "They almost led me away in handcuffs," Duke reported proudly. "But then I remembered the right thing to say. I looked the cop straight in the eye and said, 'Officer Henry, take me to your commanding officer.' "

We left the crime scene and returned to our secure apartment. "I want to live someplace normal," I sighed.

"Oh honey," Duke laughed. "There are strange people everywhere."

CHAPTER
EIGHTEEN

I T SEEMED LIKE the job would never end. All that was actually left to do was tie up the loose ends, but given Hal's innate resistance to finishing things, the house had more loose ends than a fringed jacket. Brandon had drawn up an insanely specific "punch list" with such trifles as: trim nail point extruding from dining room bay window, install one bulb at track light, seal fireplace tile, tighten loose bolt on shear panel, and provide cover plate at refrigerator's plug. But no sooner did an item get crossed off the list than another mysteriously appeared.

Week Ten began like many others. At 7:30 A.M., Hal buzzed the apartment. I rolled out of bed and went to the intercom to see what was the matter. Hal couldn't find our house key, and the piano movers were waiting outside. I pulled on my jeans and rushed over to write the moving guys a check—all the while trying not to worry about the implications of a missing house key on Venice Beach. I made a mental note to call a locksmith and have the locks changed.

The poor dismembered baby grand was lying precariously on its side, swaddled in blankets, on the squalid kitchen floor. I shuddered to think of the tuning costs. "You promise you won't scratch the wood floors?" I asked fretfully. I loved the floors more than anything else in the house.

"We don't promise nothing, lady," the mover said. He handed me a release to sign that absolved him of all responsibility. I said a silent prayer to the floor god as the mover casually tossed down a few furniture pads, strapped the piano onto a rickety dolly, and shoved it in place. (Little did I know, but at that very minute Dexter was dragging a heavy compressor across the shiny bedroom floorboards, with just a T-shirt underneath it for protection.)

"Which way do you want the piano facing?" asked the mover.

Who knew? I'm not good at visualizing where furniture should go. I have to see it in place. This isn't a problem if you have the ability to subsequently move it, which in this case we did not.

The mover was positive that the keyboard should face east. "That way, it shows its best side to the room," he explained. It seemed logical. His helpers struggled to hold the hulking instrument up while he screwed on the legs. It didn't look bad facing east. Then again, it didn't look good either. I'd grown accustomed to the empty space, and it made me uneasy to fill it. I summoned Duke, who is more adept at arranging furniture. He announced with more certainty than I ever feel about anything that the keys should face southwest. The movers grimaced, stuck a pad under each leg, and swerved the piano around. It loomed over the room. With equal conviction, Duke suggested northwest. It blocked the door. Duke suggested west.

"You only get one more move, lady," snarled the mover, who automatically blamed me, the female, for the indecisiveness. "We got other jobs." I had this vision of these guys dashing around Los Angeles, collecting large checks to move pianos eight feet.

"Put it back to east," I said firmly. I didn't want any hostile piano mover taking his aggressions out on my floor. As it was they skulked out without connecting the sustaining pedal. A few days later, I almost murdered my father-in-law, Earl, when he carelessly slid the piano bench across the room, leaving a two-foot scar.

Alas, the extent to which you identify with a house is the extent that it drives you insane. Nothing stays perfect for long. For twenty-four hours I reveled in the flawlessness of freshly painted walls. Then Hal yanked off a misaligned baseboard and tore off a sizable chunk of paint. I was demoralized when I saw the wound. At that moment, I realized that no matter how much energy or cash I put into this house, it would never, ever be right.

"You've broken my heart," I said sadly.

"It wouldn't have happened if the painter had sanded the baseboards," Hal muttered under his breath.

He touched up the paint, but there was no touching up the psychic wound. I was laden with guilt, because everybody else was enchanted with the job. My husband was delirious with pride of ownership. The house he had bought in the neighborhood of his choice had been marvelously transformed with a minimal effort on his part. Passersby peered in the windows and squealed, "Ooh, this place is so adorable." Not a day passed when someone didn't inquire if it was for rent. (I took their phone numbers.) "You must be so thrilled," said an envious neighbor who shared a tiny studio apartment with her three-year-old daughter. I knew I was lucky to have a house, and I was ashamed to complain when, a block away, there were scores of homeless people sleeping on the beach. But thrilled I was not. Friends told me that I'd change my mind when the aggravation was over.

I couldn't imagine the aggravation ever being over.

"We have a problem with the bedroom fixture," Dexter reported after the piano movers had gone. The ceiling fan looked terrific, but it was making an ominous ticking sound, which according to Dexter could result in my future decapitation. I called the Lighting Palace. After insisting that no one in the recorded history of man had ever had a problem with this type of fan, the King of Lamps conceded that maybe a screw in the motor was loose. Dexter promised to check it out. But an hour later, Hal gravely informed me that the fan couldn't be fixed. "You'll have to go get another one," he said.

In the final week of the job I'd had an epiphany. If I limited the hours that I devoted to being a job-site slave (to, say, all morning), I would actually have time to write. With that in mind, I told the contractor that if the fan was ready to go before noon, I'd be pleased to run it to the store. Otherwise, it would have to wait until the following day.

Hal sighed deeply and rubbed his temples. "But I called for the inspection tomorrow afternoon," he said, sounding pained. "And I can't pass without lights." More important, he wouldn't get any money until he passed.

I stood my ground. It was only ten o'clock. The contractor would have two hours to take the fan down, a process that would take fifteen minutes, at most. Hal promised to get right on it. "Just as soon as I put this magnetic catch on the kitchen cabinet and install an insect screen on the fireplace air intake."

Not for the first time, I wished that my brother-in-law lived closer than Chicago. The Shark knows how to keep workers in line. "I argued over charges that I wasn't sure were in my domain," he told me. "I argued over things that I didn't think were done in a craftsmanlike manner. The guy who laid down the tile left grout splattered all over the place. He said, 'It will come up.' I said, 'It's not coming up on my time. It's not something I'm going to clean up with Fantastik.' I argued because they painted the windows closed. The contractor said, 'We weren't even supposed to paint the windows. I did it as an extra, and I only charged you what it cost me.' I said, 'If you charged me and you did it wrong, then it ain't no deal.' "

The shell-shocked contractor finally gave the Shark $250. "He said,

'This is to cover anything else that you think I should have done. Don't ever call me again.' He said I was the most difficult person that he'd ever met."

And Hal thought *I* was troublesome?

At eleven-thirty, when I went back to the house, the fan was still hanging from the ceiling. According to the message penciled on a scrap of two-by-four, Hal had gone to the store to buy a GFCI plug, a special outlet for the bathroom that prevented accidental electrocution. Meanwhile, Dexter was having his way with the three-way light switch in the bedroom. We used to be able to turn it on and off from either side of the room, but ever since Dexter got his hands on it, only one position worked. "It's hot," he assured me. "I can feel electricity going through it, but when you flip the switch, it doesn't go on."

I was reminded of a chilling tale that Dexter told me about how he used to stall helicopters for fun when he was in Vietnam. He seemed more intrigued by the risk element of electricity than the nuances of the system. I warned him to be careful. He chuckled demonically.

"When guys put in big electrical panels, the way they see if there's too much voltage is, they lick their two fingers," Dexter said, his eyes glowing. "If their hand goes flying back, then it's the right amount. But if their hand just gets pushed back a little, they need to work on it."

He couldn't say how long it would take him to fix the switch, or how much it would cost ("You'll have to talk to Hal about that"). But he had decided that the fan was too heavy for the ceiling junction box. He suggested that instead of replacing it I buy a simple dome that he could install quickly. I got the impression that Dexter didn't want to reassemble another fan, but he assured me that he had my best interests at heart.

"You wouldn't want the fan to fall in an earthquake," Dexter said. "Especially since it's over the bed." I recalled a horror story posted on America Online about an incompetent "all around handyman" who installed fifty-two-inch, five-blade ceiling fans in five rooms of the correspondent's house. Within a week several began to squeal, creak, and vibrate abnormally. "The climax was that the master bedroom fan, located directly over my bed, fell out of the ceiling from a four-foot downrod. Good thing I wasn't in it at the time."

At one o'clock, Hal called: The fan was ready. I weighed the advantage of enforcing my work schedule versus the inevitable implication that I was causing him financial hardship if I refused to go. Hal put the fan in the trunk. "Is the box in there too?" I asked. (Dexter had refused to take the fan apart and repackage it.)

"Everything is in the trunk," he said.

I drove seven miles to the Lighting Palace, circled the parking lot three times looking for a space, gave up, parked a block away, walked to the store, and asked if someone could give me a hand. The King of Lamps was having an animated phone conversation about why O.J. was innocent and pretended that he didn't hear me. I walked back to my car, hoisted the heavy fixture out of the trunk, and staggered back. The King didn't lift a finger to help. He did put his phone pal on hold long enough to ask me where the box was. As if I could possibly carry both the box and the fan.

I returned to the car. The box wasn't there. The King refused to take the fan back without the original packing and continued elucidating how O.J. was set up by the mob.

I threatened to cry. It wasn't my proudest feminist moment, but it worked. The King reluctantly agreed to let me exchange the fan for a fixture of equal or greater value. The fan cost twice what I wanted to pay for a plain bedroom fixture, but I craned my neck for an hour and a half until I came up with two items that used up most of my credit—an Art Deco–inspired plastic dome that cost around $2 a watt and a fluorescent kitchen fixture so bright you could use it for surgery. I still hadn't spent enough, so I bought an alarmingly priced halogen bulb for the sconce we'd bought a week before. The bulb looked kind of large, but the King insisted that it would fit. He was equivocating, but I didn't realize that until after I returned home.

Hal helped me carry the new fixtures inside. "Did you get a floodlight for the can light?" he asked.

"Aren't you supposed to buy that?"

"No, you are," he said testily, brandishing Brandon's punch list. *GET FLOOD LIGHT* was written in italics, indicating it was the owner's responsibility.

I felt like screaming, "Then why didn't you tell me before?" I reminded myself that the job was almost over and tramped back to the car.

As I pulled out, Hal came running after me carrying the box for the fan.

"Here," he said. "You forgot this."

Remodeling is the sum of everybody's mistakes. As the end approached, I couldn't relax and admire the dramatic cathedral ceilings, the elegant master bathroom, or the spacious extra kitchen cabinet that meant I could finally get my good dishes down from the attic where they'd been in a carton collecting dust for the past eight years. I was totally fixated on the holes from the old towel bars that the painter forgot to spackle, the loose floorboard the floor guy missed, the absent telephone junction box, and the infinitesimal splotch of drywall in the bathroom that needed smoothing. Brandon was having second thoughts about the red trim in the kitchen. I was kicking myself for not realizing that the top of the picture window in the great room needed obscure glass (I would later cover it with Frosty, a film that I bought at the hardware store for a dollar a yard). Never have I spent so much money and gotten so little gratification in exchange.

"The lights in the bedroom are a mystery to us," Hal announced next. "Dexter went and got the diagrams of every possible way to do a three-way switch, but it doesn't work the way it's supposed to work. If you want, we can get a continuity checker and pull out all the wires and maybe label them. Hopefully, it won't take a lot of time."

We'd previously shelled out $80 for Dexter to fix a short in the kitchen light fixture that I was fairly certain he'd caused. "Aim for minimal," I said.

Hal pursed his lips and shook his head. "I'm more than willing to change a wire out, but I can't get into rewiring the whole house."

"Believe it or not, we're not trying to take advantage of you," I snapped.

The tension went out of Hal's face. He smiled at me. "I know you're not," he said gruffly. It occurred to me that it must be terribly stressful to be responsible for a job.

I was on my way out for my yearly mammogram, a terrifying prospect to a breast cancer veteran, when I got an urgent call from Brandon. "What do you want to do about the light switches and the plugs?" he asked. The old ones were ivory, and Hal wanted $15 each to replace them with white ones. It would cost $300.

Nothing like a mammogram to put the potential trauma of the wrong-colored light switches in perspective. "Just change the plugs on the white walls," I said hurriedly. "The ones on the yellow walls won't show."

The next day, Hal came up with a price to fix the faulty bedroom switch: $150. I told him to forget it. (We spent a maddening month not knowing what would happen when we turned the bedroom switch on. Sometimes, a light in another room would go on. Sometimes, a light in another room would go off. Sometimes, a circuit breaker would blow and the back of the house would be plunged into darkness. Sometimes the washing machine would stop midcycle. It was like living in the Amityville Horror. Eventually, we paid our neighbor, Jeffrey, a real electrician, $88 to repair the damage. "Whoever did this connected two hot wires," he said incredulously. "He obviously didn't know what the hell he was doing.")

Every five minutes, a new expense appeared on the horizon. "The painter threw out the old light plates," Hal said as I was rushing out. "Do you want me to pick up some more and you can just reimburse me? They'll be about a buck."

I accepted gratefully.

I turned down his offer to pick up the tile sealer. We'd already had a bad scare. I'd gone to the house when Alfonso was finished tiling. To my horror, the fireplace tiles were Da-Glo orange instead of rosy pink. "I like it better orange," said Brandon, but Duke agreed that it looked like a Taco Bell.

A new message floated up in the Eight Ball window. "Outlook not so good."

We called Shoshanna at Ceramic City. She blamed the tile guy for using an oil-based sealer. "He should have checked with you to see what kind of finish you wanted," she said. (It wouldn't have killed her to warn us that the tile could change color.)

Brandon thought we might be able to remove the orange color with a caustic, oil-based stripper, which required the use of goggles and gloves. Hal promised to get back to us with a price. I figured he'd get back to us around the millennium, but an hour later Hal phoned with good news: Alfonso hadn't sealed the tiles. He'd merely washed off the grout with water. Hal promised that the tiles would dry pink. (They dried a little less orange.)

We paid a final call on Ceramic City. Brandon had instructed us to buy a special sealant for the pavers and another for the bathroom tile. Shoshanna's helper claimed that the bathroom tile was glazed, so it didn't need to be sealed. "Are you sure?" we asked. It was unlike Brandon to make such a mistake. Again and again, the helper insisted that a sealer was unnecessary. Duke finally thought to ask about the grout.

"Oh, well, grout, sure, *that* needs to be sealed," he said. We wrote another check.

"I guess a lot of people buy tile and don't use grout," Duke sneered. "You must see that every day." I dragged him out of the store.

Despite all the chaos, we easily passed our final inspection. Building inspector Percy Chang signed our official Certificate of Occupancy card, our record that everything on the job was up to code.

"You didn't lose any sleep over this one," the inspector said. "Usually remodeling is the hardest thing you do in your life." (Illness is hard. Unemployment is hard. Remodeling is just aggravating, unless your job lasts more than three months, in which case, it's masochistic.) "You have to make a million decisions, and you don't know how to make them because you don't know what you're talking about."

We were lucky there. We had Brandon. He couldn't have made it any easier for us unless he'd paid for it himself.

"A lot of architects just build monuments to their ego," Percy said. "They take the client's money and go."

"This one was about as hands-on as you could have hoped for," Hal said, rolling his eyes.

Percy smiled at me. "These guys would tell you that you're an easy customer," he said. I must have looked incredulous, because the inspector pointed to a heating vent. "Some women, they'd look at the paint around this heating vent and notice that it's not straight. They can't take that. Some women, they'd go bananas if the floors weren't level. Some women really care about their homes."

I looked at Hal and Dexter, and to my astonishment they nodded in agreement. "Some women wind up crying, arguing with everybody, screaming," Dexter said.

Sometimes, I wanted to do that. I guess I'm glad I didn't.

"You're not perfect," said Hal. "But you know that. And you said at the beginning that you just wanted the house to look better, and you pretty much stuck with that. Most people, as it gets better and better, they want to keep going."

We were lucky there too. The bedroom was like a stop-loss order. We couldn't fix it without spending a hundred thousand dollars. And that was more than I wanted to commit to this house.

"Now all you have to do is get rid of this place," Percy chortled as he drove away.

Hal solemnly presented me with all the permits and a bill for the lights and receptacles. "How much did I say I'd charge you for the light plates?"

I froze. "A dollar," I said. "What is it now? Nine?"

"Fifteen," Hal chuckled. "But I have to get one more." I wasn't surprised. Hal always left a little something to do later. Whenever I thought he had all the light plates on, I'd go into the house and discover he'd taken another one off because he didn't like the size. Still, now that the job was almost over Hal seemed serene and sanguine. Perhaps he had kept himself motivated by imagining personal slights and potential financial disaster. He shambled around surveying his handiwork, and his face lit up.

"The house really got a genuine face-lift," Hal said. "Before it was kind of dreary." (The end of a remodel is much like the end of a successful diet. Friends say, "Oh, you look so trim now," as if you looked like hell before. Friends who used to tell me the house was cute now referred to it as, "that hole in the wall.")

I asked Hal if he had enjoyed the job. He had to think about it. "You like to make a difference," he said finally. "We did a kitchen in a house once. When we walked in, the kitchen was perfectly fine, it looked like new. The lady didn't like her cabinets, so we took it all apart and put it back together. It looked good, but I didn't find that satisfying. But here we made a big difference."

I thanked him for doing a beautiful job and wrote a check for the base shoes, receptacles, and new switches. He wanted the rest of his final payment, but Brandon calculated that there was still $1,500 worth of work that hadn't been done. Hal didn't put up much fuss.

How could he? The security bars for the windows were lying on the ground. The bathroom and fireplace hadn't been sealed. Three light switches needed plates. We were still missing a grid for a window in the great room that Hal had been promising for the last six weeks. And of course the house was still a pigsty.

"How much do you charge to do the cleanup?" I asked.

"Two hundred and fifty dollars."

I weighed what he would do for $250 versus what Lupe, my housekeeper, would do. I suggested we make a deal.

"I wouldn't want to pay for the whole cleanup," Hal said.

"Believe me," I said. "You won't." It wound up taking Lupe and her sister, Maria, *Las Hermanas Dinamicas,* six days, twenty-two rolls of paper towels, three jumbo bottles of Windex, four cans of Ajax, five cans of Pledge, two huge bottles of Soft Scrub, and six gallons of Fantastik to clean our house. And this wasn't counting the two and a half hours that I spent on my hands and knees, scrubbing the filthy kitchen floor with three boxes of Brillo, the only thing that would cut through the grime. (The white floor was never white again.)

"How much will it cost to put our door knocker on?" I asked. We'd bought the heavy bronze hand-of-Salamanca door knocker in Grenada, on our honeymoon. Hal had originally promised to install it as part of our contract, but despite numerous reminders, he hadn't gotten around to it.

"That's a freebie," Hal grinned. I grinned back. He slipped Sophie a Dorito. We were friends again.

The next couple of days were reminiscent of the last days of summer camp. I loathed Camp Kinni Kinnic, but I always felt nostalgic when it was time to pack for home. Hal dashed about turning the hot water on, organizing a tile sample box, repairing nail holes, dusting the lenses of the skylights, installing the smoke detectors, and replacing the security bars. Thursday afternoon he sealed the fireplace tiles—the pink tiles turned pale salmon, but there was nothing we could do. Brandon pronounced that the job was finished, save for the missing window grid, which Hal swore would be in the following week (and to our astonishment, it was). I handed the contractor his final check and thanked him again. I was not brokenhearted to see him drive away.

On the other hand, I got misty saying good-bye to Brandon. If only I could turn my life over to him, and have him make me detailed priority lists and solve my problems. He asked if he could leave his sign up for a while, and I said okay. I asked if he was content with the job. "The great room turned out great," he said thoughtfully. "It's a nice little blend of modern and the kind of attitude the beach house originally had. I like the way the space feels right without being too high or too light." I asked if he was satisfied with Hal. "He needs to charge more so he can carry a job if it runs over and not keep begging," Brandon said. "But he basically did a good job."

The architect reminded me that the work was guaranteed for ninety days. "Be sure to call Hal if anything goes wrong." (Nothing but the electricity did.) Brandon promised to send me the lien releases so we'd be protected in case a worker decided to sue. (No one did.) Then he climbed on his shiny red bicycle and pedaled away.

I sat alone in the empty house, enjoying the silence. It was hard to believe we were done. Actually, with a home, you are never done. The front walk needed repair. I made a mental note to call the concrete man from Tonga (the Friendly Island) whom I'd hired the year before to build a wall in my front yard. The only thing I'd ever heard about Tonga was that the king is so fat that when he went to Prince Charles and Lady Diana's wedding he had to bring along a special reinforced chair. But when I went outside with the pugs to see how the wall was progressing, I learned

something else. "We eat those," the Friendly Islander said, pointing to my now dear departed pug, Bess, who was sniffing the freshly dug trench.

"Really?" I said, surreptitiously trying to coax her back into the house.

"They're delicious," he said, mouth watering. "First, we dig a pit." (The Friendly Islander would later greet Clara and Sophie with enthusiasm. "Young dogs," he'd exclaim. "Very fresh.")

I'd also have to get the gardener to replace all the plants that had been trampled. And we needed to buy blinds for the front windows. And replace the yellowed kitchen floor. But the repairs would have to wait until we refilled our coffers.

Our original budget had been $20,000. We wound up spending almost twice that, but we cleaned up every room. My mother, a tough critic, would later refer to the house as "a perfect little jewel." On an intellectual level, I was proud that I had transformed our house into a sunnier, cheerier, more comfortable and inviting space. Emotionally, I was bereft. It was like trying to save a relationship when the sex is lousy. I still didn't want to live in the place.

Over the weekend, Duke changed the locks. We ran into Spiro, the Cypriot who owns the Deadbeat Arms next door. He complimented us on the remodel, which of course he had inspected. Then he shook his head. "You shouldn't be living there," he said. "In my homeland, Turks, they shoot at me, I'm not afraid, but the people in my building scare me."

I'd heard rumors that the police had visited his building the night before to deal with a suicide attempt in one of the units. Possibly the same unit as the Realtor love-triangle shooting a few years ago, or was it the cherry-bomb throwers? "Where do you find these people?"

"Sometimes you make a mistake," Spiro sighed. Then he brightened. "You know what I would do if I were in your shoes? I would sell this place, while it still looks fresh."

It was my turn to brighten.

"It's a thought," Duke said.

We had three weeks left on our apartment lease. Duke suggested that I take a break before I organized the move. As the days passed, my dread mounted. One day I biked up to Malibu. On my way home, I ran into Jerry, a dedicated anti–nuclear weapons protester left stranded without a cause by the end of the cold war. He offered to rubber-stamp a peace symbol on my hand (I passed) and asked me to sign his latest petition. A neighborhood committee had recently proposed a $10 million plan to make over the cracked asphalt Venice Boardwalk with attractive brick, which was anathema to Jerry. "Help stop Venice from becoming an upscale yuppie mall," he said, holding out his petition.

I shook my head. "They can't make this an upscale yuppie mall fast enough for me."

My husband maintained that I would feel better about the house when I started decorating. I was reminded of the waning days of my previous marriage. It was in December when I told my former husband, Richard, that I was unhappy and wanted to leave. Richard maintained that I was just depressed about Christmas. He insisted that I'd feel better by the time the Rose Bowl parade rolled down Colorado Boulevard on New Year's Day. On January 2, I said good-bye.

I spent a delightful hour in Bed, Bath and Beyond buying towels and choosing a black-and-white batik shower curtain for the new master bathroom. But when I went to put them in the lovely bathroom, a little voice urgently cried, "Run away!"

"You need to burn sage, to get rid of the evil spirits," said my friend Debbie, explaining that it was a Native American cleansing ritual. They were having a sale on sage and lavender smudge sticks at the Psychic Eye, the metaphysical bookstore around the corner. I lit the stick and carried it from room to room, watching the fragrant smoke swirl around, hopefully changing the atmosphere. It set off every smoke alarm in the house.

My negative feelings remained.

"Maybe you need an exorcist," said Debbie, who of course knew two. One had retired to Palm Springs. The other told me she only did ghosts. I didn't have ghosts, just creepy neighbors. The exorcist told me to put salt on the windowsills and the ghosts would stay away.

"Maybe you need a geomancer," said Debbie, whose Rolodex naturally included a card for a feng shui guy. (Typical feng shui remedies involve strategically placed mirrors, plants, stones, and the ultimate feng shui cure, a fish tank.) I didn't need someone skilled in the ancient Chinese art of placement to come and tell me if my house was aligned for optimum energy flow. Or that money and good luck would blow right out my doors because my house was in the wrong place.

I already knew my house was in the wrong place.

What I really needed was a Realtor.

I called Artemis, the unrecognized artist who had quite a large following as a Realtor. I told her that I was thinking of selling. "Your timing is perfect," Artemis said excitedly. "The market is on the upswing." She hurried over in her new hunter-green Mercedes S600 (only $138,000!). She toured the property with giddy enthusiasm.

"You couldn't have done it better," Artemis marveled. "You did absolutely everything right." My spirits lifted as she ticked off the selling points: the cathedral ceiling, the tiled bathrooms, the new kitchen appliances, the brilliant floors, the colorful paint job. "If you did this in any other neighborhood, you would have lost all your money, but this is perfect for Venice. It will sell really fast."

Artemis gave me a printout of all the properties that she had recently sold near the beach. She said she would list the house for more than twice what we owed on it.

"If she can get that, tell her to go ahead," Duke said.

But was there anything on the market for us to buy? A week later, Artemis picked me up in her gorgeous car and chauffeured me around. I saw a "Storybook Cottage," ten feet from Santa Monica Beach, that was almost a clone of our house before the remodel. It had one tatty bathroom, a maze of dark, itsy-bitsy rooms, and a loft that Artemis recommended I convert into a master bedroom. It needed at least $200,000 worth of improvements, but the asking price was $600,000.

"They already turned down five fifty," Artemis said. "I told them they were out of their minds."

I grew increasingly despondent as we toured "Steal This Bauhaus," a

charmless boxy foreclosure in Santa Monica Canyon that was advantageously priced at only $750,000; "Fairytale Castle," a sleazy bachelor pad
on the canals that should have been called "Castle Fuck," and "Beach-
comber's Delight," a sleek, perfectly decorated two-bedroom townhouse
on the sand in Marina del Rey. (*Only* $800,000, and they didn't accept
dogs.)

Finally, Artemis drove up to "Needs Tender Loving Care," a hundred-
year-old, baby blue, two-story clapboard house in Santa Monica that was
actually within our price range. "This needs a lot of work," she warned
me.

A lot was an understatement. At the very least, the house needed a new
roof, a foundation, and a kitchen. But remodeling is empowering. Having done it once, you know you can manifest change. I was wildly aroused
by the possibilities. The living room had an ocean view. There was even
an attic, so we could raise the roof to the rafters. The sprawling backyard
had weeping willows and avocado trees and, best of all, no encroaching
neighbors. Granted, the house was three blocks, instead of half a block,
from the ocean, but when Duke saw it, he readily agreed to walk the extra
distance to swim.

"It's a nice housey house," Duke said, and I loved him for understanding.

I called Brandon, gave him the address, and asked if he could bicycle
over.

"Be sure to bring your sketch pad," I said.

ABOUT THE AUTHOR

MARGO KAUFMAN is the author of *1-800-Am-I-Nuts?*
Her work has appeared in *The New York Times,* the *Los
Angeles Times, Redbook, Good Housekeeping,* and *Cos-
mopolitan.* She is the Hollywood correspondent for
the award-winning *Pug Talk* magazine and can be
heard weekly on KABC talk radio as "The Gripe
Lady" on the *Ken & Barkley* show. She lives with her
husband and two pugs in Venice, California, in an old
beach bungalow—at least, until the real estate market
rebounds.